Michael Jordan's
50
Greatest Games

Michael Jordan's 50 Greatest Games

From His NCAA Championship to Six NBA Titles

BOB CONDOR

A Citadel Press Book
Published by Carol Publishing Group

For Mary, Arthur, and Lana—
they fill the empty spaces of my heart
and form the family of my dreams.

A Citadel Press Book
Published by Carol Publishing Group
Citadel Press is a registered trademark of Carol Communications, Inc.

Editorial, sales and distribution, and rights and permissions inquiries should be addressed to Carol Publishing Group, 120 Enterprise Avenue, Secaucus, N.J. 07094.

In Canada: Canadian Manda Group, One Atlantic Avenue, Suite 105, Toronto, Ontario M6K 3E7

Carol Publishing Group books may be purchased in bulk at special discounts for sales promotion, fund-raising, or educational purposes. Special editions can be created to specifications. For details, contact Special Sales Department, Carol Publishing Group, 120 Enterprise Avenue, Secaucus, N.J. 07094.

Manufactured in the United States of America
10 9 8 7 6 5 4 3 2 1

Library of Congress Cataloging-in-Publication Data

Condor, Bob.
    Michael Jordan's 50 greatest games : from his NCAA championship to six NBA titles / Robert Condor.
        p.   cm.
    "A Citadel Press book."
    ISBN 0–8065–2030–2 (pbk.)
    1. Jordan, Michael, 1963–   . 2. Basketball players—United States—Biography. 3. Chicago Bulls (Basketball team) I. Title.
GV884.J67C65 1998
796.323'092—dc21   98–30392
[B]   CIP

Contents

Acknowledgments

*T*he sportswriter covering a professional sports team holds a daily conversation with readers, who are fans and self-appointed experts. The better writers answer your questions about a team or game almost before you can ask or even wonder about an issue.

Covering the Chicago Bulls means you have plenty of readers and even more expert opinions. It allows you a front-row seat for some portion of Michael Jordan's own brand of masterpiece theater.

While serving as sports editor of the *Chicago Tribune*, I had the pleasure of working with the three beat writers who have covered the championship years of the 1990s. Sam Smith is a widely-read journalist who has strung together countless worthwhile conversations with readers, liberally spiced with insider information and never lacking for opinions of his own. His columns have become mandatory reading for any serious Bulls or NBA fan.

Melissa Isaacson carried out the difficult task of succeeding Sam with the fluidity of a Jordan jumper. She brought the instincts of a former player and a thirst for good stories that never waned over what can be a grueling season. Terry Armour continued the *Tribune* tradition with his unique version of Bulls give-and-take with readers. Anyone who knows Terry knows it is just a matter of time before he gets his own talk show.

The insights of these writers are woven into the fabric of

this book, along with those of Bob Sakamoto, who covered the early Jordan years in Chicago with enthusiasm and with a keen eye for the personal details of a legend in the making. I am indebted to these beat writers for their bodies of work and their friendship.

Columnists also hold daily conversations with sports fans. Bernie Lincicome and Bob Verdi never seemed to miss a single opportunity to enlighten and entertain. Their takes on Jordan were indispensable in shaping this book. Mike Conklin also contributed more material than he might imagine, and writers like Skip Myslenski, K. C. Johnson, Paul Sullivan, Fred Mitchell, Robert Markus, Andrew Bagnato, and Ed Sherman also showed up in the several thousand news clippings used in my research.

As it turns out, John Jackson, the *Chicago Sun-Times* Bulls reporter during the later championship years, is a former colleague from our New York days. I have enjoyed his emergence in the Chicago market, and this book is better due to his own Jordan interpretations.

I consider it a distinct privilege to work at the *Chicago Tribune*. As a Chicagoan, it was a thrill to put out a sports section that recorded many highlights from the Jordan years, especially that magical "three-peat" of 1991, 1992, and 1993. I work for many talented editors, including Howard Tyner, Ann Marie Lipinski, Gerry Kern, and Janet Franz. I appreciate their guidance and leadership, and thanks goes to Dick Ciccone and Dick Leslie for believing in me during those nearly breathless deadline nights of the first title runs.

Of course, this book has its own coach. Jim Ellison at Carol Publishing Group has supplied more than his share of enthusiasm, patience, professionalism, and good ideas to the project, with always the fan in mind. I thank him for his many kindnesses. Andrew Richter was an invaluable editor and swingman at Carol, and I thank production editors Bob Berkel and Steve Palmé for their attention to detail. A fast-break outlet pass also need go to Jim Donovan, the literary agent who proposed this book to me. He was most valuable in the book's early development. Curtis Pesmen, a dear friend and colleague, also helped greatly during the formative stages.

On a personal note, I stopped playing organized basketball after a glorious undefeated season as an eighth-grader. What I learned that winter was much more than the joy of winning a championship; I learned basketball is a team game staked on defense and hustle. My coach, Andy Scianna, turned on a lightbulb that has never burned out in my years of watching Michael Jordan play a team game so brilliantly. I believe Coach Scianna has been admiring the Jordan years as much as I have.

There's also a man in Ames, Iowa, who knows about the art of checking your ego at the door. Tom Emmerson, my mentor, is a writer, editor, and Iowa State professor who is genuine, warmhearted, intelligent, and one tireless teacher. His biggest lesson? Be comfortable with yourself. That's when freedom and creativity show up big in your life. It is an absolute joy to call him a friend.

The most brilliant truth in my life goes on every day at home. My wife and soulmate, Mary, supported the late nights and lost weekends of this project. We always found the time to be with our precious angel-babies, Lana and Arthur, but sometimes this book's research and writing boxed out those quiet moments when the kids were tucked in for the night.

On the other hand, Mary regularly volunteered her thoughts about how Jordan's games should be ranked and helped me wrestle with the larger question of measuring greatness. She listened to me, encouraged me, and lifted my spirits at just the right times. Mary transformed the sometimes lonely task of writing a book into a sense of togetherness, even when I was downstairs in the middle of the night writing about the Pistons or Knicks or Michael's knack for big fourth-quarter performances.

Life, you see, is a team sport, too.

Pregame

*I*n my favorite memory of Michael Jordan, he isn't playing
basketball. He is standing on top of the scorer's table at the
old Chicago Stadium, wearing a newly creased Back-to-
Back ball cap minutes after the Chicago Bulls defeated the
Portland Trail Blazers to clinch their second consecutive
National Basketball Association (NBA) championship in 1992
and the first one before the hometown crowd.

With a spontaneity usually displayed by the youngest of
children, Michael leaps up on the press row with the NBA
championship trophy clenched to his champagne-soaked
jersey. His smile is ear to ear. He yells, "Two! Two! Two of
them!" He cradles the game ball in his other arm, and his
jersey is half out of his baggy shorts.

Jordan dances without a care. For once, Michael isn't perfectly dressed. He breaks his custom of showing up for
postgame interviews amazingly without a bead of sweat on the
most famous of all cleanly shaven heads. (Another time that
he appeared so delightfully disheveled was after winning the
Bulls' fifth title in 1997, waving at the assembled media throng
and smiling as he said, "Hi, guys!" before sitting down for what
turned more like a porch chat rather than a press conference.)
Appearances were secondary; emotions were primary. Joy to
the basketball world.

The national television cameras were already turned off
on that 1992 championship night, after an official blast of

whooping and trophy-accepting downstairs in the locker room, but Chicagoans could still view the scene and catch the fever on local stations. What they saw was Jordan linking arms with teammates, cheering back at the more than 18,000 fans who showered the Bulls, especially and most of all the loyalist Jordan, with a standing ovation and a love-in that lasted the good part of an hour. People in living rooms were linking arms, too. Cars on Michigan Avenue and Austin Boulevard and 63rd Street were honking their horns all night long.

Favorite Michael Jordan moments are personal treasures. We eagerly share them with family and friends, or even total strangers at an airport. You want to hear other people's stories, compare notes, relive the excitement. There are so many great moments—so many great games—from which to choose that the material always seems fresh. Lots of new memories were spun on title night, and plenty of old ones were rethreaded.

"I'm just so glad Chicago drafted me eight years ago," Jordan would say later, still in full uniform but shoeless while holding a lit victory cigar. "If they didn't, I don't think I could do what I did, being a part of back-to-back championships. This is a great town to play for. I love it—and I hope to play here forever."

One could easily flash back to more frustrating seasons for Jordan and the Bulls franchise, when Michael's sensational play drew worldwide raves and three-game sweeps at the hands of the Celtics. Reporters once asked Jordan if he ever longed to take the usual superstar bypass route, demanding a trade to one of the coasts, say, play for the Knicks or Lakers.

Michael politely and firmly said, no, we'll get the job done here. "We're going to hit," he said. "Just give us time." He planned to do it in Chicago, for the team that drafted him, the NBA city that first believed in him.

Indeed, the greatness of Michael Jordan extends far beyond the rather confining dimensions of a basketball court or the Chicago city limits. His stature is certainly greater than the sum of his individual talents and accomplishments. He, of course, redefined the sport into a vertical game for all comers, not just big guys with seven-foot resumés. Then he switched gears to become one of the league's all-time premier shooters, developing a fadeaway jump shot that none other than the great scorer and creative shot-maker Julius "Dr. J" Erving calls unstoppable. While Jordan and the Bulls were running for a sixth title in 1998, Erving said Michael's superior play was matched only by his "bionic" energy.

Perhaps most remarkable about Jordan's redefinition of basketball is how he outworked every team, every pro player, to become the first man ever to lead the league in scoring *and* be named Defensive Player of the Year. He also hired a personal trainer, Tim Grover, to supremely prepare an already conditioned body for the long, pounding nights on the NBA backboards and in the free-throw lane. In the agreement, Jordan set a precedent for professional athletes.

Ultimately, he shredded the flimsy label of being a great solo player who couldn't lead his team to a title. He especially made room for teammate and pal Scottie Pippen on the award podium, literally asking Pippen to help him hold the 1997 NBA Finals Most Valuable Player (MVP) trophy aloft (and later giving him keys to the vehicle awarded with the honor).

It was just another side of the multidimensional Jordan. Greatly supported with a one-of-a-kind smile and unwavering integrity, his persona off the court has expanded the NBA's reach to all points of the globe. There isn't a country in the world that doesn't have its share of people wearing Bulls caps or a No. 23 jersey. Only Muhammad Ali rivals this North Carolina country kid for name recognition, and Jordan clearly is a role model for youngsters from Boston to Bangkok, Southern California to South Africa. Even Knicks fans tell their kids to be like Mike. In fact, Michael's greatness is confined only by the word itself. Calling him a superstar is understating the case, and insulting the intelligence of the knowledgeable fan.

Yet on that June night in 1992, the super-extraordinary, globally colossal Michael Jordan appeared to be just another ordinary human being. He smiled and laughed, screamed, shouted, hugged, laughed some more, mouthed a cigar, perspired on more than a few people, sprayed champagne, kissed his wife and kids, tugged on a ball cap, complimented his bosses, high-fived his neighbors, ran around in his socks, prayed with gratitude for his blessings, shook his head in amazement, and smiled and laughed some more. He was simply one of us, and it was great.

Introduction:
Sizing Up Greatness

With the 1990s mostly in our collective rearview mirror, it seems hard to believe that Michael Jordan's unique talents as a basketball player were not wholly and instantly apparent. At one time, though, as kids everywhere who have struggled with their own athletic shortcomings know, Jordan was cut from his high school basketball team during sophomore year back in Wilmington, North Carolina. His coach kept a taller player on the team. Michael's lesson to the basketball world was about to begin.

Even general managers, coaches, and scouts for pro teams were not convinced of Michael's singular date with greatness, six years later. Jordan was drafted third in the 1984 selection of college players, behind two centers, the University of Houston's Hakeem Olajuwon and the University of Kentucky's Sam Bowie. Somehow hitting the game-winning shot as a freshman in the 1982 National Collegiate Athletic Association (NCAA) championship game, then being twice named Player of the Year before coming out of school a year early, was not enough to guarantee that he was the player who should have been chosen first.

Bulls general manager Rod Thorn lamented the choice of Jordan—a chance that, to their credit, was cheered by local fans attending the draft process at Bulls headquarters. "We wish he were seven feet tall, but he isn't," said Thorn. "There wasn't a center available. What can you do?" Maybe allow Michael to reinvent the jumping order of the NBA, a feat he accomplished despite some initial misgivings of Bulls management, which didn't even send a car for him when he arrived at O'Hare International Airport en route to his first pro training camp.

If there is any uncertainty about Michael's ability to sky, check the number of championship trophies held aloft by Jordan compared to Olajuwon (don't even mention Bowie), and remember that Hakeem won those NBA titles in 1994 and 1995, when Michael was on his baseball sabbatical.

Maybe the proof comes more from Michael's peers. Dirk Minniefield, a close friend and Kentucky teammate of Bowie, was in the Bulls camp for a tryout during Jordan's rookie season. Minniefield was cut late, but stuck around long enough to observe what Bulls teammate Sidney Green called "the truth, the whole truth, and nothing but the truth."

"Houston and Portland are both going to be sorry they didn't draft him," reported Minniefield.

Look up *understatement* in the dictionary.

Phil Jackson, his coach through the glory years and a member of two championship New York Knicks teams during an era than included Bill Russell, Wilt Chamberlain, Oscar Robertson, and Jerry West (the past NBA star Jordan has said he would most like to play one-on-one), says flat-out that no one compares to Jordan no matter what the draft years.

"There's no doubt about the fact he's the greatest player who has ever played this game," explains Jackson. "There are guys as physically talented as he is, guys who are better shooters; there are more physical players, but no one has had as big an impact on both ends of the court, offense and defense, played a more complete game and had a more dramatic effect on the game than Michael Jordan."

Michael's ascension to the NBA stratosphere started long before Nike launched the first Air Jordan campaign. He showed a knack for saving his best for the last. His 1982 NCAA game-winning shot against Georgetown and Patrick Ewing was part of what University of North Carolina coach Dean Smith called "Michael's best overall game by far that year."

Jordan's work habits didn't change despite the more than $200 million in contracts and endorsements he has earned since joining the league in 1984.

"Because of Michael's competitiveness," says Jerry Krause, Bulls general manager, "we've had to build with different types of individuals. We've brought in some players who weren't tough enough to compete with him in practice. We had to get rid of them."

Krause says Jordan's talents are unsurpassed, and he is maybe even more impressed with the marquee player's focus and intensity. Krause recalls a respected Bull from a previous era who went on to be revered as an NBA coach in Utah. "I never thought I would see anyone play as hard in practice as Jerry Sloan," said Krause, who has watched probably close to two thousand Bulls workouts. "But Michael does. He's uncompromising."

Jordan was the runaway—make that flyaway—winner of Rookie-of-the-Year honors for the 1984–85 season, but in his second season he broke his left ankle three games into the season. The highly competitive Jordan returned in time for the playoff stretch run, against team owner Jerry Reinsdorf's wishes, to help the Bulls eke out the final postseason position opposite the mighty Boston Celtics.

Though Reinsdorf didn't know it at the time, and it wasn't necessary to convince more knowledgeable basketball fans, the playoff series against the Celtics dynasty would be a milestone. Jordan scored 49 points in the first game and then a breath-taking 63 in the second game, a 135–131 double-overtime thriller. Chicago lost all three games of the first-round series, but Jordan won over millions of new fans who would watch the NBA Finals and other playoff rounds simply because No. 23 was suited up. Sales of Jordan paraphernalia dramatically jumped during the off-season.

The 63-point game is the one most often mentioned first by confidants and teammates asked to identify Michael's greatest games. The young Michael Jordan, who weaved and criss-crossed and soared that Sunday afternoon in Boston, forever stays in the mind. Each shot seemed more improbable than the next, as the likes of Larry Bird, Kevin McHale, Robert Parish, Dennis Johnson, and Bill Walton were left in his wake.

"Right here in Boston, in the Garden, on national TV, God came down disguised as Michael Jordan," said an awed Larry Bird in the locker room.

"The 63-point game was a big exposure game," recalls Phil Jackson, who was not with the Bulls at the time. "Chicago was a nowheresville team that year, with forty wins and no chance of beating the Celtics, which was still a dynasty team. That effort Michael put forth was dramatic."

Pick One, Pick a Hundred

What Jackson came to appreciate most about Jordan—and what makes picking 50 of his greatest games a steep challenge—was MJ's knack for playing best during the postseason.

"If you look at every playoff game in which he has performed for this franchise, you could pick out one hundred games and say they're the most outstanding and unique."

"It's difficult to pick any one game," says John Paxson, Jordan's backcourt mate during the first three championship Bulls runs and now a team broadcaster. "It's hard to pick fifty. Michael has just been so consistently good for so long, particularly during the playoffs when everyone is watching and opponents are bearing down on you. There are so many great moments I remember from the postseason."

For his part, Jordan says April, May, and June are his favorite months to put the ball through the net and the pedal to his internal accelerator.

"It's a challenge to come out and play your best basketball at the best times, the most crucial times," says Jordan.

For his defensive efforts, he also spends extra hours in the film room studying opponents. On offense he trusts his instincts: "It's personal with me. Mentally, I am going to find a way to beat this guy. He knows what I did last time, so he's going to anticipate me doing the same thing. So I have to change my game somehow. I never really know how I'm going to do it until game time, until I see the way he sets up."

None of this is to say Jordan eases up during the regular season, a common trait among many of today's NBA stars. His competitive nature is second to none. Note in these greatest games of all-time, call them the Jordan 50, there are regular-season contests in the top ten and even an exhibition game, one practice, and two All-Star Games.

"I always want to play well every game because there will be people in the arena who would be seeing me play for the first and only time ever," Jordan once explained. "I don't want to disappoint them."

True enough. One Saturday night in February 1998, the Bulls suited up against the lowly Sacramento Kings at United Center. Rather than coast to a sure victory, Jordan set a personal challenge to duel on both ends of the court with Kings star Mitch Richmond. The Bulls won; Michael scored 28 points and impressed one young fan.

"I love the Bulls," wrote twelve-year-old fan Stefan in a thank-you letter to someone who gave his family tickets to the Sacramento game. "I have to watch them on TV because tickets are so hard to get. The security guard let us go down by the court to see the guys warming up. We got so close to them. It was like a dream, seeing some of the best basketball players in the world four feet in front of me.

"Personally, basketball is my favorite sport to watch and play. It was such a special night. That night was probably the last time I will ever see Michael Jordan play. I will remember it forever. It was such an amazing night. Thank you for making that night happen."

"He didn't miss games," says Jackson. "He played hurt, with pain, when he was sick. He came out and performed at an intense level. I don't think anybody ever went away disappointed after watching Michael."

All Sides of Great

After winning some championships alongside Jordan, teammates like Dennis Rodman and Ron Harper, who had watched him score game-winners over them when they played for foes, came to understand more deeply (and gladly) the superlative and always consistent Jordan tenacity.

Rodman, who played for Detroit Pistons teams that defeated the Bulls in key playoff series during the formative postseasons of 1989 and 1990, scoffs at any debate about basketball's greatest all-time player. Michael is the best, and you can credit ego and competitiveness even more than talent.

"Michael is a guy who doesn't want to lose," says Rodman. "That's the bottom line. If he feels threatened that he's going to fail, he takes it up a notch. A lot of players can't do that in this league."

"MJ brings a character and style of going out and playing hard every night," says Harper. "He comes out to compete every day and brings his heart to the team. He makes everybody's game go up to a higher level.

"I appreciated him before I became a Bull, but I really appreciate him now. You see him as a basketball player or as a fan and you appreciate him. Now that I'm on this team I see the way he carries himself, and it is unreal."

Jordan's defensive abilities are now paramount. John Bach, the Bulls assistant coach who built the defense based on Phil Jackson's concepts during the first three title seasons, benefited from Michael's cooperation and willingness to play tirelessly in a trap-pressure scheme.

"I think he is an unbelievable person as well as a phenomenal basketball player," says Bach. "It seems he can handle well all the demands on his time that fall to a superstar, and handle the game on the floor. What's amazing is the vitality he brings to practice. He could be snobby about the whole affair, but he doesn't let his money belt weigh him down.

"Anything you want [as a coach], he does. He's not shirking it, saying, 'I'm too tired, I'll just play offense.' That's what makes it nice to be with the Air Jordan airline. It flies every night."

Jack Ramsay, now a commentator who won an NBA championship with a Portland Trail Blazers team sparked by big man Bill Walton, has seen untold numbers of pro basketball games spanning the league's five-plus decades. Though people want to discuss how today's league is watered down, or apples and oranges while comparing guards and centers, Ramsay is firm on Jordan as the league's all-time top player. He has an impressive vote of confirmation from one of the NBA's most competitive legendary players who also developed into one of the league's best-ever general managers.

"Jerry West once told me, 'Michael Jordan is just the best ever,' " Ramsay told the *Chicago Tribune*. "I'm talking about Jerry West, who was a great player himself. We both agreed that, night after night, Michael Jordan is unbelievable."

Making His Points

The question remains, how to take the consistently unbelievable—the unreal—and divide it into only fifty deserving segments? You can debate the spectacular dunks compared to sinister defense. Make a case for the young Michael or the wiser Michael. Vote for championship runs rather than nights when MJ scored more than half his team's points.

The common denominator—and place to start—is scoring. Throughout his career, Michael has hovered around the 30-points-per-game mark. He has more regular-season scoring titles than any other player, and tied Wilt Chamberlain's mark for most consecutive seasons leading the league in points. Only Chamberlain and Rick Barry join Jordan as players who averaged 35 points or more per game for an entire year.

Yet until Michael came along, only one player since 1950 led the NBA in scoring the same season his team won the championship. Kareem Abdul-Jabbar did it with the Milwaukee Bucks in 1970–71. In fact, only one player (Barry with the

Golden State Warriors in 1974–75) has finished as high as second in league scoring while playing for an NBA champ. The Boston Celtics never had a scoring champion during their dynasty years in both the Russell and Bird eras.

Every year the Bulls won the title, MJ led the league in scoring. He just kept knocking down roughly 30 points each night—give or take a few baskets. He has played in nearly a thousand straight games without dipping below double figures on the stat sheet.

So forget about picking the Jordan fifty on points alone. He has scored 50 or more points more than thirty times. He has more than thirty *playoff* games at the 40-plus mark, and nearly 150 when the regular season is included. There is much more than numbers when judging his greatest games.

In fact, here's a sneak preview and one indicator of MJ's unique brand of greatness. Two games in which Michael scored more than 60 points didn't make the cut for the Jordan 50. In one of those games, a loss to Atlanta, he scored 23 straight Bulls points during a eight-and-a-half minute stretch of the second quarter and third quarter breaking his own NBA mark of 18 earlier in the same season.

Geometry Lesson

A remarkable part of Michael's scoring achievements has been his nightly responsibility to a disciplined "triangle offense" scheme, installed by Bulls coach Phil Jackson and assistant Tex Winter for the 1989–90 season. It frequently requires several touches of the ball by different players, prompting Jordan to once call it "our equal opportunity offense."

Jackson believed the triangle system, combined with a pressure defense led by Jordan, Scottie Pippen, and Horace Grant, was the secret to success. The first step was getting Michael's on-floor endorsement.

"It was, 'Maybe you don't win a scoring championship. Maybe you're not going to get as many shots,' " recalls Jackson. "That didn't mean that it had to be exclusive, but these are some of the things that needed to happen if this was going to be a better team, and Michael was willing to make that adjustment."

Another thing, says Red Kerr, the Bulls first-ever coach and longtime broadcaster: "Michael has probably rested in more fourth quarters during sure wins than any other star player in history. He put up a lot of those 30-point nights in three quarters."

Bill Walton, the former University of California at Los Angeles (UCLA) and pro center not unaccustomed to being double- or triple-teamed during his own glory days, says Jordan has no peers hitting baskets and drawing fouls versus defensive alignments stacked against him. "I mean, those players are coming straight at him," said Walton, now a commentator, during his playing days with the Boston Celtics. "After you've been around, you become numbed to the spectacular in this league. I watch Larry Bird every day in practice, but Jordan, he is the best at scoring against two or three guys."

Jordan might also be the greatest intimidator, inch for inch, who has ever played the game. His mental toughness is legendary. "Most guys in the league don't even want to talk about him with reporters, especially the young guys," says Red Kerr. "They are afraid of saying anything to displease Michael. That's respect in the form of fear."

Phil Jackson says the turning point of Michael's near-consensus, best-ever-to-play status may very well be a game not listed in the Jordan 50. The Bulls were playing the Utah Jazz during their 1990–91 title season. Jazz guard John Stockton kept switching off to double-team Jordan, leaving John Paxson wide open. Michael decided to keep feeding Paxson the ball, and Jordan's longtime backcourt mate tallied 20 points in the second half.

Jackson said the game opened new possibilities for the ever-creative Jordan, marking the "beginning of his transformation from a gifted solo artist into a selfless team player."

Winning three straight championships certainly rested any notions that Jordan couldn't improve the players around him or fit his rather extensive palate of skills into a team format. Then he retired and eventually returned to lead a new group—Jackson and Scottie Pippen were vital holdovers—to the best regular-season record put up by any team, any dynasty, anywhere. The 1995–96 team won seventy-two games and lost only ten before steamrolling over every foe in sight during the playoffs.

Top Teammates

After years of hearing that he couldn't improve the players around him, Michael can't help but smile every time he remembers that Scottie Pippen was named by the league as one of the NBA's fifty greatest players.

Sam Smith, the *Chicago Tribune* reporter and columnist who wrote the bestseller *The Jordan Rules*, tells a wonderful story about the early days of kinship between the already world-famous Jordan and the gangly kid from central Arkansas who was team manager at the National Association of Inter-collegiate Athletics (NAIA) school as a freshman. In his second pro season, Pippen was still struggling to beat out Brad Sellers in the Bulls' starting lineup.

Jordan and Pippen were huddled before a playoff game in a far corner of the Bulls' basement locker room at old Chicago Stadium. "What you do when you go to the basket is you lean in to create the contact and three-point play," Jordan explained to Pippen. They were talking about an April game against Detroit, when Pippen's last-second shot didn't fall and the Bulls lost. MJ said that Pippen should have made it his business to draw a foul on the play.

"When I go to the basket, I'm off-balance, that's why I lean so much when I'm going to the hole," continued Jordan. "I'm anticipating the defense knocking me back on balance to even a better position from when I started. Then I'm in a good position to shoot and I've made contact for the foul."

Pippen could only think Michael was kidding, merely pulling a gag on a young, naive player.

"You can do that because of your jumping ability, MJ." Pippen answered. "I can't."

"Sure you can," said Jordan. "You're a good jumper."

Pippen has soared in the years since. So have many others—from John Paxson to Steve Kerr, Bill Cartwright to Bill Wennington, and nearly two dozen others. They all own championship rings, endorse products, and have detailed stories to tell their kids about the greatest basketball player of all time. They have their own favorite memories, tucked in a mental scrapbook. They might not agree on which particular game was the absolute best—or whether it's possible to select only fifty of Jordan's greatest (Cartwright, for one, says it is a crazy endeavor), but they know greatness when they see it, when they have played side by side with it.

"There will never be a better player than Michael," says Pippen. "There will never be a better teammate."

Tipoff:
The Great Game Index

There is a well-worn cliché in sports about "giving 110 percent." Somehow 110 percent, as unarithmetical as it might be, still doesn't seem high enough to measure the performance level of Michael Jordan's greatest games.

So with apologies to a couple of all-world mathematicians in their own day, Euclid (300 B.C.) and Descartes (early 1600s), this book hatches an entirely new measurement called the Great Game Index. It has a base of 100 percent plus 23 percent more (get it?) for the unique Jordanian system. After all, math was Michael's favorite subject in school, and, judging from his numbers in the record books, NBA championships, turnstile receipts, endorsement deals, and a billion-some fans, that aptitude hasn't changed.

The Great Game Index—the GGI—awards points in ten categories to every one of the more than 1,200 games Michael has played on the pro, college, and Olympic levels. Each category has its own maximum point value, derived from numerous interviews with basketball players, coaches, and commentators, plus (probably) too many hours dissecting Jordan's career with media colleagues. The GGI also factors in countless conversations about Michael's greatness with his fans, which pretty much covers everyone I've met in the 1990s, including young French children wearing Chicago Bulls hats in the Alps and one doctor who talked about his favorite player while performing an open-heart surgery I was observing for an assignment.

Michael Jordan's best fifty games were judged on ten cri-
teria weighed for significance. Appendix I explains the Great
Games Index in detail—and perhaps provides fodder for bar-
room debates or online chats. Here's what you need to know as
we head into the rankings: Each game is scored on a 123-point
maximum scale over ten categories (listed below with their
maximum values):

Scoring (33 possible points)
Game Importance (20)
Opponent Strength (20)
Historical Significance (10)
Legendary Intangibles (10)
Pressure Points (10)
Defense (5)
Other Offensive Contributions (5)
MJ's Physical Condition (5)
Long odds (5)

GAME TIME

-1-

June 14, 1998

Bulls at Utah Jazz Game 6 Clincher, NBA Finals

Jordan steals victory in the final minute; Chicago makes it six.

T his hang time was of a different sort. After Michael Jordan launched his game-winning eighteen-foot jump shot with 5.2 seconds left—every player, every coach, every fan knew it was good—the NBA's star of the ages stood near the top of the key admiring his work. Jordan froze for just a second or two in follow-through position, as if to linger over his greatest moment on a basketball court.

There was enough time remaining for Utah's rock-steady John Stockton to put up his own shot at legendary status, albeit with Ron Harper's hand in his face, but Jordan said later he knew that the Bulls defense would clamp the 87–86 victory shut. Forget his 45 points. Jordan was saying that stopping the other team is what has won six titles in the last six full seasons he had played.

"Our defense held up strong the whole series," said Jordan after the game, explaining why he knew his jumper was the

As Michael Jordan sank the series-winning jumper, it seemed that only his early retirement had kept him from winning eight straight titles. *Agence France Press/Corbis-Bettmann*

Game 1: Bulls 87, Jazz 86

Bulls	Min	FG-att	FT-att	Reb	Ast	Fls	Pts
Pippen	26	4-7	0-0	3	4	2	8
Kukoc	42	7-14	0-0	3	4	3	15
Longley	14	0-1	0-0	2	0	4	0
Jordan	44	15-35	12-15	1	1	2	45
Harper	29	3-4	2-2	3	3	2	8
Rodman	39	3-3	1-2	8	1	5	7
Burrell	10	0-1	0-0	0	0	0	0
Wennington	4	1-1	0-0	0	0	1	0
Kerr	24	0-0	0-0	0	3	3	0
Buechler	8	1-1	0-0	2	1	1	2
Totals	**240**	**34-67**	**15-19**	**22**	**17**	**23**	**87**

Percentages: FG .507, FT .789. **Three-point goals:** 4-10, .400 (Jordan 3-7, Kukoc 1-2, Harper 0-1). **Team rebounds:** 13. **Blocked shots:** 4 (Harper, 2, Pippen, Rodman). **Turnovers:** 9 (Pippen 2, Rodman 2, Wennington 2, Kerr, Harper, Jordan). **Steals:** 11 (Jordan 4, Pippen 2, Rodman 2, Longley, Harper, Kerr). **Technical fouls:** Illegal defense, 3:42 first; illegal defense, 1:01 first; Illegal defense, 10:58 second. **Illegal defense:** 1.

Jazz	Min	FG-att	FT-att	Reb	Ast	Fls	Pts
Russell	37	2-5	3-4	4	2	2	7
Malone	43	11-19	9-11	11	7	2	31
Keefe	14	1-3	0-0	1	0	1	2
Hornaeck	37	6-12	4-4	6	0	0	17
Stockton	33	4-10	1-2	3	5	4	10
Carr	26	4-7	1-2	3	5	4	9
Eisley	15	1-1	1-1	2	3	1	3
Morris	16	1-3	0-0	2	1	4	2
Anderson	16	2-4	1-1	1	1	0	5
Foster	3	0-0	0-0	0	0	1	0
Totals	**240**	**32-64**	**20-25**	**33**	**19**	**19**	**86**

Percentages: FG .500, FT .800. **Three-point goals:** 2-10, .200 (Hornaeck 1-3, Stockton 1-4, Morris 0-1, Russell 0-2). **Team rebounds:** 6. **Blocked shots:** 0. **Turnovers:** 14 (Malone 5, Horaneck 3, Stockton 3, Foster 2, Russell). **Steals:** 4 (Malone, Keefe, Hornaeck, Foster). **Technical fouls:** Coach Sloan, 3:42 first. **Illegal defense:** None.

Bulls	22	23	16	26	87
Jazz	25	24	17	20	86

A: 19,911. **T:** 2:32. **Officials:** Dick Bavetta, Hue Hollins, Danny Crawford.

title-winner. "We would have never been in this scenario if it hadn't been for defense."

Indeed, Chicago held the Jazz to 81.8 per game, the lowest average ever for a six-game series. The antizenith was a 96–54 suffocation in Game 3, but most remarkable was the defensive play of basketball's most creative offensive player of all time. Michael finished the series with a team-high 11 steals, including 4 in Game 6.

None was bigger than cleanly swiping the ball from Karl Malone's huge palms, with the Bulls down one point and about twenty seconds left on the fourth-quarter clock. Jordan moved over on a double-team. Malone, likely forming a thought about sweet revenge and Game 7, was just starting to uncoil a post-position move over nemesis Dennis Rodman, but Michael had other instincts and faster hands.

"Karl never saw me coming," Jordan said later. One glimpse at Malone's face confirmed that statement.

From there, Jordan experienced what Bulls coach Phil Jackson might relate to Zen Buddhism and which most of us can only envy or marvel at, or both. Time slowed down just for Michael, and the right path opened up before his highly conscious eyes.

"It was a do-or-die situation," recalled Jordan, about taking the ball down the floor while glancing at a game clock showing 18.5 seconds. "So I let the time tick to where I felt like I had the court right where I wanted it to be."

That included John Stockton to the far right side guarding Steve Kerr, and not about to leave for a double-team on Jordan, because Kerr hit the winning shot in 1997's Game 6 clincher. Utah coach Jerry Sloan, the hard-nosed Bull of yesteryear, stuck to his series-long decision to play the young and talented Bryon Russell straight up on Jordan.

"That's when the moment becomes the moment for me," said Jordan. "Once you get in the moment, you know you're there. Things start to move slowly, you start to see the court very well. You start reading what the defense is trying to do. I saw that; I saw that moment. Russell reached and I took advantage of the moment."

Michael feinted right, then left, then right again before leaning left to set up his jump shot. Russell sprawled backwards somewhere in the series of a fakes and a slight nudge from Jordan in contact, common for practically every NBA move to the basket. Jordan had what players like to call "a good look," and that was all he and millions of Bulls fans needed. He finished with more than half of his team's points.

"One thing we try to do with Michael is give him a tough time," said Sloan, a renowned defensive player in his day. "We could have gone and doubled him, but we want to force him into the middle [where other Utah players are closer by to help out]. Those are things you have to be able to do. That's our philosophy. It's been our philosophy for thirteen years here, and we have to continue to try to make those things work.

"You have to give him credit. All your philosophies you can throw out the window. You can double him, you can force him in the middle, but great players make great plays."

Phil Jackson agreed with his opposite number: "Michael is a guy who always comes through. He is always a winner. Michael is a real-life hero."

From his more-than-formidable viewpoint, Jackson said this game—widely speculated and debated as Jordan's finale—was a case of saving the very best for the very last.

"Last year," Jackson said, "the fifth game here [during the 1997 Finals, when Michael was sick from food poisoning], I didn't think you could top that performance, but he topped it tonight. I don't know if anybody could write a scenario that's quite as dramatic as that was."

The dramatics seemed to tilt in Utah's favor during the early part of the last minute of play. Stockton drained a three-pointer after a precision crosscourt pass from Malone. The Jazz were up 86–83 with forty-two seconds remaining. The Delta Center crowd roared its approval as the Bulls huddled for a time-out.

Jackson called the likely play: Michael would drive to the basket as quickly as an opening developed, the Bulls didn't want to run much clock, and MJ could at least draw a foul. He was a perfect 8 of 8 from the free-throw line in the fourth quarter, when he scored 16 overall.

Michael sliced by Russell for a lightning-quick layup. It

took only five seconds. Utah still appeared in control of its own destiny—which looked brighter than ever for a decisive Game 7 as Scottie Pippen hobbled around the court with a painful, spastic back—but Jordan swiped the dream.

"Of all the championships we won, this was the toughest," said Jordan.

The Bulls megastar was referring to a season of injuries (especially to Scottie Pippen and Steve Kerr), controversy (always Dennis Rodman), and uncertainty (whether Michael, Scottie, Dennis, and Phil would return for another try if they won the sixth title). But MJ could have been talking about his shooting night. He was 15 for 35 in the game, and 4 for 9 in the final quarter.

Michael struggled, but kept his poise. There was perhaps no greater example of this admirable trait than when he shorted a three-pointer inside the three-minute mark. Rather than stand disappointed for even a split second too long, Jordan hustled back on defense. He was the only Bull downcourt, which allowed him to leap with all of his might—Michael was nearly gassed from playing so hard to cover Pippen's gap in play—to steal a long outlet pass intended for Malone that could have put the Jazz up by four points.

"I think everybody knows how he should be remembered, as the greatest player that has ever played," said Sloan. "I hope he continues to play."

No Chicago fan could have said it any better.

Number 1: Great Game Index

GG1 Score (119 of a possible 123)   Tiebreaker is opponent strength.

Scoring (33 of a possible 33)   It's hard to bicker with 45 points, even if MJ missed twenty field-goal attempts. He scored four key baskets down the stretch and drained 8 of 8 pressurized free throws in the fourth quarter for a vital 16 points.

Perhaps as importantly, Michael notched 15 points in the

second quarter when the Bulls were struggling to stay even. Scottie Pippen was back in the locker room, out for the half with his bad back. MJ hit 6 of 11 from the floor, including 2 of 4 three-pointers. The Bulls stayed within four points at halftime and clung that close until Jordan's last-minute heroics.

Game Importance (20 of 20)   For the Bulls' purposes, this was Game 7. No one could predict if Pippen's back would allow him to play three nights later, and the Delta Center in Salt Lake City was the toughest place to earn a win during the 1997–98 season.

Opponent Strength (20 of 20)   Utah was one year wiser and more prepared for the Bulls. Karl Malone (39 points, 11 rebounds in Game 6) played a significantly better Final in 1998 than in the previous June. Bryon Russell, as noted by defensive whiz Scottie Pippen, played a more mature series while guarding Jordan.

Historical Significance (10 of 10)   Six titles put the Bulls only second behind the Boston Celtics among NBA dynasties. During one postgame interview, Jordan revealed his historical—and competitive—leanings: "Magic [Johnson] won five rings [with the Los Angeles Lakers]; we won six." MJ also won his sixth Finals MVP award to match a half dozen regular season MVP honors.

Legendary Intangibles (10 of 10)   Game-winning shot. Last-minute steal from the other team's star player. Clutch free throws. Smiling after the Bulls' two losses in this series, putting his teammates at ease. At halftime of Game 6, Jordan assured his teammates they would win.

   "I never doubted the whole game," said Jordan.

   "Michael carried us on his back," said Phil Jackson at the championship rally in Chicago's Grant Park, "and we rode him home."

Pressure Points (10 of 10)   Nothing but net in the final minute, plus all eight free throws in the fourth quarter (12 of 15 for the game). MJ called his final eighteen-footer an "easy shot."

Defense (5 of 5)   There was no defensive letup in Jordan's game-high forty-four minutes. His 4 steals matched Utah's team total. The Bulls recorded 60 steals in six games compared to 38 for the Jazz. Michael's defense turned the game—and the basketball world—around in the late stages.

Other Offensive Contributions (2 of 5)   Jackson asked Jordan if he could possibly go forty-eight minutes if necessary, since the Bulls already knew Pippen was far less than 100 percent. Jordan said, "I'll do what I can," but realized he would have to get some rest even while on the court. He sacrificed in rebounding and assists, finishing with a mere one of each. But he had just one turnover while Malone (5), John Stockton (3), and Jordan's defensive assignment, Jeff Hornacek (3), each coughed up the ball more.

MJ's Physical Condition (4 of 5)   Michael was physically tired, which will happen when you average more minutes in your thirteenth season than in your rookie year and play one-hundred-plus games for the third straight season. The loss of Pippen, along with a stomach virus that greatly slowed Ron Harper, made Jordan work that much harder, yet he managed to stay strong mentally and emotionally.

Long Odds (5 of 5)   Michael is predictably great, but no one was expecting such a high-drama outcome. In fact, for first time since the inaugural title run against Los Angeles in 1991, the Bulls were not favored in the NBA Finals. Even most of the Chicago media was predicting Utah as the new world champions.

"Michael was laughing about us being the underdogs," said Chicago teammate Steve Kerr. Probably because Jordan knew he had everyone—including John Stockton and Bryon Russell—right where he wanted them.

Michael showed the world why people call him Superman by scoring 38
points and guiding the Bulls to victory while on the verge of collapse.
Agence France Press/Corbis-Bettmann

-2-

Bulls at Utah Jazz Game 5, NBA Finals

Michael rises from a sickbed, and puts the Bulls in position to win their fifth title.

Michael Jordan calls them "chill bumps." You may know them as "goose flesh," "goose bumps," or "the chills."

No matter what the description, it is an all-too-common tingly feeling fans get when watching one of Jordan's great games or miracle moments. This 1997 late-spring night in Salt Lake City had more than its share of chill bumps. More than even Michael himself bargained for.

Michael woke up on the morning of Game 5 with a horrible case of food poisoning from a bad room-service pizza, completely fatigued, and nauseous after a fitful night. He didn't feel much better as the day progressed. He missed the Bulls shoot-around, stayed in bed until the team bus departed for the Delta Center, and generally made his coaches and teammates queasy about the prospect of playing without Jordan in a critical fifth game of the NBA Finals. In the hour before the game, he stretched out in a dark room with a bucket nearby for his nausea.

Game 2: Bulls 90, Jazz 88

Bulls	Min	FG-att	FT-att	Reb	Ast	Fls	Pts
Pippen	45	5-17	7-9	10	5	4	17
Rodman	23	1-1	0-2	7	1	6	2
Longley	26	6-7	0-1	4	2	1	12
Jordan	44	13-27	10-12	7	5	3	38
Harper	24	2-4	0-0	4	1	3	5
Williams	23	2-8	3-6	4	0	2	7
Kerr	24	0-3	0-0	2	1	1	0
Kukoc	24	3-5	0-0	4	2	2	9
Buechler	4	0-0	0-0	0	0	1	0
Caffey	3	0-0	0-0	0	0	2	0
Totals	240	33-72	20-30	42	17	25	90

Percentages: FG .444, FT .667. **Three-point goals:** 6-15, .400 (Kukoc 3-4, Jordan 2-5, Harper 1-1, Kerr 0-2, Pippen 0-3). **Team rebounds:** 7. **Blocked shots:** 5 (Kukoc 3, Longley, Jordan). **Turnovers:** 8 (Pippen 3, Jordan 3, Kerr, Kukoc). **Steals:** 8 (Jordan 3, Williams 2, Pippen, Longley, Harper). **Technical fouls:** Williams, 4:15 third; Kerr, 7:43 fourth. **Illegal defense:** 1.

Jazz	Min	FG-att	FT-att	Reb	Ast	Fls	Pts
Russell	40	4-10	0-0	7	1	2	11
Malone	34	7-17	5-9	7	6	5	19
Ostertag	34	5-8	3-4	15	0	3	13
Hornaeck	29	2-11	2-3	5	2	4	7
Stockton	36	5-10	2-3	3	5	3	13
Anderson	13	1-2	0-0	0	0	2	2
Eisley	12	1-3	0-0	0	4	0	2
Morris	14	4-7	0-0	2	0	0	11
Foster	16	0-3	6-6	6	1	3	6
Carr	11	2-4	0-0	0	2	3	4
Keefe	1	0-0	0-0	0	0	0	0
Totals	240	31-75	18-25	45	21	25	88

Percentages: FG .413, FT .720. **Three-point goals:** 8-19, .421 (Russell 3-5, Morris 3-5, Hornacek 1-4, Stockton 1-4, Malone 0-1). **Team rebounds:** 7. **Blocked shots:** 5 (Ostertag 3, Malone, Morris). **Turnovers:** 11 (Stockton 3, Malone 2, Ostertag 2, Hornacek 2, Foster, Carr). **Steals:** 4 (Stockton, Anderson, Eisley, Morris). **Technical fouls:** Stockton, 7:43 fourth. **Illegal Defense:** None.

Bulls	16	33	18	23	90
Jazz	29	24	19	16	88

A: 19,911 (19,911). **T:** 2:30. **Officials:** Bill Oakes, Hugh Evans, Danny Crawford

The series was tied 2–2. Utah was proving arguably the Bulls' most formidable challenge of their title years, and playing Utah in their noisy home arena is never easy (Dennis

Rodman revved up the degree of difficulty with some inflammatory comments about Mormons).

"We thought maybe we would have to win without him," said Bulls coach Phil Jackson." Someone might have to fill the gap. Michael didn't have to fill any gap; he filled all the holes."

"I've played many seasons with Michael," said Scottie Pippen. "I've never seen him this sick. It was to the point where I didn't think he was even going to be able to put his uniform on."

Slide on the No. 23 jersey he did, though taking long pauses between each article of clothing and lacing his world-famous sneakers. He took a few half-hearted shots during warmups, then went to the bench to sit down while his teammates kept shooting.

On the court for the game, one look told Bulls fans all they needed to dread the worst. Even the usual cynics on press row acknowledged that Michael was undoubtedly sick. His clear eyes were glazed over, the heat-of-battle-isn't-this-great smile had disappeared, and no tongue jabbed out on MJ's field goal attempts.

Yet Michael scored 38 points as the Bulls took command of the series, which ended three days later with Chicago's fifth title. He played forty-four of the most gutsy minutes ever punched on a scoreboard clock in sports history. Only Pippen played more, just one minute more. MJ hit the winning three-pointer with twenty-five seconds remaining in a 90–88 thriller. He even summoned the energy to haul down 7 rebounds (the same number credited to Dennis Rodman and Utah star power forward Karl Malone, and dish out 5 assists (equal to Pippen and Utah star point guard John Stockton).

The Jazz luck had played out like a tune in the jukebox. Michael orchestrated the first defeat of Utah on its home floor in twenty-four games. He was everybody's most valuable maestro this night, even if Malone had won the regular season Most Valuable Player award.

"He was dehydrated," said Pippen. "At times he felt like he was going to pass out. [Trainer Chip Schaefer and staff] were feeding him fluids and giving him cold towels and things of that nature, but he really just came out and gave us the performance we needed. There's nothing else to say."

Except this: "He's the greatest, and he's the MVP in my eyes," added Pippen.

Anyone who remembers this game—figure that to be tens of millions of people—will no doubt recall the image of Jordan falling into Pippen's arms near the end of the game as both headed to the bench for a time-out. He dropped his head to Scottie's shoulder as if their long-held roles as big brother–little brother had reversed. Michael hugged tight for more than few seconds.

During play, it was the Bulls who leaned on Jordan. Their star teammate hit his usual assortment of fadeaway jumpers and slashing drives to the basket. His scoring line was 13 of 27 from the field, 10 of 12 free throws. On defense, he squeezed and strong-armed his way through picks. He recorded a game-high 3 steals and blocked a shot. He left Utah players as the ones who were ill.

"Obviously, we have our work cut out for us," said Malone.

The Jazz took a 84–81 lead with 3:07 left on a nifty pass from Malone to Stockton, who promptly rippled a three-pointer, but Michael roared back down the court, pulled up in the lane, and swished a short jumper to make it 84–83 and much less deafening in Delta Center.

With 46.5 seconds remaining, Jordan stood at the free-throw line with the Bulls behind by a point. It took all of Michael's stamina to simply remain upright while waiting for the referee to hand him the ball. He sank the first free throw but badly missed the second, barely clanging the front of the rim. In a furious scramble of bodies, the Bulls' slender Toni Kukoc kept the rebound alive until Jordan—naturally—controlled the loose ball.

The Bulls reset their offense, developing a play for Pippen to isolate against the smaller Jeff Hornacek. Utah's Bryon Russell made the mistake of switching off Jordan to help double-team the more fortified Pippen. But Scottie knew better. He quickly passed the ball to Jordan, who drilled a three-pointer. Open looks at the basket late in a critical games are the best medicine for great players.

"I feel better now that we won," said an exhausted Jordan in brief comments before skipping the usual postgame press conference to get back to a warm bed. "I endured it, and it went to a good cause. Now we want to go home and accomplish what we want to accomplish: Get one win."

Michael said he felt "very queasy, low on energy" during his brilliant forty-four-minute performance and second-best game in the Jordan 50.

"Once I got out there and started sweating, I was out and I really didn't want to sit down. I knew I had to play in spurts, with bursts of energy, then rest for two minutes and do what I had to do."

Funny, nobody, especially the Jazz, figured Michael should be putting in for sick time.

Number 2: Great Game Index

GGI Score (119 of a possible 123)

Scoring (32 of possible 33)   Michael scored 21 points in the first half to keep the Bulls close. He then conserved energy for the fourth quarter, when he hit four of first five shots. He notched 16 for the quarter, including the key three-pointer to tie the game at 77 and the big long-range jumper to win it.

Game Importance (20 of 20)   The turning point of this Finals. Utah was left with the tough task of winning two straight in Chicago. Bulls coach Phil Jackson said, "This [game] was as big as any win we've had in a playoff situation."

Opponent Strength (19 of 20)   Utah's Karl Malone and John Stockton have been perennial all-stars and longtime teammates who know each other's every move. Michael referred to the Jazz as the most talented and mature team the Bulls faced in Finals play.

Historical Significance (10 of 10)   Nobody forgets this one.

Legendary Intangibles (10 of 10)   In his career, Michael played through many injuries and flu bugs, always delivering due to unsurpassed concentration. The Jazz players publicly claimed not to know Jordan was ill. Don't believe it.

Pressure Points (10 of 10)   MJ scored 16 of his team's 23 fourth-quarter points, while Utah's Karl Malone had one lonely free throw and only 5 points the entire second half. MJ hit the game-winning shot by keeping his composure—and grabbing a loose-ball rebound—after missing his second foul shot that would have put Bulls ahead by one with forty-six seconds left. Despite overwhelming sickness, he did sink the first free throw to tie the game at that point, 85–85.

Defense (4 of 5)   Michael had to ease up some time on the floor, but didn't take too many breathers. He finished with a game-high 3 steals and a block.

Other Offensive Contributions (4 of 5)   Seven rebounds and 5 assists put him on par with other stars of the game.

MJ's Physical Condition (5 of 5)   This game was Michael's lowest physical point for any game, anywhere. No one who has ever experienced food poisoning can believe this type of effort is possible, even two days later.

Long Odds (5 of 5)   Walking out for the opening tip-off, no Bulls player ever imagined such production, even from Michael. They thought they had seen it all. They, of course, were wrong.

-3-

April 20, 1986

Bulls at Boston Celtics Game 2, First-Round Playoff Series

MJ scores an unprecedented 63 points against the Celts dynasty.

T his vibrant afternoon on the parquet floor of Boston Garden had all the makings of an NBA classic. A young Michael Jordan almost singlehandedly took on the latest version of the Celtics dynasty, featuring the incomparable play of Larry Bird, with no small contributions from Kevin McHale, Robert Parish, Dennis Johnson, and even Bill Walton to further glitz the mix. The game went into first overtime because MJ sank two free throws at the buzzer. It entered a second overtime when Michael could not drop a jumper from about the same place on the court that he hit the winning shot for North Carolina in the 1982 NCAA championship game. The loaded Celtics finally won the game, 135–131, but not before Jordan scored 63 points and made an indelible impression.

No one who saw it at the Garden or on national TV will ever forget this game. Michael is not one to dissect which of his games are the greatest—he leaves that to the historians and

17

Game 3: Celtics 135, Bulls 131

Bulls	Min	FG-att	FT-att	Reb	Ast	Fls	Pts
Woolridge	54	9-27	6-8	9	2	5	24
Oakley	33	3-5	4-6	14	0	5	10
Corzine	39	4-7	0-0	7	1	5	8
Jordan	53	22-41	19-21	5	6	4	63
Macy	28	3-4	1-1	1	2	4	7
Green	19	2-8	3-4	5	0	4	7
Banks	25	3-7	2-4	3	3	2	8
Smrek	2	0-0	0-0	0	0	1	0
Gervin	5	0-0	0-0	0	1	1	0
Paxson	32	1-3	2-2	0	3	2	4
Totals	**290**	**47-102**	**37-46**	**44**	**15**	**34**	**131**

Percentages: FG .461, FT .804. **Team rebounds:** 12. **Turnovers:** 11 for 11 points [Jordan 4, Corzine 2, Oakley 2. Banks, Paxson, Woolridge]. **Steals:** 9 [Jordan 3, Oakley 3, Paxson 2, Woolridge]. **Blocked shots:** 4 [Jordan 2, Corzine. Green].

Celtics	Min	FG-att	FT-att	Reb	Ast	Fls	Pts
McHale	51	10-22	7-8	15	4	4	27
Bird	56	14-27	6-7	12	8	5	36
Parish	31	4-11	5-6	9	0	5	13
Johnson	44	4-14	7-9	4	8	6	15
Ainge	47	8-13	7-9	4	5	5	24
Walton	25	4-8	2-2	15	2	6	10
Sichting	22	4-5	0-1	0	4	1	8
Wedman	11	1-3	0-0	0	0	0	2
Carlisle	3	0-0	0-0	0	0	0	0
Totals	**290**	**49-103**	**34-42**	**59**	**31**	**32**	**135**

Percentages: FG .476, FT .809. **Team rebounds:** 11. **Turnovers:** 16 for 19 points (Bird 4, McHale 4, Parish 4, Johnson 2, Ainge, Walton). **Steals:** 7 (Ainge 3, Johnson 2, Bird, Parish). **Blocked shots:** 12 (McHale 6, Bird 2, Parish 2, Johnson, Walton).

Bulls	33	25	33	25	9	6	131
Celtics	25	26	37	28	9	10	135

A: 14,890. **T:** Bulls (illegal defense). Ainge. **Officials:** Jake O'Donnell, Ed Middleton.

won't even allow talk that he is the best basketball player of all time, allowing that you can't fairly compare competitors from different eras. Nonetheless, MJ never neglects to mention this game when asked about the highlights of his career. There is a certain smile on his face when the 63 points are mentioned,

At the height of his Celtic team's greatness, not even the legendary Larry Bird could stop Jordan from pouring in 63 points. *UPI/Corbis-Bettmann* though he still wonders how this playoff series (a three-game Boston sweep) might have turned out if he had made that shot at the end of the first overtime.

Larry Bird is glad he didn't have to live through that particular challenge. People might not remember that Jordan scored 49 points in the first game of the series, indeed eclipsing back-to-back performances against superior Boston teams of any player in previous NBA eras, from Wilt Chamberlain to Oscar Robertson to Jerry West to Elgin Baylor (who held the previous one-game mark with 61 against the Celts in 1962).

Jordan's 63 points were divided into six periods: 17 points in the first quarter, 6 in the second, 13 in the third, 18 in the fourth, then 5 in the first overtime, and 4 in the double overtime. He hit 22 of 41 shots from the field, added 19 of 21 free throws (including the pressure-packed pair with no time on the clock in regulation), 5 rebounds, 6 assists, 3 steals, and 2 blocked shots.

"I couldn't believe anybody could do that against the Boston Celtics," said Bird, who sat at his locker for nearly an hour after the game to discuss the marvels of Jordan's performance. "I couldn't believe he missed as many shots as he did. No question, he had control of the game. He had to have one of the greatest feelings you can ever have. It's actually fun playing against the guy."

Playing with Jordan was equally gratifying to teammate Orlando Woolridge, who was the other player in Bulls coach Stan Albeck's game plan to effectively reduce the contest to a two-on-two matchup. Albeck figured he would let Jordan and Woolridge dominate the ballhandling on offense, and take his chances. It almost worked.

"It was incredible," said Woolridge, who scored 24 points and pulled down 9 rebounds. "I just wish I could have been a spectator and sat back and watched. Being on the court with him, you could tell there was something magical happening."

Jordan admitted he thought his 49-point night in the first game of the series was his best effort ever on a basketball court.

"I keep pushing myself, " he said. "When I reach a point where I think I may not go any further, I go further. I surprised myself."

Pushing past even superhuman limits of greatness is Michael's forte. To prove the point, his all-time best game would come almost a decade—and lots of basketball—later against the Utah Jazz in the 1998 NBA Finals.

On this Sunday afternoon, Jordan's line against the Celtics was made more impressive by his recovery from a broken foot early in the same season. While owner Jerry Reinsdorf preferred his young star take the rest of the season off—critics say to ensure a high draft pick—Jordan wanted only to return for a playoff run.

"One thing I really like about Michael is that he was ready to play, even though management said no," said an admiring Bird, who knows plenty about performing despite pain and injury. "There was no question management wanted to get in the draft lottery. I think that takes a lot of guts. It shows you what kind of a person he is. You've got to feel happy for people like that."

While Michael was winning over hard-nosed competitors like Bird, NBA general managers were likely taking copious notes on how maybe, just maybe, the future of basketball was less about seven-foot centers and more about "big guards" who defied precise categorization.

One sequence stands out in the minds of those pro team executives watching that day: MJ dribbling between his legs and around Bird, stutter-dribbling by Johnson, scaling over McHale, and double-pumping a layup past Parish. The six-foot, six-inch Jordan had just chopped more than twenty-six feet of Celtic green.

Jordan's heroics put the Bulls up by 7 at halftime. Both Boston big men, Parish and Walton, already had three fouls in attempts to slow down a whirring Michael. The Celts rallied in the third quarter, riding the sometimes cranky back of Bird (who scored 36, boarded 12, and dished out 8 assists), but Jordan stood tallest. Chicago led, 91–88 going into the fourth quarter.

You could see the worry in the faces of the Celtics players and coach K. C. Jones, who was finding few takers on the bench who wanted to guard Jordan. Jones offered a down-to-earth description: "Want to know how great Jordan is? Normally, the guys on the bench are leaning forward and making eye contact with me to get into the game. When they saw what Jordan was doing, nobody wanted to guard him. I'd look down the bench and they were all leaning way back. So I leaned back, too. When somebody finally went in, it took so long for their warmups to come off."

Remember, this was only Michael's second season, and he had missed sixty-four games with the foot injury.

Boston threw everything at the ultra-underdog Bulls, yet when Jordan dunked with 3:40 left, the mighty Celtics were up only 108–107. The game seesawed from there. McHale made it 116–113 with forty-five seconds left. Bulls forward Charles Oakley hit one of two free throws to make it a 2-point game with thirty-three ticks remaining. On the Boston possession, Bird missed a shot, but Parish yanked down the rebound to seemingly keep the game in hand—until Michael knocked the ball loose. Oakley grabbed it and Chicago called a time-out with six seconds left.

Of course, Jordan took the last shot, a three-pointer that bounced off the rim, but not before McHale fouled Jordan on the release. MJ calmly drained both free throws—distilling 14,890 screaming fans and even McHale, who was waving his arms to incite the crowd—and probably would have hit the third of what is now considered a three-shot foul.

In the first overtime, Michael missed a fifteen-footer with three seconds left. He also overlooked a wide-open Oakley under the hoop, a mistake he certainly didn't make later in his career, when he passed NBA title-game-winners to the likes of John Paxson and Steve Kerr.

Other lessons were learned for Bulls title runs of the 1990s. Probably what most impressed the Celtics—with at least five future Hall of Famers—was Jordan scoring 63 points within the context of the Chicago team offense. Bird was critical of

Michael's 49 points in Game 1 of the series, writing it off as the Bulls simply clearing out of the way so Jordan could perform in the 19-point loss. Sunday afternoon was more fundamental and frightful.

"He was getting his points right in the flow of the game," said Bird. "When he does that, it is scary."

Parish mentioned the same thing, adding, "There's no telling what he would have done with another five minutes" of third overtime, which the Celtics narrowly avoided.

"I was watching and all I could see was this giant Jordan," said K. C. Jones, who played alongside Bill Russell and faced Wilt Chamberlain more times than he cared to count. "Everyone else is sort of in the background."

Number 3: Great Game Index

GGI Score (118 of a possible 123).

Scoring (33 of possible 33)   What's to argue with 63 points against one of the all-time great NBA squads? It broke an all-time playoff high against Boston, and gave Jordan 112 points in two games. Nearly 44 percent of his scoring came in the fourth quarter and overtimes. He was double- and triple-teamed all afternoon, and still shot 53 percent from the floor. He was impressive under pressure, with 19 of 21 from the free-throw line.

Game Importance (17 of 20)   The Bulls were undermatched and didn't figure to win the series no matter what happened in this game, but Jordan argues that Chicago would have won the series if this game's outcome were reversed.

Opponent Strength (20 of 20)   The Celtics were filled with big stars who played as a team. That is the key ingredient of any dynasty. Just ask guys like Jordan, Scottie Pippen, and Dennis Rodman.

Historical Significance (10 of 10)   The 63 points is always part of any Jordan memory collection. While nearly 15,000 attended the game at Boston Garden, chances are 150,000 Celtic diehards claim to have been there that day. This game is a sentimental favorite with longtime Jordan fans, including many teammates who had yet to don a Bulls uniform and other contemporary players throughout the NBA, including some younger stars who were teenagers in 1986.

Legendary Intangibles (10 of 10)　When Larry the Legend claims God played in disguise as Michael Jordan, there is nothing more legendary. Should almost get extra points here.

Pressure Points (10 of 10)　Two free throws were needed for a tie, with no time on the clock, and millions of eyes watching on national TV.

Defense (4 of 5)　Michael had yet to reach Defensive Player of the Year form, but 3 steals and 2 blocks indicate prowess— and no coasting when Boston had the ball.

Other Offensive Contributions (4 of 5)　Michael's role in the game plan was scoring, but he still dished out 6 assists and grabbed 5 boards.

MJ's Physical Condition (5 of 5)　He came back from a broken foot that might have kept other players in street clothes. It's one thing to heal the bone; it's another to play fearlessly against the Celtics in Boston.

Long Odds (5 of 5)　After scoring 49 points in Game 1 of the series, reporters asked Michael what he could possibly do for an encore. "Maybe score fifty," he said, smiling. Nobody believed it, and certainly no one anticipated he would put up 63 after torching the Celts in the opening game. No player had ever scored so prodigiously in back-to-back games against Boston, and MJ was little more experienced than a rookie.

-4-

Bulls at Cleveland Cavaliers
Game 5, First-Round Playoff Series

Michael hits The Shot in a make-or-break game.

A mong the Jordan 50, this game was the most gripping. In Chicago—and among Jordanphiles all over the hoops planet—fan shorthand for this performance is simply, The Shot.

In a postseason that eventually promoted the Bulls to the conference finals for the first time in the Jordan era, and only the second time in club history, Michael's heroics in make-or-break Game 5 of the opening series against the Cleveland Cavaliers was the turning point.

Make-or-break is an understatement. The Bulls and Cavs exchanged leads nine times in the last three minutes of the game at Richfield Coliseum. MJ hit a twelve-foot jumper from the right side to put Chicago up, 99–98, with six seconds remaining.

Game 4: Bulls 101, Cavaliers 100

Bulls	Min	FG-att	FT-att	Reb	Ast	Fls	Pts
Pippen	42	4-14	3-8	10	2	4	13
Grant	28	6-10	0-0	5	1	6	12
Cartwright	31	6-7	4-5	5	1	4	16
Jordan	44	17-32	9-13	9	6	3	44
Hodges	42	4-12	0-0	2	4	4	10
Sellers	25	1-3	0-0	3	3	3	2
Corzine	16	1-4	0-0	3	1	0	2
Vincent	8	1-1	0-0	3	1	0	2
Davis	4	0-0	0-0	0	0	0	0
Totals	240	40-83	16-26	37	20	24	101

Percentages: FG .482, FT .615. **Three-point goals:** 5-11, .455 (Hodges 2-4, Pippen 2-6, Jordan 1-1). **Team rebounds:** 13. **Blocked shots:** 3 (Cartwright, Pippen, Sellers). **Turnovers:** 13 (Grant 3, Cartwright 3, Hodges 3, Jordan 2, Pippen, Sellers). **Steals:** 7 (Cartwright 2, Hodges 2, Grant, Pippen, Jordan). **Technical fouls:** None. **Illegal defense:** 1.

Cavaliers	Min	FG-att	FT-att	Reb	Ast	Fls	Pts
Williams	32	2-5	3-4	6	3	2	7
Nance	38	5-11	6-7	7	1	3	16
Daugherty	33	3-9	2-2	11	6	4	8
Harper	44	9-16	4-5	2	6	4	22
Price	40	8-14	4-4	6	7	1	23
Ehlo	27	9-15	2-2	2	4	1	24
Rollins	15	0-1	0-0	0	0	2	0
Sanders	5	0-0	0-0	0	0	1	0
Valentine	6	0-0	0-0	0	1	2	0
Totals	240	36-71	21-24	34	28	20	100

Percentages: FG .507, FT .875. **Three-point goals:** 7-12, .583 (Ehlo 4-7; Price 3-4, Harper 0-1). **Team rebounds:** 7. **Blocked shots:** 7 (Williams 2, Harper 2, Nance 2, Daugherty). **Turnovers:** 18 (Price 7, Nance 4, Daugherty 3, Williams, Harper, Sanders, team). **Steals:** 7 (Daugherty 2, Harper 2, Williams, Nance, Price). **Technical fouls:** None. **Illegal defense:** None.

Bulls	24	22	23	32	101
Cavaliers	28	20	27	25	100

A: 20,273. **T:** 2:23. **Officials:** Jake O'Donnell, Jack Madden, Hugh Evans.

Cleveland came right back with a perfect inbounds play, as Craig Ehlo shook free from a screened Craig Hodges to sink an easy layup. One could only imagine the hundreds of thousands of heads instantly buried in hands back in Chicago.

In retrospect, Ehlo's move did feature one flaw. It required only 3 seconds, leaving three more precious ticks of the clock for Michael Time. Ever notice how, even at the most pressure-filled moments, Jordan always looks like he has all the time in the world?

In this instance, a Bulls' time-out allowed for everyone to catch their collective breaths. Michael used the opportunity to assure Hodges not to fret about allowing the last basket.

"Michael came up to me and said, 'Don't worry,' " Hodges recalled. "He said he was going to hit the shot. So I said, 'Go ahead and do it.' "

That was before the Bulls even huddled to discuss options. Chicago coach Doug Collins outlined two: Brad Sellers would throw the ball into play from mid-court, first looking for MJ running away from Craig Ehlo on a back screen from Bill Cartwright. If that didn't work, then Scottie Pippen was told to set a pick for Craig Hodges, who would shoot from the corner.

Sellers, not always a fan favorite in Chicago, made the historic correct play with split-second execution. Jordan did not get totally free of Ehlo or the intimidating Larry Nance, but squeezed his way to the free-throw line from a low position near the basket, and Sellers delivered a perfectly timed pass.

"From there, we figured Michael could shoot or take it to the hoop," said Collins.

Yet Jordan wasn't entirely confident in his free-throw capabilities. He was notably human in both Game 5 (9 of 13) and Game 4 (22 of 27, including a pair of misses in the final minute of the close loss). MJ was thinking jump shot.

The Cavs and 20,273 rowdy fans were thinking, No way. Ehlo swiped at the ball as Michael gathered the inbounds pass. Fatal mistake.

"It allowed me a step when he went for the ball," said Jordan. "So I came across [right to left], went up, hung, and then shot."

In what seemed an instant to Jordan, the ball's flight lasted far too long for Cleveland. The double-pumped fifteen-footer dramatically rippled the net for a 101–100 Bulls victory and a series knockout punch. Some reports called it sixteen feet, others eighteen feet, but what's a few feet when you are measuring miracles?

Michael's hang time is legendary, and was painfully apparent to Cavs center Brad Daugherty. "I just can't believe he made that shot," Daugherty said in a quiet, dejected Cleveland locker room. "We did everything right. I just can't believe it. "I don't see how he stayed in the air that long. It's the most outstanding shot I've ever seen."

The winning shot, the final two of MJ's 44 points, was not unlike the one he had missed at the buzzer in Game 4 two nights earlier at Chicago Stadium. Michael also missed those two late free throws, either of which would have the prevented the overtime period that Cleveland won to force a fifth deciding game.

Cleveland was 37–4 at home during the regular season and sported the league's second-best record. The impressive home record included six straight defeats of the Bulls before Michael and his teammates—the other eleven Chicago players called "dross" by one Cleveland columnist—snapped the spell in Game 1 of the postseason series. Worse, Michael had guaranteed his team would advance in four games.

"This is probably the biggest shot I've hit in the NBA, mainly because I put my credibility on the line," said Jordan. "I thought we could beat this team, but when we lost Friday after I missed that last free throw and last shot, it was the lowest I've ever felt in basketball. "Like when I was cut from my high school team [sophomore year], I was disappointed in myself. There were tears in my eyes. I had to swallow my pride, my words."

Inspiration came in those teardrops—and the shower. Civil rights leader Jesse Jackson, a Chicagoan and loyal fan, actually appeared while Michael was lathering up. Jackson told MJ to forget what happened and concentrate on Sunday.

"I had never been cheered up in the shower by a presidential candidate before," quipped a now smiling Jordan on Sunday.

Michael received even more consolation from his late father, who stayed by his side most every waking hour until game time in Richfield. MJ was most bothered—and even admitted a bit of fear—about missing the free throws on Friday night. He struggled at the line on Sunday, especially when you consider that most of his makes clanged around the rim before settling in the hoop.

"If I had taken it to the hole and got fouled, I didn't want to be at the free-throw line."

Honest talk, and hard to believe one decade and countless clutch free throws later. If somehow The Shot didn't fall, Jordan would have been left to brood all summer about missed chances to win the series in both Game 4 and Game 5.

More significantly, would such failure ever so subtly degenerate the unmatched Jordan confidence that fully manifested itself in the 1990s? No need to answer. Moot point. Instead, Jordan celebrated his game-winner in uncharacteristic fashion. He waved and pumped his fist at the Cleveland crowd, even yelling "Go home!"

Michael had been provoked. The Cavs fans were taunting him for predicting that the Bulls would win in four games, taunting his free-throw shooting, and mentioning the most dreaded word in sports, *choke,* maybe 25,000 times in the two and a half hours of this playoff thriller before Michael buried his jumper—from the free-throw stripe of all places.

"I shouldn't have yelled that," said Jordan later, "but they were telling me to set up my tee times and everything. "It's a lot of vindication."

To that point, The Shot was simply the most memorable clutch shot of Jordan's career. He told the media it was better than even his game-winner in the 1982 NCAA championship game for his beloved North Carolina Tar Heels. Since he came into the NBA, MJ has always worn a pair of powder-blue UNC shorts under his uniform each game for luck.

"I was unknown and a kid [in '82]," said Jordan. "I couldn't appreciate it."

Fame no longer eluded Michael. This game—and The

Shot—put him squarely in line for the coming glory years of the 1990s.

Number 4: Great Game Index

GGI Score (115 of a possible 123).

Scoring (33 of a possible 33)   His 44 points were almost half of the team's total. He hit makeable jumpers in the final minutes that other pros miss in such situations. The game-winning shot speaks volumes.

Game Importance (20 of 20)   Can't ask for more. It was the deciding final seconds of the deciding game of the series.

Opponent Strength (19 of 20)   Cleveland was the league's second-best team during the regular season.

Historical Significance (10 of 10)   The game-winner still stands as one of the top five Jordan shots of all time. The series victory jump-started the future Bulls championship teams and deflated a formidable rival in the process.

Legendary Intangibles (10 of 10)   Up to now, Jordan's long hang time came in spectacular slam dunks. The Shot was a more subtle—and ultimately more resounding—example of Michael's incomparable vertical jump.

Pressure Points (10 of 10)   Three seconds left in the do-or-die final game of a playoff series, after Michael had missed a similar shot in the previous game loss. Enough said.

Defense (3 of 5)   Nothing spectacular, but solid.

Other Offensive Contributions (4 of 5)   Michael was making sure other Bulls were in the flow of offense. He was active on the boards.

MJ's Physical Condition (1 of 5)   Not a factor.

Long Odds (5 of 5)   The Bulls had lost seven of their last eight meetings at Richfield Coliseum. The crowd was frenzied. The Cavs were matching the Bulls blow for blow in the series.

-5-

March 28, 1995

Bulls at New York Knicks Regular Season

Big hit in the Big Apple: Michael bags 55 early in a comeback.

New York is crammed with big names and bigger performances, but this town always finds extra room when Michael Jordan checks in at Madison Square Garden. In only his fifth game since making his comeback after self-induced retirement, Michael lit up the Knicks for 55 bright lights. The usually tough New York crowd could only applaud with mouths agape.

Michael racked up the most single-game points and field goals of the 1994–95 season while breaking his own Garden record for points scored by a Knicks opponent, and all this after four games and eight practices. As a bonus, he helped the again-proud Bulls beat the Knicks for the first time since Game 5 of the 1993 NBA Finals. While Jordan was chasing baseball dreams, his teammates were whiffing against rival New York. The momentum was most certainly shifting.

"I'm here to win, to enjoy the game, and win championships," he explained in a standing-room-only press room after his Garden coming-back-out party. "I'm not here to chase

Game 5: Bulls 113, Knicks 111

Bulls	Min	FG-att	FT-att	Reb	Ast	Fls	Pts
Kukoc	30	1-6	0-0	9	1	6	3
Pippen	41	7-12	4-5	9	8	4	19
Perdue	21	3-4	0-0	2	0	6	6
Armstrong	42	4-5	6-7	1	2	2	16
Jordan	39	21-37	10-11	4	2	3	55
Blount	15	1-1	0-0	4	0	4	2
Myers	5	0-1	0-0	1	0	0	0
Krystkowiak	6	0-0	0-0	0	0	0	0
Longley	22	2-6	1-2	5	0	6	5
Kerr	14	2-5	0-0	0	0	1	5
Wennington	5	1-1	0-0	0	0	3	2
Totals	**240**	**42-78**	**21-25**	**35**	**13**	**35**	**113**

Percentages: FG. 538, FT .840. **Three-point goals:** 8-15, 533 (Jordan 3-4, Armstrong 2-2, Kukoc 1-2, Kerr 1-3, Pippen 1-4). **Team rebounds:** 6. **Blocked shots:** 4 (Perdue 2, Longley 2). **Turnovers:** 16 (Kukoc 5, Blount 3, Armstrong 2, Jordan 2, Pippen, Myers, Krystkowiak, Longley). **Steals:** 6 (Pippen 2, Kukoc, Armstrong, Jordan, Krystkowiak). **Technical fouls:** None. **Illegal defense:** None.

Knicks	Min	FG-att	FT-att	Reb	Ast	Fls	Pts
Bonner	27	4-6	4-4	5	3	3	12
Oakley	25	4-5	0-0	8	2	4	8
Ewing	42	10-21	16-23	7	2	3	36
Harper	37	7-11	0-0	3	7	2	14
Starks	34	4-10	5-6	3	4	5	14
Smith	22	3-6	2-5	3	2	3	8
Mason	22	3-3	4-6	5	4	1	10
Davis	14	2-3	0-0	1	1	0	4
Anthony	11	1-2	0-0	0	1	3	3
H. Williams	6	1-4	0-0	1	0	1	2
Totals	**240**	**39-71**	**31-44**	**13-36**	**26**	**25**	**111**

Percentages: FG .549, FT .705. **Three-point goals:** 2-11, .182 (Anthony 1-1, Starks 1-7, Smith 0-1, Harper 0-2). **Team rebounds:** 8. **Blocked shots:** 5 (Ewing 4, H. Williams). **Turnovers:** 14 (Bonner 3, Starks 3, Oakley 2, Ewing, Davis, Anthony, H. Williams). **Steals:** 10 (Bonner 3, Ewing 3, Smith 2, Oakley, Mason). **Technical fouls:** Oakley, 5:35 1st; Harper, 5:19 3rd; illegal defense 6:53 1st. **Illegal defense:** 1.

Bulls	31	19	32	31	113
Knicks	34	22	26	29	111

A: 19,763 (19,763). **T:** 2:27. **Officials:** Bennett Salvatore, Lee Jones, Monte McCutchen

individual accolades. I want to win another title; I want to win for Chicago."

Earl Monroe, the Knicks star who played on championship teams with Bulls coach Phil Jackson, watched from the front row. He registered the noise made each time Jordan drained another jumper or drove from all areas of the Bulls upcourt. He appreciated the unique Jordan rhythm that was returning to the NBA jukebox.

"It's like he never left," Monroe said.

Mike Lupica, the *New York Daily News* columnist and sports voice for the whole city, realized this game was about more than 55 points and a 113–111 Bulls victory.

"This was more than Jordan coming back to Madison Square Garden and a rivalry with the Knicks," Lupica wrote. "This was Jordan showing he still is in the business of wonder. The only game in town now was Jordan against himself. We know Jordan's best move now. The best move was simply coming back to nights like this."

Mark Kriegel, another *Daily News* columnist, added: "A few weeks ago, Michael Jordan was a minor leaguer. Tuesday night, he was the national pastime."

Beside relighting a countrywide flame, Jordan scorched John Starks for 20 of his team's 31 points in the first quarter on 9-for-11 shooting. He had 35 by the half, making 14 of 19. He added 20 points in the second half, as the Bulls stayed even with a team nine games ahead of them in the conference standings.

The performance marked the thirty-fourth time Michael had busted the 50-point barrier in his career, but it didn't even make his top ten scoring nights. Nobody on the Bulls bench was complaining, and Knicks coach Pat Riley put the scoring total in perspective after seeing his team lose.

"There are some players that are simply unique and transcend every aspect of the game," said Riley. "Michael's the only one in the history of the game who has had the impact he has had, all the way around."

Michael carried the team that night on his ever-broader shoulders (he added about ten pounds of muscle to a near fat-free body during his flirtation with baseball)—but he stuck to team values in the end.

His last field goal was a clutch jump shot with less than a half-minute left to put the Bulls up, 111–109.

The Knicks tied it on a pair of Starks free throws, but even Pat Riley knew too much time—14.6 seconds—remained on the clock. No one needed a stat sheet to gauge Jordan's offensive output.

The Bulls huddled during a time-out to plot strategy, which resulted in a familiar one for coach Phil Jackson in recent days: put the ball in Michael's hands.

Jordan took the inbounds pass, then dribbled toward the expectant Knicks. He started to drive the lane, whisking past an outmatched John Starks. Star center Patrick Ewing was waiting. He stepped over to block the anticipated shot, but Michael's basketball mind was already in peak shape. He found Ewing's forgotten assignment, Bulls reserve center Bill Wennington, who promptly dunked for his first points of the night and a 113–111 lead.

No one was watching Wennington, except perhaps a few buddies from his St. John's University playing days.

"I would be lying if I said I came out to pass the ball," explained Jordan later, "but they had to stop me from shooting and they did. But I was able to move the ball to an open man."

Jordan had learned from an earlier encounter in the game, showing his penchant for never giving an opponent the same move twice.

"I just remedied a situation [that happened] previously when I seemed to have Starks beat and Patrick came over [to block the shot]."

The Knicks did have one last gasp in the final 3.1 seconds, but Jordan—who else?—forced Starks to mishandle an inbounds pass. The game was over, and the Bulls had improved to their best record of the season, something that would become a habit during the last twelve games with Jordan in the lineup.

"Jordan will change the Bulls," concluded Pat Riley after the 55-point viewing. "He'll change their whole approach, their belief pattern. They'll become a more enthusiastic team. They'll believe they have a chance. I think that's what his power is. Anyone who's around him believes they can conquer anybody."

Just ask the well-traveled Wennington, someone who has always fought to keep his job in every training camp of his NBA career but rose to cult status in Chicago, even having McDonald's name a sandwich after him. When Jordan sat down for a breather during the first half of this magnificent Knicks game, he plopped next to Wennington and looked him square in the eye. "I hate losing," Jordan said to his new teammate.

Wennington was getting the idea.

Number 5: Great Game Index

GGI Score (114 of a possible 123).

Scoring (33 of 33)   Michael scored on six of his first seven field-goal attempts. He was 9 of 11 in the first quarter for 20 points, then 14 of 19 by halftime for 35. After three quarters, he already had 49 points and no opponent would be thinking about the proffered theory that maybe MJ had lost his jump-shooting touch. Michael finished the night 21 of 37 from the floor, plus 10 for 11 at the free-throw line and 3 for 4 behind the three-point arc. He hit a pivotal sixteen-footer for the lead with 25.8 seconds left and acted as a decoy on the game-winner. Fans who paid scalpers as much as $1,500 per seat were not disappointed (that's a little more than $27 per point).

Game Importance (17 of 20)   The Bulls were attempting to make up some ground in the Eastern Conference standings now that Jordan was back for the playoff run.

Opponent Strength (18 of 20)   The Knicks were about at the height of their abilities as a team during the Ewing era.

Historical Significance (10 of 10)   Michael convinced himself—erasing what were minuscule doubts—that he was ready to return as the NBA's dominant force. More importantly, he inspired his (mostly new) teammates.

Legendary Intangibles (10 of 10)   New York and Michael Jordan are a sublime combination, and this is the best of Michael's many Garden appearances. He revels in the big-crowd, all-eyes-watching atmosphere, and appreciates Knicks fans' knowledge of the game.

Pressure Points (10 of 10)   MJ had been struggling with his outside shooting. People were whispering that maybe he should have waited until the following fall to return, if at all. The Bulls needed every one of Michael's field goals to win this game in an arena that stifles more than one NBA superstar.

Defense (4 of 5)   High-energy night, highlighted by knocking the ball from John Starks's hands with the game in the balance.

Other Offensive Contributions (3 of 5)   Michael had only two assists, but one marked the game-winning play. His rebounds were minimal, at 4, but he had only 2 turnovers.

MJ's Physical Condition (5 of 5)   He came into New York with little more than a week of practices and games to round into shape. He logged thirty-nine electrifying minutes; only Pippen and Ewing played more. MJ was playing with sore ankles, still catching up to the demanding moves of being Michael Jordan.

Long Odds (4 of 5)   He scored 50 points before at the new Garden, and he would do it again (once in 1998 while wearing his retro-1984 Air Jordan shoes on national TV), but hitting those numbers—and dishing off the game-winning assist—is not the usual outcome when a player returns after a near two-season layoff.

-6-

March 29, 1982

North Carolina vs. Georgetown, NCAA Championship Game

Freshman Jordan sinks the game-winner.

*T*he origins of this pinnacle night in Michael's college career started in fall practice, when the freshman from Wilmington, North Carolina, played his way onto the starting five of what would become a top-ranked North Carolina team. James Worthy and Sam Perkins were the acclaimed stars, but Jordan turned the head of legendary coach Dean Smith during the first few workouts, especially during one-on-one drills.

"We didn't have anybody who could guard him," recalls Smith.

Georgetown coach John Thompson was probably thinking the same thing in the frenetic final minutes of the 1982 title game, which resulted in the closest outcome of the previous two decades. MJ hit three of Carolina's last five field goals and set up the other two with a rebound and a steal. He scored 12 of his 16 points in the second half.

Game 6: North Carolina 63, Georgetown 62

Georgetown	Min	FG-att	FT-att	Ast	Reb	Fls	Pts
Smith	35	6-8	2-2	5	3	5	14
Hancock	8	0-2	0-0	0	0	1	0
Ewing	37	10-15	3-3	1	11	4	23
Brown	29	1-2	2-2	5	2	4	4
Floyd	39	9-17	0-0	5	3	2	18
Spriggs	30	0-2	1-2	0	1	2	1
Jones	10	1-3	0-0	0	0	0	2
Martin	5	0-2	0-0	0	0	1	0
Smith	7	0-0	0-0	0	0	1	0
Totals	**200**	**27-51**	**8-9**	**16**	**22**	**20**	**62**

Percentages: FG. 529, FT .889. **Team rebounds:** 2. **Turnovers:** 12 (Brown 4). **Steals:** 11 (Floyd 4, Ewing 3). **Blocked shots:** 2 (Ewing).

North Carolina	Min	FG-att	FT-att	Ast	Reb	Fls	Pts
Doherty	39	1-3	2-3	1	3	0	4
Worthy	38	13-17	2-7	0	4	3	28
Perkins	38	3-7	2-6	1	7	2	10
Black	38	1-4	2-2	7	3	2	4
Jordan	39	7-13	2-2	2	9	2	16
Peterson	7	0-3	0-0	1	1	0	0
Braddock	2	0-0	0-0	1	0	1	0
Brust	4	0-0	1-2	1	1	1	1
Totals	**200**	**25-47**	**13-22**	**14**	**30**	**11**	**63**

Percentages: FG .532, FT .591. **Team rebounds:** 2. **Turnovers:** 13 (Doherty, Worthy, Jordan 3). **Steals:** 7 (Worthy 3). **Blocked shots:** 1 (Perkins).

Georgetown	32	30	62
North Carolina	31	32	63

Officials: John Dabrow (Big Eight); Bobby Dibbler (WAC); Hank Nichols (Metro).
A: 61,612. **Tournament MVP:** Worthy.

Of course, the shot everyone remembers was the last attempt, from about sixteen feet out with fifteen seconds left. The now-famous Jordan swish put the Tar Heels back in the lead, 63–62, against Georgetown and another impressive freshman named Patrick Ewing. It held as the final score when Hoya guard Fred Brown mistakenly passed to Worthy, thinking he was teammate Eric "Sleepy" Floyd.

"Left corner, sixty-three thousand fans," remembered Jordan nearly ten years later when returning to the Superdome in New Orleans for an exhibition with the newly crowned world champion Bulls. "I feel the shot propelled my career."

While Worthy, who scored 28 points in the championship final, was named Most Valuable Player of the NCAA tourney, Jordan was the most influential Tar Heel in the game's last dozen possessions. Twice he pulled down rebounds of missed Carolina free throws; he had 9 rebounds on the night.

With 2:30 left, Michael shot a rainbow over the looming, outstretched arm of Ewing to give North Carolina a 3-point cushion, but Georgetown roared back to go up, 62–61 with just less than a minute remaining. North Carolina worked the ball up-court, then called a time-out with thirty-two ticks left on the clock.

In the team huddle, Smith considered his options. Worthy and Perkins were sure targets of Georgetown coach John Thompson's defensive schemes. Ewing was an intimidating force in the middle. So the veteran coach, in his sixth trip to the Final Four with North Carolina teams—and in a fourth title game—put his hopes of winning his first NCAA championship in the hands of a freshman.

North Carolina guard Jimmy Black explained the plan: "Against their zone, we wanted to swing the zone to my side and pass crosscourt to Michael, where he could have a fifteen-foot jump shot."

The play worked to perfection, as Black and Jordan traded passes for several seconds. Then Black whipped a bullet to a cutting Matt Doherty, who promptly returned it to Black, who made the crosscourt feed to Michael. The freshman didn't disappoint Smith for believing in him.

"James Worthy told me he was in position to tap it in if it had been missed," said Jordan after the game, "but it felt good all the way."

The shot marked what has turned out to be an unparalleled career in hitting pressure shots in big games. For his part, Jordan appeared well past his first-half nervousness, which prompted Smith to later note that Jordan "made some good plays" and "some mistakes."

"Pressure? You don't think about it then," said Jordan.

What Michael has thought about over the years was the success of the game-winning shot. Bulls coach Phil Jackson, who encourages his players to use visualization techniques to "see" and imagine success before competition, says that Jordan has used the 1982 title game for reassurance during tight moments of NBA playoff games. Jackson explains it less as actual visualization and more of a "Okay, I've been here before" approach.

Smith tells a revealing story about the time-out discussions to set up the Tar Heels' final play: "We knew Georgetown was going to be in a zone. [Sam] Perkins and [James] Worthy were the two key guys. They covered Worthy, but Perkins was wide open on the other side." The ball, however, ended up in Jordan's hands, and he had the confidence to take the available shot as the precious seconds ticked down. Smith himself planted the seed, pulling his freshman guard aside before the time-out ended. "If it comes to you, knock it in, Michael," said Smith.

Jordan was appreciatively all-ears and remained so years later.

"I guess maybe the first time you're nervous, but once you get more successful, you get more confident at it," said Jordan one time when asked about his ability to stay calm in the most pressurized junctures of a game. "My biggest confidence came with Coach Smith telling me, 'If you're open, take it. Don't think about it.' That's all you need. I could live with the consequences because I had his endorsement."

Smith, no easy touch, was most impressed with Jordan's work habits. It is a sentiment echoed by every coach and teammate who has ever worked with Jordan in the gym when no fans or even media are watching.

"He was just remarkable as a practice player," says Smith. "From his sophomore year on, every team we put him on would win."

Jordan said he actually had a premonition about taking the decisive shot before ever stepping foot on the court. By the night's end, he didn't need to imagine a single thing. He knew his career would be taking off. The only question was how fast and how far.

Number 6: Great Game Index

GGI Score (112 of a possible 123).

Scoring (32 of possible 33)   Michael was the difference down the stretch for North Carolina—and he didn't miss when it counted.

Game Importance (20 of 20)   Doesn't get any more vital.

Opponent Strength (16 of 20)   Georgetown was a solid college team with budding superstar Ewing, but they still would have lost on most nights in the NBA. North Carolina clearly met its match in one of the best NCAA finals ever.

Historical Significance (10 of 10)   Michael's first championship night, Michael's introduction to the American public, Dean Smith's first national title—and the beginning of long series of frustrations for Ewing against Jordan.

Legendary Intangibles (10 of 10)   Smith pulled Jordan aside and told him he could do it. Michael was anything but nervous. The pep talk only inspired him.

Pressure Points (10 of 10)   Not only was this a nationally televised game for the national title but more than 61,000 fans attended the Superdome event. That's a lot of eyes on your shot for the trophy.

Defense (4 of 5)   Jordan and Ewing were the best defensive players on the floor in the second half. A key Jordan steal set up a late North Carolina basket.

Other Offensive Contributions (4 of 5)   Jordan's 9 rebounds included several that kept offensive possessions alive. Michael's play during the Atlantic Coast Conference tournament forced opposing coaches to spread out defensive maneuvers beyond Worthy and Perkins.

MJ's Physical Condition (1 of 5)   Not a factor.

Long Odds (5 of 5)   Two years earlier, Jordan attended summer basketball camps and went unnoticed by Division I coaches and scouts. One year earlier, he didn't make a popular list of the top three hundred college basketball prospects. Michael wrote UCLA about a possible scholarship and received no answer. A similar letter to the University of Virginia produced only the standard undergraduate student application. His own high school principal urged him to attend the U.S. Air Force Academy to at least get a good education.

-7-

June 5, 1991

Los Angeles Lakers at Bulls Game 2, NBA Finals

━━━━━━

Jordan spurs the Bulls to even the series, and makes an impossible shot.

━━━━━━

Flight 7:47 took off with just under 8 minutes left in this critical game of the Bulls' first-ever NBA Finals. It was a fitting liftoff time for a shot people still talk about at sports bars, sweaty gyms, playgrounds, family rooms, and wherever else basketball has rocketed its way to ultimate popularity by flying in Michael Jordan's airspace.

In the midst of a 15–2 Bull run that sunk the Lakers like cement in their sneakers (for the series, it turned out), Jordan scored on an incredible, seemingly unmakeable, wouldn't-believe-it-unless-I-saw-it-with-my-own-eyes shot.

Michael started by flying in the air down the offensive lane on one of his resounding slam dunks, but North Carolina alum and ex-teammate Sam Perkins stepped in Jordan's path. So MJ adjusted like no other gravity-bound player on this planet: As his body soared upward, he brought the ball down while switching it from his right hand to his left. Then he rotated his

Game 7: Bulls 107, Lakers 86

Lakers	Min	FG-att	FT-att	Reb	Ast	Fls	Pts
Perkins	35	4-8	2-2	6	0	2	11
Worthy	40	9-17	5-6	5	1	1	24
Divac	41	7-11	2-2	5	5	2	16
Scott	26	2-2	0-0	0	2	4	5
Johnson	43	4-13	6-6	7	10	2	14
Thompson	10	0-3	0-0	0	0	1	0
Green	22	2-11	0-0	7	0	2	6
Teagle	14	0-2	6-6	1	1	1	6
Drew	5	2-4	0-0	1	0	0	4
Campbell	4	0-2	0-0	2	0	0	0
Totals	240	30-73	21-22	34	19	15	86

Percentages: FG .411. FT .955. **Three-point goals:** 5-12, .417. **Team rebounds:** 5. **Blocked shots:** 2 (Divac, Campbell). **Turnovers:** 17 (Worthy 4, Johnson 4, Perkins 3, Divac 2, Teagle 2, Thompson, Campbell). **Steals:** 8 (Divac 3, Johnson 2, Scott, Green Campbell). **Technical fouls:** 1, illegal defense, 9:40. 4th quarter. **Flagrant fouls:** Scott. 8:05, 3rd quarter.

Bulls	Min	FG-att	FT-att	Reb	Ast	Fls	Pts
Pippen	44	8-16	4-4	5	10	4	20
Grant	40	10-13	0-0	5	1	1	20
Cartwright	24	6-9	0-0	5	1	1	12
Paxson	25	8-8	0-0	0	6	2	16
Jordan	36	15-18	3-4	7	13	4	33
Levingston	22	0-2	0-0	1	2	4	0
Hodges	11	1-6	0-0	1	0	1	2
Perdue	11	1-3	0-0	7	1	0	2
Armstrong	7	0-2	0-0	1	1	0	0
Williams	15	1-1	0-0	3	0	2	2
King	3	0-3	0-0	1	0	1	0
Hopson	2	0-0	0-0	0	0	0	0
Totals	240	50-81	7-8	36	35	20	107

Percentages: FG .617, FT .875. **Three-point goals:** 0-5, .000. **Team rebounds:** 1. **Blocked shots:** 1 (Jordan). **Turnovers:** 14 (Pippen 5, Jordan 4, Cartwright 2, Grant, Perdue, King.) **Steals:** 10 (Grant 2, Cartwright 2, Jordan 2, Levingston 2, Pippen, Paxson). **Technical fouls:** None. **Illegal defense:** 1.

Lakers	23	20	26	17	86
Bulls	28	20	38	21	107

A: 18,676. **T:** 2:10. **Officials:** J. Kersey, M. Mathis, J. O'Donnell.

body in mid-dunk, twisting it to avoid Perkins and keep his balance, before banking the ball off the glass for two points before landing.

Though it is difficult for an artist to recall exactly how masterpieces are created, Jordan attempted to explain the play to reporters after the 107–86 wipeout. He talked about improvising.

"I first intended to dunk the ball," Jordan said, "but once I got up in the air I didn't think I had enough room. I thought I was going to fall short of the rim, so I switched hands and laid it in. I probably couldn't duplicate if I tried. It was just one of those things."

"He did the impossible, the unbelievable," said Magic Johnson, simply and honestly with more than a hint of awe in his voice.

The rest of Michael's night wasn't any less spectacular. After a Game 1 loss, the Bulls were looking to regain their momentum before heading out to L.A. for three games. Michael finished with 15-of-18 shooting—10 of 11 in the second half—and 33 points overall.

At one point, MJ, who is no shy talker on the court, even glared at the Lakers' bench and raised his palms as if to say, "You got anybody who can beat me?"

Jordan didn't stop at near-perfect shooting. He handed out 13 assists, getting teammates involved in the resurrection of championship-level ball. John Paxson, a perfect 8 for 8 from the field, was the biggest beneficiary. Michael also hauled down 7 rebounds and played ferocious defense (he finished with 2 steals and a block).

"I was surprised we won by the margin we did," said Jordan after the game. "But we reverted to what we had been doing the twelve playoff games before Game 1 [of the NBA Finals]. We picked up our defensive intensity and got everyone involved."

Perhaps more tellingly, Jordan's teammates recognized Michael's renewed competitive intensity—he did a lot of glaring in this game, especially in the early minutes—well enough to know it was time to pump up the volume. While Michael scored only 2 points in the opening quarter, the team raced to 28–23 advantage.

The Lakers clawed back to take a 36–35 lead with just less

than five minutes left in the first half, but MJ proceeded to score 8 straight for the Bulls, securing a halftime margin that only expanded in the second half. Jordan put on a coaches' clinic by finding every seam in the Lakers' defense, but he saved his best demonstration for the runway special with 7:47 remaining in the game.

"They plain ol' whipped us," said Magic Johnson, a decidedly lesser light in this installment of the ballyhooed Michael-Magic Show.

"When Michael gets going, he can roll over the top of teams," said Bulls coach Phil Jackson.

Number 7: Great Game Index

GGI Score (111 of a possible 123)   The tiebreaker is opponent strength.

Scoring (32 of a possible 33)   MJ scored when the Bulls needed him most, hitting eight straight to keep the lead at halftime, then pouring in 14 points during a third quarter in which Chicago outscored L.A. 38–26. Jordan shot 83 percent for night, including the almost perfect 10 for 11 in the second half.

Game Importance (19 of 20)   Losing the first two games at home in the 2-3-2 NBA Finals format was a disadvantage even Michael Jordan didn't want to have to overcome.

Opponent Strength (19 of 20)   This was an unflappable Lakers team that wavered from Jordan's knockout blows.

Historical Significance (9 of 10)   The game put the Bulls back in a confident, winning state of mind. Nobody forgets the 7:47 move.

Legendary Intangibles (10 of 10)   Michael's midair switching from a slam dunk to a bank shot would be called a miracle if any other player pulled off the same thing (that includes you,

Magic, and Dr. J, and Kobe, for that matter), but with Michael, the unbelievable is believable.

Pressure Points (9 of 10)   When the game was in doubt in the second quarter—and the Bulls team psyche was on the ropes—Jordan rode to the rescue.

Defense (3 of 5)   Another solid night that included a block, 2 steals, and several frustrated Lakers stars.

Other Offensive Contributions (5 of 5)   Thirteen assists and 7 rebounds were both game highs. Most importantly, Jordan made sure every fellow starter got in the offensive flow. The first five all recorded double-figures scoring for the night.

MJ's Physical Condition (1 of 5)   Not a factor.

Long Odds (4 of 5)   Shooting 15 of 18 is tough on any court—but this was the NBA Finals.

-8-

June 16, 1993

Phoenix Suns at Bulls Game 4, NBA Finals

━━━━━━

Jordan hits 55, including the game-winner, as the Bulls take command.

━━━━━━

F ans at Chicago Stadium were all feeling a little younger after this victory. How could they not, as they watched Michael Jordan play a game more characteristic of his earlier days in the NBA? He came out slashing to the basket from the opening tip, consistently scoring on drives to the hoop in the first half. The punctuation point was a soaring one-handed jam over a beleaguered and seemingly feet-glued-to-the-floor Danny Ainge with fifty seconds remaining before intermission.

The entire Suns team had to be trying to shake off Michael's retro show. Jordan scored 33 points in the first half against Phoenix guard Kevin Johnson on 14-of-20 shooting. He nailed 22 points in the second quarter alone, including a run of 16 straight Bulls points.

Check the calendar—was it 1993? Because it sure looked a lot like Air Jordan, circa 1988 or 1989.

The Bulls had dropped a triple overtime loss to the Suns and Charles Barkley in Game 3 to allow Phoenix back into the

Game 8: Bulls 111, Suns 105

Suns	Min	FG-att	FT-att	Reb	Ast	Fls	Pts
Dumas	25	8-11	1-1	1	0	3	17
Barkley	46	10-19	12-15	12	10	1	32
West	19	3-5	2-2	4	0	6	8
K. Johnson	43	7-16	5-6	3	4	3	19
Majerle	46	3-9	1-3	5	3	1	14
Miller	14	1-3	0-0	2	1	5	2
Chambers	23	1-9	5-6	4	0	4	7
Ainge	21	1-5	0-0	3	2	3	2
F. Johnson	3	2-2	0-0	0	0	2	4
Totals	**240**	**38-79**	**26-33**	**34**	**20**	**28**	**105**

Percentages: FG .481, FT .788. **Three-point goals** 3-8, .375 (Majerle 3-5, Miller 0-1, Barkley 0-2). **Team rebounds:** 11. **Blocked shots:** 3 (Barkley, West, Majerle). **Turnovers:** 10 (K. Johnson 3, Dumas 2, Barkley, West, Miller, Chambers, Ainge). **Steals:** 6 (Barkley 3, Dumas, Miller, F. Johnson). **Technical foul:** Ainge, 2:20 4th. **Illegal defense:** 1.

Bulls	Min	FG-att	FT-att	Reb	Ast	Fls	Pts
Pippen	44	7-14	0-2	6	10	1	14
Grant	37	7-11	3-6	16	2	5	17
Cartwright	30	1-4	1-2	5	2	4	3
Armstrong	35	4-10	2-2	2	6	2	11
Jordan	46	21-37	13-18	8	4	3	56
McCray	4	0-0	0-0	1	0	0	0
Tucker	1	0-0	0-0	0	0	0	0
Paxson	18	2-5	0-0	3	1	2	6
King	9	1-1	1-2	0	0	3	3
S. Williams	14	1-1	0-0	1	0	6	2
Walker	2	0-0	0-1	0	1	0	0
Totals	**240**	**44-83**	**20-33**	**42**	**26**	**26**	**111**

Percentages: FG .550, FT .606. **Three-point goals:** 3-9 (Paxson 2-4, Armstrong 1-2, Jordan 0-1, Pippen 0-2). **Team rebounds:** 13. **Blocked shots:** 5 (Grant 3, Armstrong, S. Williams). **Turnovers:** 10 (Pippen 6, Armstrong, Jordan, McCray, Paxson). **Steals:** 8 (Grant 3, Armstrong 3, Pippen, King). **Technical foul:** Jordan, 2:20 4th. **Flagrant foul:** Armstrong, 1:19 1st. **Illegal defense:** None.

Suns	27	31	23	24	105
Bulls	31	30	25	25	111

A: 18,676. **T:** 2:41. **Officials:** Hugh Evans, Bill Oakes, Ed T. Rush.

series. Johnson boasted about taking away Michael's first step on drives, explaining how he held Jordan to "only" 44 points in the loss.

The bragging rights didn't last long. MJ freeze-dried the

Suns' Johnson—and reinforcements Dan Majerle and Richard Dumas—for 55 points on the night, which tied him with Rick Barry (1967) for second-place behind only Elgin Baylor (1962), for the highest single-game point total in a NBA Finals game. He was the fifth player in history to notch a 50-plus game in the Finals (Jerry West and Bob Pettit were the others). It was a superior show from a star who admitted to "losing his legs" in the late stages of the Game 3 loss.

No problem with the wheels in Game 4.

"I really didn't sense myself taking over the ball game," said Jordan. "I felt myself penetrating, trying to get easier baskets, and I felt myself capitalizing on the defense.

"One thing led to another. The next thing you know I was more or less in rhythm. I was really nervous about doing it, because I didn't want my teammates to get to the point where they'd start standing around."

This game remained close to the end, and Michael saved his best for last. The Suns didn't let any Bulls lead build too high.

With thirty seconds left and the Bulls clinging to a 106–105 lead, Bulls guard B. J. Armstrong stole an Ainge pass intended for Johnson and quickly moved the ball to Jordan. MJ did the rest, bringing the ball up-court and scissoring through the middle of the Suns' defense on his determined path to the hoop. He scored on the layup and got fouled.

He sank the free throw to turn out the lights on any realistic chances of the Suns winning the title. Jordan and the Bulls were one win away from three straight titles, a feat reached two nights later that was never pulled off by either Magic Johnson and the Lakers or Larry Bird and his Celtics teammates.

Even Charles Barkley looked discouraged when his buddy Michael canned the free throw for a two-possession lead. Phoenix coach Paul Westphal's postgame comments sounded suspiciously like a concession speech: "I don't think even Michael can stop Michael. It's important to acknowledge reality when it comes to guarding Michael Jordan. All you can do is try to make Michael work for his shots.

"I'm as much in awe of Michael Jordan as anyone else. He's the best offensive point guard and defensive point guard of all time, the best offensive and defensive two guard, the best offensive and defensive small forward, and he's probably right up there in the top five at power forward and center."

Number 8: Great Game Index

GGI Score (111 of a possible 123).

Scoring (33 of a possible 33)   Michael lit up the scoreboard for just under half of his team's points in the 111–105 win that put the Bulls on the brink of a third straight title. He scored at all the key times, including the Sun-scorcher in the last minute.

He had 33 of the Bulls' 61 first-half points. He finished with 21-for-37 shooting and 13 of 18 from the free-throw line (after getting many fewer calls in Game 3). His second-quarter line alone was 9 of 12 for 22 points, just 3 shy of Detroit star Isiah Thomas's Finals record for a quarter.

Game Importance (19 of 20)   Letting the Suns draw even in the series was not an option, since Games 6 and 7 would be back in Phoenix.

Opponent Strength (18 of 20)   Charles Barkley is a bona fide all-time NBA great. He notched a triple-double with 32 points, 12 rebounds, and 10 assists. His teammates were a solid, if not all-time, group. They won 2 of 3 in Chicago during these Finals.

Historical Significance (10 of 10)   Michael became one of only five players to score 50 or more points in a Finals game. Elgin Baylor, Rick Barry, Jerry West, and Bob Pettit are impressively exclusive company.

Legendary Intangibles (10 of 10)   MJ stepped up when the Bulls needed him. While the 1993 Jordan was more intent on spreading the offensive wealth—as evidenced by the output of B. J. Armstrong and John Paxson in the subsequent Game 6 clincher—no one else was up to the task this night.

Pressure Points (10 of 10)   Michael made all the plays—on offense and defense. The series outcome was in doubt before the game started. That uncertainty was cleared up.

Defense (3 of 5)   Another solid night.

Other Offensive Contributions (3 of 5)   Michael exhorted his teammates at every critical point of the game and tossed in a few assists and rebounds for good measure.

MJ's Physical Condition (1 of 5)   Not a factor.

Long Odds (4 of 5)   Even in his ninth season, Michael kept defying gravity as if he had a rookie's spring in his legs. Scoring 50 points is always rare, and even rarer in the NBA Finals.

-9-

June 13, 1997

Utah Jazz at Bulls Game 6 Clincher, NBA Finals

Jordan scores 39, but the key play is a pass to Steve Kerr.

The silence lasted a good thirty seconds. Bulls guard Steve Kerr was watching Michael Jordan during Chicago's final time-out of the 1997 playoffs. Kerr could see Michael was thinking, visualizing the next court sequence before it ever happened—sort of like Superman seeing through walls with his X-ray vision.

"Be ready," Jordan said to his teammate, "Stockton's coming off [his man Kerr]."

That's exactly what happened. Michael had the ball inside the three-point line on the left side of the court, blanketed by Utah's Bryon Russell. The All-Star Stockton raced over from the top of the key to double-team Jordan. It left Kerr wide open.

Jordan actually split the two defenders and had room to shoot, but he didn't hesitate flipping a pass to Kerr, who had struggled with his shooting touch the entire Finals. The reserve drained this wide-open seventeen-footer with 5 seconds on the game clock for the title and Michael's lifetime endorsement.

MJ may have lost the 1997 MVP vote to Karl Malone, but he came out on top when it counted most. *Reuters/Sue Ogrocki/Archive Photos*

"Steve Kerr earned his wings tonight from my perspective," said Jordan in a jubilant postgame press conference. "I don't think he would have slept this summer if he missed that shot."

Jordan was a bit sluggish himself in the early stages of this 90–86 thriller that clinched the Bulls fifth NBA title in seven years (and five of six with Michael in the playoffs). He was still recovering from a nasty bout with food poisoning that he spectacularly overcame in Game 5 (see Game No. 2 in the Jordan 50), but he dazzled the Jazz in the second half with 13 points in the third quarter and another 10 in the tense fourth quarter.

Game 9: Bulls 90, Jazz 86

Jazz	Min	FG-att	FT-att	Reb	Ast	Fls	Pts
Russell	43	5-10	2-2	3	0	4	17
Malone	44	7-15	7-15	7	2	3	21
Ostertag	21	0-2	1-2	8	2	3	1
Stockton	37	5-9	3-3	6	5	3	13
Hornacek	36	4-9	8-9	4	1	5	18
Eisley	11	2-5	2-2	0	3	1	6
Foster	5	0-1	0-0	2	0	1	0
Carr	6	1-2	0-0	0	1	1	2
Anderson	26	2-10	4-6	3	0	1	8
Morris	11	0-2	0-0	3	0	3	0
Totals	**240**	**26-65**	**27-39**	**36**	**14**	**25**	**86**

Percentages: FG .400, FT .692. **Three-point goals:** 7-15, .467 (Russell 5-8, Hornacek 2-4, Stockton 0-1, Anderson 0-1, Morris 0-1). **Team rebounds:** 16. **Blocked shots:** 6 (Ostertag 4, Stockton 2). **Turnovers:** 11 (Russell 3, Stockton 3, Malone 2, Ostertag, Eisley, Morris). **Steals:** 8 (Malone 4, Russell, Stockton, Hornacek, Anderson). **Technical fouls:** Malone, 0:0.6 2d. **Flagrant fouls:** Ostertag 5:15 3d. **Illegal defense:** 1.

Bulls	Min	FG-att	FT-att	Reb	Ast	Fls	Pts
Pippen	43	6-17	10-12	9	2	5	23
Rodman	33	0-4	1-2	11	3	4	1
Longley	14	0-4	0-0	3	0	4	0
Harper	18	1-4	0-0	3	2	3	2
Jordan	44	15-35	8-10	11	4	2	39
Williams	23	2-5	0-0	7	2	4	4
Kukoc	25	3-6	2-4	4	0	0	9
Kerr	25	3-5	2-2	1	0	3	9
Caffey	2	0-0	0-0	0	0	1	0
Buechler	8	1-1	0-0	1	1	0	3
Brown	5	0-0	0-0	0	1	2	0
Totals	**240**	**31-81**	**23-30**	**50**	**15**	**20**	**90**

Percentages: FG .383, FT .767. **Three-point goals:** 5-14, .357 (Kukoc 1-1, Buechler 1-1, Kerr 1-2, Pippen 1-4, Jordan 1-4, Rodman 0-1, Harper 0-1). **Team rebounds:** 6. **Blocked shots:** 4 (Pippen 3, Jordan). **Turnovers:** 13 (Pippen 5, Longley 4, Rodman, Jordan, Williams, Kukoc). **Steals:** 7 (Pippen 2, Rodman, Longley, Jordan, Williams, Kukoc). **Technical fouls:** Williams, 4:22 first; Rodman 0:0.6 second; illegal defense, 11:50 4th. **Illegal defense:** 1.

Jazz	23	21	26	16	86
Bulls	17	20	27	26	90

A: 24,544. **T:** 2:33. **Officials:** Bennett Salvatore, Joe Crawford, Steve Javie.

With five minutes left in the game, MJ hit a twelve-footer to put the Bulls ahead, 82–81. A minute later, he made it 84–81 with a ten-foot fadeaway jumper at the baseline. He then traded baskets with Utah star Karl Malone before dishing out the most important assist of the night, and the series.

Perhaps as importantly, in the third quarter Jordan cleanly picked Russell for a steal and a subsequent slam dunk that energized the 24,544 United Center fans, who would soon be getting the chance to see Michael dance on the scorer's table for the second time (the Bulls won three titles at opponents' arenas).

"Chicago fans are the best fans to play for," said Jordan later with his requisite victory cigar and champagne-drenched hat. "They've stuck with me since I've been here in '84. I've never given up on them. We've gone from bottom to top as a team. Tonight the fans inspired all of us. I felt chill bumps from their cheers."

Jordan finished the night with 39 points, a game-high 11 rebounds, and one exhausted body, though—get this—he had made a golf tee time for 8:30 A.M. the next morning, long before the start of Game 6.

"If I give up, then they [Bulls teammates] give up," said Jordan, recounting his Game 5 sick-bay heroics. "No matter how sick or tired I was, I felt an obligation to the city and the team. I'm tired and I'm weak but I have a whole summer to recuperate."

The rest of the NBA didn't plan on sending any get-well cards.

Number 9: Great Game Index

GGI Score (110 of a possible 123)   Tiebreaker is game importance.

Scoring (30 of a possible 33)   In a key five-minute stretch of the fourth quarter, Jordan scored 10 of the Bulls' 11 points. He matched everything Utah leaders Karl Malone and John Stockton could throw at him. He finished the Finals with a 32.2 points per game average.

Game Importance (20 of 20)   The Bulls had margin for error, but no one was looking to play the Jazz in a Game 7.

Opponent Strength (19 of 20)   Utah was a poised basket-ball team coached by another Bulls legend, Jerry Sloan. Malone and Stockton were both named to the NBA's fifty greatest players team.

Historical Significance (10 of 10)   Five championships created talk that the Bulls were in the same dynasty class as the Lakers and the Celtics. Most experts said Boston first, Chicago second, and the Lakers third, but qualifying Michael Jordan's superiority puts one on shaky ground—and in position to have to revise the analysis someday.

Legendary Intangibles (10 of 10)   Michael knew Steve Kerr had the best look, and a lifetime of driveway jump shots in his past. It was one reason why Jordan earned his fifth Finals MVP award in five tries.

Pressure Points (10 of 10)   This game was in doubt until the last horn. MJ controlled the action and tempo down the stretch.

Defense (4 of 5)   Michael crashed the boards and played his usual hard-nosed, suffocating defense.

Other Offensive Contributions (4 of 5)   The last assist was plenty, but he was moved the ball around to teammates all night.

MJ's Physical Condition (1 of 5)   Not a factor.

Long Odds (2 of 5)   It was almost ho-hum that Jordan orchestrated the game-winner.

-10-

June 3, 1992

Portland Trail Blazers at Bulls
Game 1, NBA Finals

MJ hits a record six three-pointers and 35 points in the first half.

Note to all of you sharpshooters out there: There's always value in more practice.

Michael proved that point on the morning of the first game of the 1992 NBA Finals. At the Bulls Berto Center practice facility in suburban Deerfield, he stuck around for some extra shooting long after his teammates, the media, and even the ball boys had cleared out. It was just MJ and the hoop; he had to chase down his own makes and misses. He practiced hundreds of shots from beyond the three-point arc.

That night at Chicago Stadium, just when sportswriters and commentators thought they had defined all facets of Michael Jordan's much varied high-level game, along appeared this memorable showing.

MJ hit six three-pointers in an eighteen-minute stretch in the first half. He finished the half with a record 35 points—and one enormous message sent to Portland.

After hitting six 3-pointers in eighteen minutes, even Michael couldn't believe his own exploits. *Reuters/Mike Blake/Archive Photos*

As if to make it officially historic, after draining one of the six bombs, Jordan ran past the national TV network announcers at courtside, holding up his palms as if to say, "I can't believe it myself." He was gesturing to none other than Magic Johnson in the NBC Sports blazer while one pretty fair NBA player, Clyde Drexler, was shaking his head on the court.

"I thought I was playing pretty good defense," said Drexler. "The guy had an incredible scoring spree. There's nothing you can do about it. [Beyond the three-point line] is where we wanted him to shoot."

"The only way you can stop Michael is to take him off the court," said Drexler's Portland teammate Cliff Robinson.

Game 10: Bulls 122, Trail Blazers 89

Trail Blazers	Min	FG-att	FT-att	Reb	Ast	Fls	Pts
Kersey	27	3-8	1-1	7	3	3	7
Williams	18	1-1	1-2	2	0	4	3
Duckworth	25	3-5	1-1	5	2	3	7
Drexler	31	5-14	6-7	5	7	4	16
Porter	32	5-9	3-4	6	2	2	13
Robinson	24	7-14	2-2	2	0	5	16
Bryant	21	5-8	0-0	5	0	1	10
Ainge	22	3-8	1-2	0	1	1	8
Whatley	13	2-5	0-0	1	0	1	4
Pack	13	1-5	2-2	1	1	1	4
Cooper	8	0-0	0-0	2	0	1	0
Abdelnaby	6	0-1	1-2	2	0	0	1
Totals	**240**	**35-78**	**18-23**	**38**	**16**	**26**	**89**

Percentages: FG .449, FT .783. **Three-point goals:** 1-6, .167 (Ainge 1-2, Drexler 0-2, Porter 0-2). **Team rebounds:** 5. **Blocked shots:** 4 (Cooper 2, Duckworth, Ainge). **Turnovers:** 21 (Kersey 5, B. Williams 4, Drexler 4, Duckworth 2, Bryant 2, Porter, Ainge, Pack Abdelnaby). **Steals:** 7 (Drexler 2, Whatley 2, B. Williams, Ainge, Pack). **Illegal defense:** 1.

Bulls	Min	FG-att	FT-att	Reb	Ast	Fls	Pts
Pippen	33	8-14	8-9	9	10	2	24
Grant	31	5-8	1-2	7	2	0	11
Cartwright	16	1-4	3-4	5	0	3	5
Paxson	19	2-4	0-0	0	5	4	4
Jordan	34	16-27	1-1	3	11	0	39
Williams	28	6-6	0-0	9	1	4	12
Armstrong	29	5-11	0-0	3	6	3	11
Hansen	14	2-4	1-2	1	2	1	5
Levingston	15	4-7	0-0	3	1	1	8
King	15	0-3	1-2	2	0	2	1
Perdue	6	1-3	0-2	2	0	1	2
Totals	**240**	**50-91**	**15-22**	**44**	**38**	**21**	**122**

Percentages: FG .549, FT .682. **Three-point goals:** 7-15, .467 (Jordan 6-10, Armstrong 1-1, Pippen 0-1, Paxson 0-1, Hansen 0-1, Levingston 0-1). **Team rebounds:** 9. **Blocked shots:** 7 (Grant 3, S. Williams 2, Pippen, King). **Turnovers:** 11 (Armstrong 3, Cartwright 2, S. Williams 2, Pippen, Jordan, Levingston, King). **Steals:** 7 (Pippen 2, Jordan 2, Grant, Paxson, King). **Illegal defense:** 1.

Trail Blazers	30	21	17	21	89
Bulls	33	33	38	18	122

A: 18,676.

"I was in a zone," said Jordan. "My threes felt like free throws. I didn't know what I was doing, but they were going in."

After the game, a 122–89 breeze for the Bulls, reporters told Jordan his six three-pointers for the night tied a Finals record held by the Los Angeles Lakers' Michael Cooper and Bill Laimbeer of the fierce rival Detroit Pistons.

"If you would've told me that," said Jordan, beginning to smile, "I'd have shot more."

MJ finished with 39 points in thirty-four minutes, as the Bulls led by 15 at the half and 37 after three quarters. His three-point totals were 6 of 9 in the opening half and 6 of 10 for the game, but he mixed in an impressive number of slams and alley-oops in the first-half flurry.

Portland's Danny Ainge tried a different sort of defensive tactic.

"I was talking to him about golf," admitted Ainge. "I was trying to distract him. I reminded him that the last time we played, I beat him."

For his part, Jordan figured it was all in a night's work, albeit remarkable and great enough to make his top ten games ever played.

"Right now, it's not going to have any impact unless we win it all," said Jordan after the game. "It's something I'll remember for a long time but not right now."

Number 10: Great Game Index

GGI Score (110 of a possible 123)   Tiebreaker is MJ's total game performance of scoring, defense, and other offensive contributions.

Scoring (33 of a possible 33)   Michael's first-half performance was spectacular and showed a whole new side to his game. It was the result of years of hard work on his outside shooting. He finished 16 of 27 for the night (14 of 21 in the opening half), and scored 53 percent of the Bulls' first-half points.

Game Importance (19 of 20)   Every first game is a key game.

Opponent Strength (17 of 20)   The Blazers were a bit thin in individual talent after Clyde Drexler, but proved formidable as a team.

Historical Significance (10 of 10)   Wiping Elgin Baylor from the record books (he had the previous record of 33 points in one half) was no small accomplishment.

Legendary Intangibles (10 of 10)   Staging your own morning shoot-around after the team work is a lesson to anyone who is tempted to be overconfident.

Pressure Points (8 of 10)   Michael's barrage relieved most of the game pressure, but remember this was still the first game of the NBA Finals, and the Trail Blazers hung tough for the first quarter.

Defense (3 of 5)   The Bulls' defense was stifling and sent a message just as palpable as MJ's three-pointers. As usual, Jordan was at the heart of the defensive machinations, with two steals.

Other Offensive Contributions (4 of 5)   Michael dished out 11 assists, including some nifty passes during a third quarter in which the Bulls outscored Portland, 38–17.

MJ's Physical Condition (1 of 5)   Not a factor.

Long Odds (5 of 5)   Nobody would have ever guessed MJ would hit so many treys, including himself and the entire Portland traveling squad.

-11-

May 25, 1991
Bulls at Detroit Pistons Game 3, Eastern Conference Finals

Michael drills 14 in the fourth quarter, putting the Pistons' reign on life support.

Forget his scoring, which was formidable and game-high among all players, as usual. This playoff series—and the ensuing first-ever NBA Finals appearance for the Bulls franchise—was turned around by Michael Jordan on defense.

"One of the great stops of all time," said Chicago coach Phil Jackson, succinctly and admiringly after his team won, 113–107, to take a commanding 3–0 lead in the Eastern Conference finals.

The situation: less than two minutes to play, the Bulls were up by five, but Detroit forced a turnover. Mark Aguirre stole a Scottie Pippen pass and swatted the ball ahead to Vinnie Johnson, who sprinted downcourt with Pistons teammate Joe Dumars running step for step on his right wing. It was two on one; MJ was the only Bull who could recover in time.

Johnson looked back at Jordan in hot pursuit, expecting to

With the key defensive play and 14 points in the fourth quarter, MJ showed how grace and athleticism could overcome the bruising style of the Pistons' "Bad Boys." *UPI/Corbis-Bettmann*

be fouled rather than allowed an uncontested layup. Michael had other thoughts.

"I wasn't going to foul him," Jordan recalled later. "I had four fouls. I was going to give him the layup. I basically had to maneuver defensively to confuse him."

Indeed, Johnson, known as the Microwave for his instantly hot shooting touch off the bench, short-circuited on this sequence. Jordan's hustle and guile prompted Johnson to throw a weak pass to Dumars.

Game 11: Bulls 113, Pistons 107

Bulls	Min	FG-att	FT-att	Reb	Ast	Fls	Pts
Pippen	38	10-16	6-6	10	4	4	26
Grant	44	8-13	1-3	8	3	4	17
Cartwright	40	6-10	1-2	4	1	4	13
Paxson	26	2-5	2-2	1	3	5	6
Jordan	46	11-19	11-12	7	7	4	33
Hodges	16	2-3	2-2	0	1	5	6
Armstrong	18	2-4	2-2	1	2	0	7
Perdue	6	1-1	0-02	5	0	2	2
Levingston	4	0-2	0-0	2	0	1	0
Williams	2	0-0	3-4	1	0	1	3
Totals	240	42-73	28-35	39	21	30	113

Percentages: FG .575, FT .800. Three-point goals: 1-4, .200 (Armstrong 1-1, Pippen 0-1, Paxson 0-1, Hodges 0-1). Team rebounds: 17. Blocked shots: 9 (Jordan 5, Cartwright 3, Pippen). Turnovers: 14 (Pippen 6, Armstrong 2, Perdue 2, Grant, Cartwright, Jordan, Hodges). Steals: 9 (Jordan 3, Grant 2, Hodges 2, Cartwright, Armstrong). Technical fouls: Chicago illegal defense, 1:07 4th. Flagrant fouls: Williams, 11:14 3rd. Illegal defense: 1.

Pistons	Min	FG-att	FT-att	Reb	Ast	Fls	Pts
Rodman	21	0-3	0-0	7	0	5	0
Edwards	9	1-2	0-0	0	0	3	2
Laimbeer	19	5-7	0-0	7	0	2	10
Dumars	47	3-10	5-7	3	1	5	11
Thomas	47	9-22	11-15	7	6	3	29
Aguirre	37	7-17	2-2	4	0	5	17
Salley	22	4-6	5-7	4	0	6	13
Johnson	36	11-17	3-5	7	5	4	25
Henderson	1	0-1	0-0	0	1	0	0
Rollins	1	0-0	0-0	0	0	0	0
Totals	240	40-85	26-36	39	13	33	107

Percentages: FG .471, FT .722. Three-point goals: 1-7, .143 (Aguirre 1-3, Dumars 0-2, Thomas 0-1, Henderson 0-1). Team rebounds: 8. Blocked shots: 2 (Rodman, Dumars). Turnovers: 15 (Thomas 4, Edwards 3, Johnson 3, Aguirre 2, Rodman 2, Laimbeer). Steals: 8 (Aguirre 3, Rodman, Dumars, Thomas, Salley, Johnson). Technical fouls: Aguirre, 9:41 1st; Rodman, 11:10 4th. Illegal defense: None.

Bulls	24	27	31	31	113
Pistons	16	27	31	33	107

A: 21,454. T: 2:35. Officials: Ed T. Rush, Bernie Fryer, Hue Hollins.

"I didn't want to foul Dumars either," said Jordan. "Dumars caught the ball kind of off balance and threw up a shot. I just went after it."

Jordan was being humble. He hurried Dumars's shot—the

veteran Detroit guard claimed he was fouled—and then grabbed the rebound. MJ quickly turned the ball up-court, where Pippen converted a fifteen-foot jumper. A potential 3-point game was astonishingly at 7, and the Pistons would get no closer than 6.

Even Jordan admitted it was probably the best play of his life without shooting the ball. "With everything at stake, maybe so," said Michael.

At issue was whether the Bulls could apply the knockout punch to Detroit's "Bad Boys," the reigning kings of the NBA at the Palace (no team had ever rebounded from such a hole). Michael supplied the answer, signaling a new dynasty and, perhaps even more satisfying to many basketball fans, a return to cleaner play and more exciting offense. More than once, Detroit practically mugged its opponents as part of its game plan, especially in the postseason.

Pistons super-sub forward John Salley, who would years later win a title ring as a spot player for the 1996 Bulls, refused to accept the idea that Chicago was some sort of finesse team.

"The Bulls stole our playbook," explained Salley, "talking junk, talking garbage, their intensity on defense, making sure there is only one shot, keeping people out of the middle, making us beat them with the jump shot. That's what we usually do."

Or usually did. The Bulls went on to sweep the Pistons in four games, finishing matters on Memorial Day. In the process, they broke a hex of six straight playoff defeats on the Pistons' home court. Detroit's "three-peat" attempt at world titles came to an end and Chicago's reign began.

"The demon isn't dead yet," said Bulls forward Horace Grant after Game 3, perhaps thinking about his team's losses in the 1989 and 1990 Eastern Conference finals at the hands of Detroit, "but we can cut off the head Monday."

"I don't think it's our quickness that is dominating games," said Pippen, who contributed 26 points and 10 rebounds in the Game 3 win. "I think we're playing a lot harder and a lot smarter than the last time we played this team [in a playoff series]. We've matured. We've learned that when they're out there throwing the cheap shots and elbows, we try to play basketball."

After the series clincher, the *Chicago Tribune* headline said it all: "Bulls End Pistons Reign of Terror." Within the day, T-shirts with the front page of the newspaper's sports section were selling fast around the city.

Long live the Bulls.

Number 11: Great Game Index

GGI Score (110 of a possible 123)   Tiebreaker is opponent's strength.

Scoring (31 of a possible 33)   Michael scored when it counted most. When Detroit was crashing the boards for 9 offensive rebounds in the fourth quarter, keeping the pressure on, Jordan was answering with a flurry of clutch jumpers and drives. He finished the game's final quarter with 14 points. He tallied 24 of his game-high 33 in the second half.

Game Importance (19 of 20)   Though the Bulls had some margin for error, eradicating the Pistons' hold on them was paramount in their championship minds. Jordan and his running mates, Pippen and Grant, had developed the necessary killer instinct, learning from the likes of Isiah Thomas, Dennis Rodman (who finally got his "three-peat" years later in Chicago), Bill Laimbeer, and Joe Dumars.

Opponent Strength (20 of 20)   The Pistons were the two-time world champs. The Bulls had lost the last two conference finals.

Historical Significance (10 of 10)   This is where the Bulls' remarkable title run went into overdrive. The confidence booster was even more vital than the indestructible 3–0 series lead. Fans rejoiced that the Wicked Beast of the East was dead, replaced by no faux Oz in Jordan.

Legendary Intangibles (10 of 10)   Only Michael could punctuate a resounding victory by making a defensive stop and key rebound. He makes everything exciting, even sitting on the bench with a Gatorade, watching the action. Detroit's Joe Dumars claimed he was fouled, and coach Chuck Daly defended his veteran guard, but the Pistons knew that play symbolized the Bulls' superior hustle.

Pressure Points (8 of 10)   Not a back-against-the wall proposition, but Detroit was applying plenty of tension by staying in the game during the fourth quarter.

Defense (5 of 5)   Besides stopping the critical two-on-one break, Jordan was his usual tireless self on the half-court press.

Other Offensive Contributions (3 of 5)   Michael dished out some key assists down the stretch, especially to Pippen, who clearly helped foil the "Jordan Rules" defense that worked so well for Detroit in the 1988, 1989, and 1990 playoffs. MJ finished with 7 assists.

MJ's Physical Condition (1 of 5)   Not a factor.

Long Odds (3 of 5)   The experts said no NBA mountain could be climbed without a dominant center. They were wrong.

-12-

June 1, 1997

Utah Jazz at Bulls Game 1, NBA Finals

Buzzer-beater and all that Jazz.

*U*tah star Karl Malone was standing at the free-throw line with two foul shots that could break an 82–82 tie with 9.2 seconds left in this opener of the 1997 NBA Finals. It was his chance to steal a game and the home-court advantage from the champion Bulls.

Malone's good friend Scottie Pippen turned up next to him.

"The Mailman doesn't deliver on Sundays," said Pippen, evoking Malone's nickname and noting the game's prime-time weekend slot.

The first free throw clanged off the rim. The second was equally heavy on the metal. Guess who grabbed the rebound? The same guy who would be getting the play designed for him in the Bulls huddle with 7.5 seconds left on the clock.

Malone could only close his eyes in disgust and more than a bit of regret. Utah coach Jerry Sloan decided to bypass a double-team on Michael, electing to put Bryon Russell on the Jordan straight-up. An inbounds pass and five dribbles later, Russell poked at the ball but found only thin air rather than Air.

Jordan's buzzer-beater in Game 1 was thrilling, but he and Scottie Pippen knew that there was much more work to be done. *Reuters/Scott Olson/Archive Photos*

Jordan broke free for a twenty-foot jumper, which caressed the net and coaxed a hard-earned Bulls victory before the buzzer sounded. MJ clenched his right fist but didn't smile. There was more championship work to be done. No need to gloat over an opponent that still needed to be beaten three

Game 12: Bulls 84, Jazz 82

Jazz	Min	FG-att	FT-att	Reb	Ast	Fls	Pts
Russell	40	2-9	2-2	6	1	2	7
Malone	41	10-22	3-6	15	3	1	23
Ostertag	18	1-4	0-0	7	0	3	2
Stockton	38	6-10	2-3	3	12	2	16
Hornaeck	32	5-9	0-0	3	1	3	11
Eisley	10	4-5	0-0	0	1	3	9
Foster	17	3-4	0-0	0	0	2	6
Anderson	19	1-3	0-0	2	1	2	2
Carr	20	3-8	0-0	7	1	4	6
Morris	5	0-2	0-0	0	0	0	0
Totals	**240**	**35-76**	**7-11**	**43**	**20**	**22**	**82**

Percentages: FG .461, FT .636. **Three-point goals:** 5-11, .455 (Stockton 2-4, Hornaeck 1-1, Eisley 1-1, Russell 1-3, Foster 0-1, Anderson 0-1). **Team rebounds:** 7. **Blocked shots:** None. **Turnovers:** 18 (Stockton 7, Malone 3, Ostertag 2, Eisley 2, Anderson 2, Russell, Anderson). **Steals:** 8 (Stockton 3, Russell 2, Ostertag 2, Morris). **Technical fouls:** None. **Illegal defense:** None.

Bulls	Min	FG-att	FT-att	Reb	Ast	Fls	Pts
Pippen	43	11-19	2-2	9	2	2	27
Rodman	33	2-7	0-2	12	1	4	4
Longley	28	3-6	0-0	2	3	2	6
Harper	29	1-6	1-2	6	3	0	4
Jordan	41	13-27	5-7	4	8	3	31
Kerr	7	0-0	0-0	0	1	1	0
Kukoc	22	2-6	0-0	1	3	0	6
Buechler	12	1-2	0-0	1	1	1	2
Williams	15	0-0	0-0	1	1	2	0
Brown	10	1-3	2-2	0	0	2	4
Totals	**240**	**34-76**	**10-15**	**36**	**23**	**17**	**84**

Percentages: FG .447, FT .667. **Three-point goals:** 6-16, .375 (Pippen 3-7, Kukoc 2-3, Harper 1-3, Buechler 0-1, Rodman 0-2). **Team rebounds:** 6. **Blocked shots:** 7 (Pippen 4, Longley, Harper, Jordan). **Turnovers:** 14 (Pippen 6, Rodman 2, Longley 2, Williams 2, Harper, Buechler). **Steals:** 9 (Pippen 3, Rodman 2, Longley 2, Harper, Brown). **Technical fouls:** Assistant coach Winter, 4:40 2nd. **Illegal defense:** 1.

Jazz	18	24	22	18	82
Bulls	17	21	24	22	84

A: 24,544. **T:** 2:12. **Officials:** Ed T. Rush, Bill Oakes, Danny Crawford.

times, especially a Jazz squad that Jordan was already labeling as the most poised of all Finals opponents.

Guard Steve Kerr raised his arms in triumph. The devilish Pippen—who also contributed 27 points, 9 rebounds, 3 steals, and 4 blocked shots on a pained left foot—and Randy Brown ran over to hug their famous teammate, who has clearly lost track of just how many game-winners he has drained.

"It was not so much a celebratory moment as matter-of-fact," said Kerr. "I was thinking, 'Get the ball to Michael.' I don't think it surprised anyone."

Pippen said Jordan "ran the play to perfection."

For his part, MJ knew that history was again in the making. He didn't back away from the eerie feeling of knowing tens of millions of eyes, from Australia to Zaire, were watching him. Malone didn't seem able to shake the now-global focus of the NBA title series, which was created by Jordan in the first place.

"Everybody watching the game in the arena and on television knows you're going to get the ball," said Jordan in the postgame press conference, another standing-room-only event prompted by Michael mania. "It's an unbelievable feeling."

Jordan matched several clutch baskets with Malone down the stretch, and made one of two free throws with 35.8 seconds remaining to tie the game at 82. Then the real Most Valuable Player stood up.

"I kept looking for the double team, but it didn't come," said Jordan, who never admitted to being bothered about not getting enough votes for regular season MVP, finishing second to Malone. "I made a crossover dribble, and [Russell] went for the steal. I knew I could get a good look with the dribble to the left."

He got more than a look, and Utah lost a game that could easily have been theirs.

Number 12: Great Game Index

GGI Score (110 of a possible 123)   The tiebreaker is opponent strength.

Scoring (33 of a possible 33)   Jordan hit a game-high 33 points and practically every key shot down the stretch. His buzzer-beater alone improved his 13-of-27 shooting night by several notches. He also answered any doubts about his status as the game's top player. Stay right where you are, Mr. Malone.

Game Importance (19 of 20)   This was Chicago's fifth different opponent of its five NBA Finals. Each foe needs to be set back on its heels, and there is no better time to start than in Game 1. Plus, the Bulls knew Utah was going to be a difficult venue.

Opponent Strength (19 of 20)   Malone and John Stockton made the Jazz perhaps the most formidable of all Finals opponents. Utah coach Jerry Sloan, a Chicago favorite, is a strategist and motivator who holds his own with Phil Jackson.

Historical Significance (8 of 10)   Just when fans were secretly wondering if Jordan and the Bulls were losing a step, this game set up the sequence for a fifth title.

Legendary Intangibles (10 of 10)   Jordan comes through in the clutch, while his opposite star number struggles with the big free throws.

Pressure Points (10 of 10)   Everyone knows you are getting the ball. A miss forces overtime and the possibility of a seven-game series.

"I don't want to be put in that situation too often," said Jordan, referring to his preference for bigger leads in the final seconds of a game, "but when I do, I want to be successful."

Defense (4 of 5)   A solid performance in a big game.

Other Offensive Contributions (4 of 5)   Eight assists spread the offense around.

MJ's Physical Condition (1 of 5)   Not a factor.

Long Odds (2 of 5)   Jordan started on the right foot toward five NBA titles and five Finals MVP awards.

-13-

June 20, 1993

Bulls at Phoenix Suns Game 6 Clincher, NBA Finals

Jordan's whole game completes the "three-peat."

The night was "three-mendous" for Jordan and his Bulls teammates, or so said the huge front-page headline of the next day's championship edition of the *Chicago Tribune*. What qualifies this historic clincher in the Jordan 50 is less Michael's total points—although another game-high 33—than the timing of his all-around talent.

With one minute left and the Bulls down by four in Game 6 of the 1993 NBA Finals, Jordan grabbed an errant Suns shot for one of his eight rebounds of the night. He sprinted the length of the court to lay his shot in (no dramatics necessary, this is all business) and douse a rowdy purple-clad crowd overheating from the notion of a decisive Game 7 on the home court of the beloved Suns.

The play is not often cited when the third title is discussed at the neighborhood bar or in front of the giant-screen TV on a Sunday afternoon, but it clearly put the Bulls in position to steal a championship and more than a few breaths from the

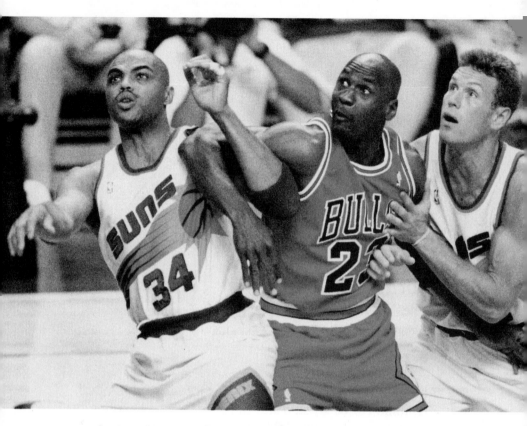

Sir Charles jousted with Michael in Game 6, but the Bulls' three-peat proved once again that the throne in the basketball kingdom belonged to Jordan. *Reuters/Neal Lauron/Archive Photos*

hometown fans. Jordan scored 9 of the Bulls' scarce 12 fourth-quarter points, including four straight baskets down the stretch.

After trading baskets in the final minute, the Bulls set up for their final possession still down by only 2. During the time-out, coach Phil Jackson had to shout to his players to be heard over the din of the Phoenix faithful.

The play, of course, was designed for Jordan, but when MJ saw no seam in the Suns' defense, he passed to Scottie Pippen, who, closely covered himself, flipped the ball to Horace Grant. The Bulls forward, playing his last Finals game as a Jordan

Game 13: Bulls 99, Suns 98

Bulls	Min	FG-att	FT-att	Reb	Ast	Fls	Pts
Grant	33	0-5	1-2	2-7	3	5	1
Pippen	43	10-22	3-7	4-12	5	3	23
Cartwright	26	1-3	0-0	0-4	1	5	2
Armstrong	41	6-10	2-2	0-0	4	5	18
Jordan	44	13-26	4-6	3-8	7	3	33
Parson	22	3-4	0-0	1-1	1	1	8
S. Williams	22	2-7	1-3	2-7	1	3	5
Tucker	7	4-4	0-0	0-0	1	1	9
King	2	0-1	0-0	0-0	1	0	0
Totals	**240**	**39-82**	**11-20**	**12-39**	**24**	**26**	**99**

Percentages: FG .486, FT .550. **Three-point goals:** 18-14, .714 (Armstrong 4-5, Jordan, 3-5, Paxon 2-3, Tucker 1-1) **Team rebounds:** 9. **Blocked shots:** 2 (Grant 2). **Turnovers:** 8 (Pippen 3, Jordan 3, Armstrong, King). **Steals:** 6 (Pippen 4, Grant, Jordan). **Technical foul:** Illegal defense, 1:08 3d. **Illegal defense:** 1.

Suns	Min	FG-att	FT-att	Reb	Ast	Fls	Pts
Barkley	44	7-18	7-10	7-17	4	5	21
Dumas	22	3-8	2-2	1-3	1	2	8
West	20	1-2	2-4	3-4	1	5	4
K. Johnson	46	6-14	7-7	2-5	10	3	19
Majerle	46	7-17	5-6	2-8	2	3	21
Miller	14	1-6	2-2	2-2	0	1	4
Ainge	30	3-6	1-1	0-3	2	0	9
Chambers	12	4-10	4-4	1-5	0	2	12
F. Johnson	6	0-3	0-0	0-0	0	0	0
Totals	**240**	**33-86**	**30-36**	**18-47**	**20**	**21**	**98**

Percentages: FG .390, FT .833. **Three-point goals:** 4-11, .364 (Ainge 2-3, Majerle 2-8) **Team rebounds:** 15. **Blocked shots:** 9 (Miller 3, West 2, Majerle 2, Dumas, Johnson). **Turnovers:** 9 (K. Johnson 3, Barkley 2, Ainge 2, Majerle, F. Johnson). **Steals:** 5 (Ainge 2, Barkley, K. Johnson, Majerle). **Technical fouls:** None. **Illegal defense:** None.

Bulls	37	19	21	12	99
Suns	28	23	28	19	98

A: 19,023. **T:** 2:37. **Officials:** Darell Garretson, Ed T. Rush, Mike Mathis.

teammate, passed up a possible shot to hand the hot potato to John Paxson behind the three-point line. The rest is memorized by Bulls fans. Pax hit the three with 3.9 seconds left. Grant blocked Kevin Johnson's desperation at the buzzer to seal the 99–98 victory.

"I put my foot in my mouth before this all started," said Jordan, perhaps talking as much to good friend and defeated opponent Charles Barkley as anyone. "I said the three-peat would be easy. After we won two, I thought the pressure was off. This was a lot harder than anything I've ever done in basketball. This game, this series represented just how hard it was."

Michael's series line showed he was up to the task. His scoring string was 31, 42, 44, 55, 41, and 33 for the six games, setting records for most points and field goals. He also averaged 8.5 rebounds and about 6 assists per game.

After lighting the victory cigar and accepting a third straight Finals MVP trophy, MJ revealed an inner flame that stoked his "three-peat" season. He was competing with the legends of the game who had once passed the NBA torch to him.

"The driving force was beating Magic," said Jordan about the Lakers star who won five rings but never three in a row. "[Larry] Bird never won three [straight] either."

Jordan, never one to call himself the greatest player of all time, was, however, willing to broach the subject of his team's place in history. "There are a lot of opinions about who the greatest team is," he said. "You look at the Boston Celtics, who won sixteen championships [eight in a row between 1959 and 1966], and they certainly have to be considered a great team, but with so much talent and parity in the league right now, we certainly feel we must be considered one of the greatest teams."

No one in Chicago—or Phoenix—was about to argue the point.

Number 13: Great Game Index

GGI Score (110 of a possible 123)   Tiebreaker is opponent strength.

Scoring (33 of a possible 33)   Michael finished off the series with enough points to set the all-time record for Finals scoring average, at 41. More importantly, he revived an unsteady Bulls team upon reentering the game with six minutes gone in the final quarter. He scored the first Chicago point of the quarter on a free throw, then hit four straight key shots to put the Bulls in position to win.

Game Importance (19 of 20)   No Bulls player or fan was fond of taking their chances in a Game 7 at the Phoenix hothouse.

Opponent Strength (18 of 20)   Charles Barkley elevated his club with his scoring, rebounding, and determination. He and his Suns teammates, like Kevin Johnson and Dan Majerle, won respect in the series.

Historical Significance (10 of 10)   Three straight titles. Magic never did it, Larry never did it, Isiah never did it. Michael smiled on the golf course all summer thinking about that.

Legendary Intangibles (9 of 10)   His hustle put the Bulls in place to benefit from John Paxson's just-in-time heroics. Equally impressive was MJ's decision not to force his own shot during the critical sequence.

Pressure Points (10 of 10)   Michael scored 75 percent of his team's fourth-quarter output. Each point was precious and necessary.

Defense (3 of 5)   A solid game, especially on the defensive boards.

Other Offensive Contributions (3 of 5)   MJ played a team-high 44 minutes, hauling down 8 rebounds and dishing out 7 assists.

MJ's Physical Condition (1 of 5)   Not a factor.

Long Odds (4 of 5)   Winning three straight titles in any sport takes much more than talent, though Jordan and his teammates (especially Pippen) had plenty of it. Michael separated himself from other NBA greats, living up to all of the advance billing.

-14-

June 12, 1992

Bulls at Portland Trail Blazers Game 5, NBA Finals

MJ scores 46 as the Bulls take command.

The Bulls jumped out to an early lead of 13 points after one quarter of play. Fueled by 46 points from Michael, Chicago extended the advantage to 20 by third-quarter's end. A nip-and-tuck series was being shredded.

Portland staged successful comebacks in Game 2 and Game 4, so no one on the Bulls squad was breathing entirely easily, Jordan included. He was playing with a painful ankle injury that limited his mobility but placed no call on his grit. What's more, MJ played most of the fourth quarter with five fouls, leaving no margin for error in this pivotal Game 5.

Never camera-shy, MJ hurt his left ankle in the second quarter tripping over a photographer positioned along the baseline. He fell hard into referee Jess Kersey, and missed the next minute and a half of game time.

Game 14: Bulls 119, Trail Blazers 106

Bulls	Min	FG-att	FT-att	Reb	Ast	Fls	Pts
Pippen	45	8-15	8-9	11	9	4	24
Grant	33	2-4	2-5	5	3	6	6
Cartwright	19	2-4	0-0	3	3	4	4
Paxson	33	6-11	0-0	1	3	2	12
Jordan	42	14-23	16-19	5	4	5	46
Williams	23	2-4	3-4	4	3	5	7
Armstrong	17	2-4	4-4	0	0	1	8
Levingston	13	2-3	2-2	3	1	1	6
King	8	1-4	2-2	1	0	4	4
Hansen	5	1-1	0-0	1	0	1	2
Hodges	1	0-0	0-0	0	0	0	0
Perdue	1	0-0	0-0	0	0	0	0
Totals	240	40-73	37-45	34	26	33	119

Percentages: FG .548, FT .822. **Three-point goals:** 2-6, .333 (Jordan 2-4, Paxson 0-1, Pippen 0-1). **Team rebounds:** 8. **Blocked shots:** 6 (Grant 4, Jordan, Levingston). **Turnovers:** 14 (Jordan 4, Pippen 3, Grant 3, Cartwright 2, Paxson, Armstrong). **Steals:** 6 (Pippen 2, Paxson 2, Grant, Cartwright).

Trail Blazers	Min	FG-att	FT-att	Reb	Ast	Fls	Pts
Kersey	36	7-17	0-0	12	3	5	14
Williams	31	3-6	0-0	7	0	3	6
Duckworth	28	3-6	7-11	7	0	5	13
Drexler	41	9-21	12-14	10	3	6	30
Porter	46	5-12	7-8	2	8	3	17
Ainge	28	5-13	3-4	3	3	5	14
Robinson	26	3-4	5-5	4	4	6	11
Whatley	1	0-0	0-0	0	0	0	0
Pack	3	0-1	1-2	0	0	1	1
Totals	240	35-80	35-44	45	21	34	106

Percentages: FG .438, FT .795. **Three-point goals:** 1-7, .143 (Ainge 1-4, Drexler 0-3). **Team rebounds:** 8. **Blocked shots:** 3 (B. Williams, Drexler, Porter). **Turnovers:** 18 (Kersey 6, Drexler 4, Duckworth 3, Porter 3, B. Williams, Ainge). **Steals:** 5 (Porter 3, Kersey 2). **Technical fouls:** B. Williams, 9:49 1st. **Illegal defense:** 1.

Bulls	39	27	28	25	119
Trail Blazers	26	28	24	28	106

A: 12,888.

There was no bruising Michael's touch around the net, though. He promptly drained a three-pointer when he returned, finishing the first half with 27 points on the strength of 8-of-13 shooting from the field and 9 of 11 at the free-throw line. The Bulls were in charge, up 19 at the break.

Before the game, Jordan was criticized in some circles for playing golf on a day off with the series still in the balance. By the late stages, he was hitting free throws to ice the game while Trail Blazers star Clyde Drexler (and his zero tee times) fouled out with more than two minutes left.

Less than forty-eight hours later, the Bulls were celebrating back-to-back championships, with MJ leading the party by dancing on the scorer's table. No pain in the ankle that Sunday night.

"I'm just so glad Chicago drafted me eight years ago," said Jordan in a show of loyalty that is disturbingly rare in sports these days. "We couldn't have done it without the fans."

Somehow the cliché didn't seem trite. The Bulls fans, who were hoarse come Monday morning from screaming in front of their TV sets, believed him. Forty-six points in pivotal Game 5 gives one plenty of credibility, and puts everyone in a comfort zone.

Number 14: Great Game Index

GGI Score (110 of a possible 123).

Scoring (32 of a possible 33)   No last-minute heroics were required, but Michael's point totals were still the most ever in the playoffs against a storied Portland franchise. The Jordan shooting line was 14 for 23 in field goals and 16 for 19 at the free-throw line. He hit 2 of 4 three-pointers.

Game Importance (19 of 20)   People tend to forget how close this series was.

Opponent Strength (17 of 20)   Portland was a solid team with only one big-name star, but plenty of playoff veterans.

Historical Significance (9 of 10)   This game set up the consecutive titles, quieting any critics who once believed Michael was a great individual player but not a team-oriented champion.

Legendary Intangibles (10 of 10)   The series was still in doubt at tip-off before a noisy Portland crowd on Memorial Day. By halftime—on the strength of Jordan's aggressive leadership and a resulting 27 points—the Blazers were simply hoping to stay respectable in defeat.

Pressure Points (10 of 10)   Big game, big shots, big stuff.

Defense (3 of 5)   A solid game. Jordan never has an off-night on the defensive end during postseason.

Other Offensive Contributions (3 of 5)   Despite foul trouble, MJ still played forty-two minutes. He pulled down 5 defensive rebounds and passed out 4 assists.

MJ's Physical Condition (5 of 5)   Only Michael can put "swollen ankle" and "46 points" in the same sentence.

Long Odds (2 of 5)   Winning back-to-back championships, once a reality only in Jordan's dreams, was now an expectation.

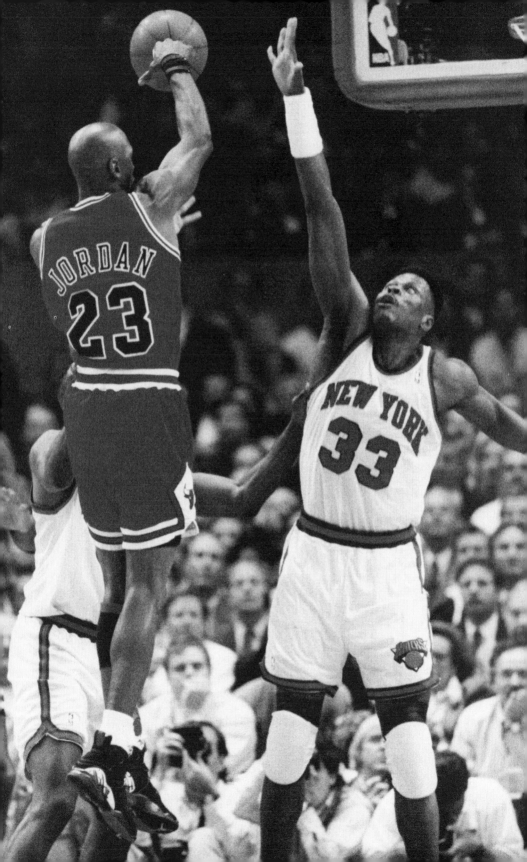

-15-

June 2, 1993

Bulls at New York Knicks
Game 5,
Eastern Conference Finals

A highly visible triple-double.

Michael snagged his second career postseason triple-double at just the right time and in the right place and under the right spotlight. A celebrity-studded Madison Square Garden crowd watched MJ hit 29 points while pulling down 10 rebounds and handing out 14 assists. Every move was needed in a hard-fought 97–94 win.

The game's biggest sequence, though, was far from glamorous. Jordan was part of a three-man buzz saw that stopped the shot of the Knicks' six-foot, ten-inch Charles Smith four times in the final seconds of regulation, when a basket would have put New York ahead.

Smith went up for the first shot. Jordan stripped the ball, but Smith recovered, only to be blocked twice by Pippen and then again by Grant, who grabbed the ball and zipped an outlet pass to Jordan. The game ended on a Jordan feed to B. J. Armstrong for an insurance layup.

Ever since their college days at North Carolina and Georgetown, respectively, Jordan always seemed to rise a notch above good friend Patrick Ewing. *Reuters/Ray Stubblebine/Archive Photos*

Game 15: Bulls 97, Knicks 94

Bulls	Min	FG-att	FT-att	Reb	Ast	Fls	Pts
Grant	35	5-9	1-2	10	1	4	11
Pippen	43	12-23	4-7	11	1	2	28
Cartwright	25	5-6	3-3	2	1	6	13
Armstrong	31	5-10	0-0	0	1	1	11
Jordan	45	11-25	7-8	10	14	2	29
S. Williams	17	1-2	1-2	7	3	4	3
Tucker	9	1-2	0-0	1	0	1	0
Paxson	15	0-2	0-0	0	0	1	0
Perque	1	0-0	0-0	0	0	0	0
King	19	1-5	0-0	6	0	4	2
Totals	**240**	**40-83**	**16-23**	**48**	**19**	**25**	**97**

Percentages: FG .482, FT .696. **Three-point goals:** 1-4, .250 (Armstrong 1-1, Pippen 0-1, Jordan 0-1, Tucker 0-1). **Team rebounds:** 6. **Blocked shots:** 3 (Grant, Jordan, S. Williams). **Turnovers:** 14 (Jordan 5, Grant 4, Pippen 2, Armstrong, S. Williams, King). **Steals:** 8 (Pippen 2, Jordan 2, King 2, Cartwright, Tucker). **Technical fouls:** Illegal defense 3, 10:29 4th; 9:47 4th; 7:27 4th. **Flagrant foul:** Cartwright 1:47 2nd. **Illegal defense:** 1.

Knicks	Min	FG-att	FT-att	Reb	Ast	Fls	Pts
Oakley	27	2-6	2-4	4	0	3	6
Smith	29	4-11	4-6	6	0	5	12
Ewing	44	12-23	8-14	9	3	3	33
Rivers	32	3-6	3-3	0	6	5	10
Starks	44	3-11	2-5	6	8	3	8
Mason	41	8-11	1-3	8	2	1	17
Blackman	7	1-1	0-0	0	0	3	2
Anthony	15	3-4	0-0	4	5	1	6
H. Williams	1	0-0	0-0	0	0	0	0
Totals	**240**	**36-73**	**20-25**	**37**	**24**	**24**	**94**

Percentages: FG .493, FT .571. **Three-point goals:** 2-6, .333 (Ewing 1-1, Rivers 1-2, Starks 0-3). **Team rebounds:** 11. **Blocked shots:** 4 (Ewing 2, Starks, Mason). **Turnovers:** 14 (Ewing 3, Starks 3, Rivers 2, Mason 2, Oakley, Smith, Blackman, Anthony). **Steals:** 3 (Starks 2, Rivers). **Technical fouls:** None. **Illegal defense:** None.

Bulls	31	24	25	17	97
Knicks	28	28	21	17	94

A: 19,763. **T:** 2:34. **Officials:** Ed T. Rush, Mike Mathis, Hue Hollins.

The game started with boos and hoots for Jordan—even before the pregame warmup—due to a recent gambling investigation. By the final buzzer, the hostile fans were once more awed by Jordan's superior performances in the most pressure-packed games. Even the stingy-to-compliment New York press was noticeably impressed.

"You get the idea Smith could go under there Thursday morning, alone in the Garden, and try to make those shots, and Jordan and Pippen would come out of nowhere and block him again," wrote *New York Daily News* columnist Mike Lupica.

Knicks coach Pat Riley was dazed and woefully aware of the uphill prospect of winning Game 6 in Chicago to earn another chance here in the Garden (which didn't happen): "All I could see was hands and arms and motion."

Michael's greatness deserves a closer examination. He started the game by making sure every other starter scored first. That's a court leader building confidence in his teammates and doubts among the defenders, and maybe fewer double-teams later in the game. His 17-point scoring streak covered the last 7 points of his team's scoring in the third quarter and the first 10 of the fourth quarter. That's a court leader who knows when shooting it yourself is the best team strategy.

Case in point: During the latter stages of the fourth quarter, Jordan swiftly moved the ball to an open B. J. Armstrong, who promptly bagged a key three-pointer. It turned out the whole thing was planned, at least that was the guess, since Jordan was remaining silent with the media due to the gambling hubbub.

"He told me to carry the load early and he would try to do something in the second half," said Pippen, who started the game a perfect 5 for 5 and finished with 28 points to Jordan's 29.

A triple-double will do.

Number 15: Great Game Index

GGI Score (109 of a possible 123) The tiebreaker is total game performance, which includes scoring, defense, and other offensive contributions.

Scoring (30 of a possible 33) When the game was tottering, Jordan balanced his teammates with 17 straight points. That's hard to do in February against a last-place team, much less in the heat of the playoffs in the Garden.

Game Importance (19 of 20)   The Bulls didn't want a repeat Game 7, as in the 1992 postseason series against New York.

Opponent Strength (19 of 20)   Patrick Ewing and the Knicks were at their pinnacle, which was never quite good enough, denying Ewing his chance for a NBA championship. The former Georgetown center had to wait for Jordan to leave school before getting a NCAA crown.

Historial Significance (9 of 10)   Big games in the Garden were becoming a habit. One could argue that the Bulls' toughest opponent during the 1993 playoffs was New York.

Legendary Intangibles (10 of 10)   Jordan took over during the 17-point streak. The Knicks never regained control.

Pressure Points (10 of 10)   Every basket counted; every miss was magnified.

Defense (5 of 5)   The Bulls-Knicks rivalry of the early 1990s was always punctuated by intense defense. Jordan and teammates Pippen and Horace Grant set the tone on the Chicago side.

Other Offensive Contributions (5 of 5)   Fourteen assists is a great day for a point guard, which Jordan is not. Ten rebounds is a good number for a power forward, which Jordan is not.

MJ's Physical Condition (1 of 5)   Not a factor.

Long Odds (1 of 5)   Jordan's triple-double, though rare enough, is feasible every time he plays a game.

-16-

June 12, 1991

Bulls at Los Angeles Lakers Game 5 Clincher, NBA Finals

Savoring the first time around.

Victory was so sweet—and required seven perspiration-dripping seasons of creating shots and boxing out and playing all-points defense to get there. Michael cried like a baby in the locker room, burying his face in his wife Juanita's arms after receiving the Finals MVP trophy. James, his father, sat at his right side and his mother, Deloris, was trying to make her way across a packed locker room. Michael sat there a good, long, well-deserved time before lifting his head to talk with reporters. His glistening eyes were red and happy. He didn't seem to care that photographers were snapping furiously.

"We started from scratch, on the bottom, not making the playoffs when I got here," he said. "It took seven years, but we won. This should get rid of the stigma of the one-man team. We have players that make us an effective basketball team."

Jordan wiped a few tears and shrugged involuntarily.

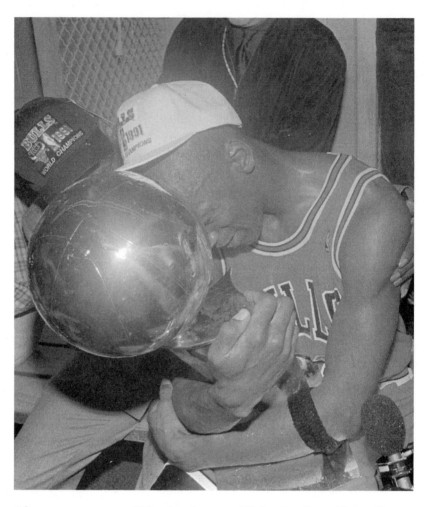

After seven seasons of blood and sweat, MJ finally allowed himself tears while embracing the Larry O'Brien trophy for the first time. *Reuters/Sam Mircovich/Archive Photos*

"I've never been this emotional publicly," said Jordan. "I don't know if I'll ever have the same feeling. What you are seeing are the emotions of hard work."

Before countless champagne soakings in the postgame celebration, Jordan spouted 30 points, shooting 12 of 23 from the floor and 6 of 8 at the free-throw line. Perhaps even more impressive were his 10 assists and 5 steals. Perspiration indeed.

Game 16: Bulls 108, Lakers 101

Bulls	Min	FG-att	FT-att	Reb	Ast	Fls	Pts
Grant	40	4-5	3-6	6	0	2	11
Pippen	48	10-22	11-12	13	7	3	32
Cartwright	33	4-11	0-0	8	7	5	8
Jordan	48	12-23	6-8	4	10	1	30
Paxson	33	9-12	2-2	3	4	3	20
Levingston	8	0-1	0-0	2	0	4	0
Williams	7	2-2	0-0	0	0	0	5
Hodges	8	0-0	0-0	1	0	2	0
Armstrong	8	1-2	0-0	0	0	0	2
Perdue	7	0-0	0-0	0	0	3	0
Totals	240	42-78	22-28	37	28	23	108

Percentages: FG .538, FT .786. **Three-point goals:** 2-3, .667 (Hodges 1-1, Pippen 1-2). **Team rebounds:** 6. **Blocked shots:** 6 (Grant 2, Jordan 2, Pippen, Williams). **Turnovers:** 18 (Pippen 7, Jordan 6, Grant 2, Paxson, Armstrong, Perdue). **Steals:** 14 (Jordan 5, Pippen 5, Grant, Cartwright, Armstrong, Paxson). **Technical fouls:** None. **Illegal defense:** 1.

Lakers	Min	FG-att	FT-att	Reb	Ast	Fls	Pts
Green	43	6-12	1-2	7	1	3	13
Perkins	37	5-12	11-13	9	3	4	22
Divac	37	4-12	0-0	7	3	2	8
Johnson	48	4-12	6-6	11	20	0	16
Teagle	18	4-8	1-2	0	0	4	9
Campbell	27	9-12	3-4	2	0	3	21
Smith	30	5-6	2-3	0	2	6	12
Totals	240	37-74	24-30	36	29	22	101

Percentages: FG .500, FT .800. **Three-point goals:** 3-11, .273 (Johnson 2-6, Perkins 1-4, Divac 0-1). **Team rebounds:** 6. **Blocked shots:** 7 (Divac 4, Perkins 2, Campbell). **Turnovers:** 22 (Johnson 6, Divac 5, Smith 4, Teagle 3, Green 2, Perkins, Campbell). **Steals:** 6 (Green 2, Campbell 2, Johnson, Smith). **Technical fouls:** None. **Flagrant fouls:** 1 (Perkins). **Illegal defense:** None.

Bulls	27	21	32	28	108
Lakers	25	24	31	21	101

A: 17,505. **T:** 2:28. **Officials:** J. O'Donnell, J. Madden, M. Mathis.

So close to his first NBA title, Michael was now wise enough to realize a hot hand when he saw one. He fed John Paxson repeatedly in the second half, including 3 key assists in the last four minutes of the game. Paxson finished with 20 points on 9-of-12 shooting, including four of five baskets in critical late stages when the game was still in doubt (Jordan scored the other jumper).

On one sequence with 3:54 remaining, MJ grabbed a Laker miss, worked the ball down the court to find Paxson for a nineteen-foot swish. He made two key steals around the six-minute mark with the game tied. The little things were adding up to something big.

As Paxson blitzed the basket in the final moments, there was irony in the outcome. This NBA Finals was promoted as the Michael and Magic Show, featuring Jordan and fellow megastar Magic Johnson. As the unsung Paxson stole center stage, Michael imitated Magic as playmaker. For his part, Johnson finished the night with 16 points, 20 assists, and 11 rebounds. Each star played the full forty-eight minutes. Jordan refused to leave the game if Magic were still on the floor.

"When I congratulated him in the locker room," said Johnson, who won five NBA titles during his Lakers years, "you could see tears in his eyes. This is a great moment for him because so much has been built on him being an individual. Now he's proved everybody wrong."

Number 16: Great Game Index

GGI Score (109 of a possible 123)   The tiebreaker is opponent strength.

Scoring (29 of a possible 33)   There is nothing shabby about 30 points on a title night. Michael shot a little better than 50 percent and didn't miss any shots. It's just that the rest of his game overshadowed his scoring.

Game Importance (19 of 20)   The Bulls had some room for error—including two more games that would be played in Chicago—but Michael was thrilled to end any suspense. Seven years is a long wait.

Opponent Strength (19 of 20)   These Lakers were glamorous and gutsy opponents. They were partly depleted by injuries to Byron Scott (shoulder) and James Worthy (ankle), which kept them out of the Game 5 finale.

Historical Significance (10 of 10) The benchmark for subsequent title years and confirmation—as if it were needed—of Jordan's greatness.

Legendary Intangibles (9 of 10) MJ found a way to win—he found Paxson the open man. He went minute-for-minute with Magic Johnson; no rest or me-first attitudes for these millionaires.

Pressure Points (8 of 10) Jordan hit the necessary shots, just not as many as usual.

Defense (5 of 5) Michael had 5 steals, showing why he is the career leader in being named to the NBA All-Defensive first team. He added 2 blocked shots.

Other Offensive Contributions (5 of 5) Ten important assists and 4 well-placed rebounds.

MJ's Physical Condition (1 of 5) Not a factor.

Long Odds (4 of 5) No one should have doubted Jordan, but they did.

-17-

May 14, 1989

New York Knicks at Bulls Game 4, Second-Round Playoff Series

Medical prognosis: Knicks in the sick bay.

Rick Pitino has earned tens of thousands of dollars making motivational speeches to business executives. The well-known basketball coach has authored a popular book on the subject.

Sometimes, though, your message can backfire.

At least that's the lesson Pitino learned back in 1989, when he was attempting to resurrect the championship-caliber years of the New York Knicks. On the eve of Game 4 of this intense conference semifinals matchup, Michael Jordan was home watching the TV sports reports like any other regular guy.

There was one particular twist: Jordan was hooked up to an electric stimulation machine for his aching groin muscle, which he had injured during that day's 111–88 Game 3 win.

Game 17: Bulls 106, Knicks 93

Knicks	Min	FG-att	FT-att	Reb	Ast	Fls	Pts
Newman	30	6-13	8-9	3	2	4	23
Oakley	34	5-13	0-0	16	1	2	10
Ewing	37	5-15	0-2	11	4	5	10
Jackson	36	6-13	0-0	4	4	1	12
G. Wilkins	22	1-7	0-0	1	5	3	2
Green	9	1-2	2-2	2	0	4	4
Tucker	21	4-9	0-0	1	1	5	11
Vandeweghe	15	3-4	2-2	3	1	1	8
Strickland	15	2-8	0-2	3	4	3	4
E. Wilkins	4	1-3	0-0	0	0	0	2
Myers	3	0-0	0-0	0	0	1	0
Walker	14	2-5	3-5	3	1	3	7
Totals	240	36-92	15-22	47	23	32	93

Percentages: FG .391, FT .682. **Three-point goals:** 6-15, .400 (Newman 3-6, Tucker 3-5, Jackson 0-3, G. Wilkins 0-1). **Team rebounds:** 6. **Blocked shots:** 2 (Ewing, Strickland). **Turnovers:** 17 (Newman 3, Oakley 3, Ewing 3, Strickland 3, Jackson 2, G. Wilkins, Green, Walker). **Steals:** 8 (Jackson 2, Newman, Oakley, Ewing, G. Wilkins, Tucker, Strickland). **Technical fouls:** None. **Illegal defense:** None.

Bulls	Min	FG-att	FT-att	Reb	Ast	Fls	Pts
Pippen	39	5-10	2-2	7	8	3	12
Grant	37	5-8	2-2	9	3	4	12
Cartwright	39	7-9	7-7	6	1	4	21
Hodges	30	0-8	2-4	2	5	3	2
Jordan	42	12-18	23-28	11	6	3	47
Davis	12	1-2	2-2	2	0	0	4
Paxson	25	3-7	0-0	2	3	2	6
Sellers	5	0-0	0-0	0	0	1	0
Perdue	8	1-1	0-0	1	1	1	2
Vincent	2	0-0	0-0	0	0	0	0
Haley	1	0-0	0-0	0	0	0	0
Totals	240	34-63	38-45	40	27	21	106

Percentages: FG .540, FT .844. **Three-point goals:** 0-7, .000 (Pippen 0-3, Hodges 0-2, Jordan 0-1, Paxson 0-1). **Team rebounds:** 6. **Blocked shots:** 3 (Jordan 2, (Cartwright). **Turnovers:** 17 (Jordan 6, Cartwright 3, Pippen 2, Paxson 2, Hodges, Team 3). **Steals:** 7 (Grant 2, Hodges 2, Cartwright, Jordan, Paxson). **Technical fouls:** None. **Illegal defense:** None.

Knicks	23	30	20	20	93
Bulls	27	28	22	29	106

A: 18,637. **T:** 2:35. **Officials:** Hue Hollins, Hugh Evans, Bernie Fryer.

Bulls trainer Mark Pfeil showed MJ how to use the device for an extended at-home treatment.

It turned out Pitino appeared on the television set, hinting that maybe Jordan was faking his injury for a little added drama and attention. Michael sat up in his chair without disconnecting any stimulation wires.

"I was pretty offended by it," said Jordan after Game 4 the next day. "He didn't know my status. I didn't think those comments should have been made. I know my body better than somebody else. So I decided to use it as energy."

If Pitino was joking, his timing was way off. Jordan scored 47 points that Sunday afternoon, basically on one leg. He also grabbed 11 rebounds as the Bulls won, 106–93, to take a commanding 3–1 lead in the series.

Something about playing against the Knicks—or Pitino?—inspired Jordan. Of the three games from this playoff series, early in his career, this is the highest-ranked to qualify among his 50 greatest games.

Pitino said he was hoping that two games in just more than twenty-four hours would wear out the less deep Bulls, especially Jordan if he really were ailing. Wrong. Michael limped through pregame warm-ups before getting better as the game progressed, and scored 18 points in the decisive fourth quarter.

"I played with Michael and know that when he's hurt, it really motivates him," said Knicks forward Charles Oakley, traded by the Bulls for center Bill Cartwright the year before. "You don't know he's hurt until you see him in a cast."

Pitino was most unhappy about Jordan's twenty-eight trips to the free-throw line. He sank twenty-three, accumulating what some starters might get in an entire postseason series or two. There could have been more Jordan free throws. Pitino only elected to put on a full-court press scheme when MJ was resting on the bench.

"When he's in there, it's difficult to guard him without fouling," noted Pitino.

Knicks star Patrick Ewing was lamenting the lost weekend and feeling a bit nervous about the looming summer vacation compliments of his off-court pal, Jordan. "Things weren't going our way," he said. "The shots weren't falling and, down the stretch, it seemed like Michael was hitting every shot."

Number 17: Great Game Index

GGI Score (109 of a possible 123)   The tiebreaker is total game performance, which includes scoring, defense, and other offensive contributions.

Scoring (33 of a possible 33)   Forty-six points on good wheels is a banner day, even for MJ. He instituted equal-opportunity scoring, hitting 8 points in the first quarter, 10 in the second, 11 in the third, and 18 of the team's 29 in the final stanza (including 8 free throws).

Game Importance (19 of 20)   This was growing-up time for a young Bulls squad, which set a precedent with New York that lasted for years.

Opponent Strength (18 of 20)   Pitino might have been a bit mouthy for Jordan's liking, but he had definitely put excitement back into Knicks basketball.

Historical Significance (8 of 10)   One link in an extensive chain of Jordan highlight games against the Knicks.

Legendary Intangibles (10 of 10)   Groin injuries are only truly appreciated by anyone who has ever suffered one. The injury alone was enough to spur Jordan's bottomless well of big-game energy; Pitino simply added a boost.

Pressure Points (9 of 10)   Down by 7 late in the third quarter, the Knicks tied it at 77–77 with 11 minutes to play. Michael didn't disappoint fans—and Scottie Pippen and Horace Grant helped on the boards. The Bulls were up by 9 with 5:32 left and the Knicks got no closer than 4. MJ notched 13 of the final 16 points.

Defense (3 of 5)   Another solid game.

Other Offensive Contributions (3 of 5)   Eleven rebounds came in handy against New York.

MJ's Physical Condition (5 of 5)   Remember, Jordan had less than a day to recover enough to play on a groin pull, then he went out and scored 46 points.

Long Odds (1 of 5)   Forty-plus scoring games were becoming a standard for Michael, even in the playoffs.

-18-

May 1, 1988

Cleveland Cavaliers at Bulls Game 2, First-Round Playoff Series

Beyond limits: MJ scores 55 on pal Harper.

Ron Harper has earned his place in Bulls lore with tenacious defense, clutch shooting, and playing through pain. He is also part of Michael Jordan's inner circle of friends and confidants. They have admired each other's style of play for more than a decade, a friendship only strengthened by on-court championships. It does, however, leave Harper vulnerable to ribbing about Game No. 18 among Michael's all-time best. Somehow, you know the subject comes up once in a while.

In the opener of this playoff series, Cleveland's Harper sat out with an ankle sprain. His replacement, Craig Ehlo, was scorched for 50 points by Jordan. Nonetheless, Jordan told reporters he thought Ehlo played better defense than Harper.

Harper was surprised and a bit bothered, especially con-

Game 18: Bulls 106, Cavaliers 101

Cavaliers	Min	FG-att	FT-att	Reb	Ast	Fls	Pts
Nance	41	11-15	5-6	6	8	3	27
Sanders	31	6-11	3-3	2	0	5	15
Daugherty	38	9-17	3-4	13	4	0	21
Harper	34	4-15	2-5	6	4	1	10
Price	37	6-12	4-4	4	6	6	19
Williams	21	1-5	0-0	5	2	3	2
Ehlo	24	2-7	1-2	5	3	3	5
Hubbard	4	0-0	0-0	0	0	0	0
Dudley	10	1-1	0-0	1	0	0	2
Totals	**240**	**40-83**	**18-24**	**42**	**27**	**21**	**101**

Percentages: FG .482, FT .750. **Three-point goals:** 3-6, .500 (Price 3-4, Sanders 0-1, Ehlo 0-1). **Team rebounds:** 7. **Blocked shots:** 8 (Daugherty 3, Nance 2, Williams 2, Harper 1). **Turnovers:** 15 (Nance 4, Ehlo 3, Sanders 2, Daugherty 2, Price 2, Harper, Williams). **Steals:** 4 (Nance, Daugherty, Harper, Williams). **Technical fouls:** None. **Illegal defense:** 1.

Bulls	Min	FG-att	FT-att	Reb	Ast	Fls	Pts
Sellers	4	0-3	0-0	2	0	2	0
Oakley	41	8-13	1-2	12	7	3	17
Corzine	33	2-9	0-0	8	1	4	4
Vincent	40	4-14	1-2	3	14	2	9
Jordan	44	24-45	7-7	6	3	4	55
Pippen	30	4-8	0-0	12	2	1	8
Grant	33	5-10	3-3	14	1	2	13
Paxson	14	0-4	0-0	0	2	2	0
Sparrow	1	0-0	0-0	0	0	0	0
Totals	**240**	**47-106**	**12-14**	**57**	**30**	**20**	**106**

Percentages: FG .443, FT .857. **Three-point goals:** 0-1, .000 (Paxson). **Team rebounds:** 4. **Blocked shots:** 2 (Jordan, Pippen). **Turnovers:** 10 (Vincent 3, Pippen 3, Corzine 2, Jordan, Paxson). **Steals:** 7 (Jordan 4, Grant, Oakley, Vincent). **Technical fouls:** None. **Illegal defense:** None.

Cavaliers	36	19	24	22	101
Bulls	23	28	28	27	106

A: 18,645. **T:** 2:19. **Officials:** Darell Garretson, Paul Mihalak.

sidering that he and Jordan had just enjoyed a friendly dinner the week before. He was determined to be ready for Game 2 of the series.

"Well, Michael never scored 50 points on me," said Harper.

"There's a first time for everything," said Jordan from the other locker room.

By the end of Game 2, Harper might have been feeling a bit like the legendary baseball manager Leo Durocher, who took over the hapless Chicago Cubs in the mid-1960s and immediately declared, "This is not an eighth-place club [in the National League]." He was right. The Cubs finished tenth and last the following season.

Harper faced similar consequences. Jordan jumped, feigned, and drove his way to 55 points against Harper and the Cavs. The Bulls won, 106–101, in a hard-fought game that went down to the final seconds. Cleveland actually led, 101–100, with just over a minute remaining. The game wasn't iced until Mark Price fouled out trying to stop Jordan with fourteen ticks left. MJ bagged both free throws.

In the scoring fest against Harper, Jordan tied Boston Celtics legend John Havlicek with a postseason record twenty-four field goals. He attempted forty-five shots and hit a perfect 7 of 7 from the free-throw line. It was the sixth time during the 1987–88 regular season and playoffs that Jordan had scored at least 50 points in a game. He broke a bunch of team records, but he had set most of them in Game 1 of this same series.

While critics continued to nudge Jordan about playing a one-man game, the star himself reasoned that dominating a game might just be one way to win. He was looking for wins, he said, not eye-opening statistics. He believed a guard could control a game the same way as a center, which was conventional basketball strategy.

"I don't live by what other people say," noted Jordan. "I live by what I do. It hasn't been done before. That's a challenge for me. No one thought we would finish second in our division [during the 1987–88 regular season], either."

For his part, Price realized this changing of the basketball guard spelled trouble for the Cavs. "They go to him every time they have to," said Price. "We've got to find a way to slow him down."

Most teams are still searching.

Number 18: Great Game Index

GGI Score (109 of a possible 123)   The tiebreaker is game importance.

Scoring (33 of a possible 33)   The Bulls needed a super-human scoring effort. Michael's 24-of-45 shooting (53 percent) helped erase a 36–23 Cleveland lead after the first quarter.

Game Importance (18 of 20)   The Bulls didn't want to lose home-court advantage in the series. Michael himself had to overcome any letdown from scoring 50 in the lopsided opener.

Opponent Strength (18 of 20)   The Cavaliers were scrappers with sound fundamentals. When Price got hot, this team could be unstoppable.

Historical Significance (9 of 10)   Scoring big and winning set a positive precedent for Jordan and Chicago.

Legendary Intangibles (10 of 10)   MJ set the trap for Ron Harper, then used for his own motivation.

Pressure Points (9 of 10)   The game was not decided until the final fourteen seconds, when Michael sank a pair of free throws.

Defense (3 of 5)   MJ had three steals and stayed defensively active the whole game.

Other Offensive Contributions (3 of 5)   Fifty-five points and forty-four minutes is just fine, thank you.

MJ's Physical Condition (1 of 5)   No factor, though Jordan was nursing some minor injuries.

Long Odds (5 of 5)   Michael, of course, owns the playoff single-game scoring record, with 63 against Boston in 1986. Only Elgin Baylor (61), Wilt Chamberlain (56), and Rick Barry (55), had scored at least 55 points in a game in past postseasons, and none did it on the heels of a 50-point game.

-19-

March 28, 1990

Bulls at Cleveland Cavaliers Regular Season

Airing it out: Jordan zooms to 69 against the Cavs.

*T*here is perhaps no more practical indicator of Michael Jordan's extraordinary basketball skills than to realize that his 69-point effort against familiar foil Cleveland ranks only nineteenth on the Great Game Index.

Michael himself called it his "best game, by far, especially because we won." Remember, this was 1990, more than a full year before the Bulls' first title run. Like everyone else, Jordan was himself a bit romanced by scoring so many points.

It marked the ninth highest total in NBA history and the most in more than ten seasons. The 69 points also came in handy, as Chicago won in overtime, 117–113, and clinched a spot in the playoffs. The victory evened the Bulls' road record at 18–18 and marked a club-record seventh straight win away from home.

Besides the Cavaliers' defense, Jordan literally ripped through the new pair of Nikes he wears for every game. It seemed that about the only shot he missed was a long three-

Air Jordan reached his zenith in a 69-point effort against the Cavaliers.
UPI/Corbis-Bettmann

Game): Bulls 117, Cavaliers 113

Bulls	Min	FG-att	FT-att	Reb	Ast	Fls	Pts
Pippen	41	3-10	1-2	8	7	5	7
Grant	40	7-14	2-4	5	4	4	16
Cartwright	39	3-7	3-4	5	1	5	9
Jordan	50	23-37	21-23	18	6	5	69
Paxson	23	1-4	0-0	0	1	6	2
Armstrong	29	2-7	2-2	1	3	5	6
Davis	11	2-3	0-0	2	1	2	5
Perdue	12	0-0	0-0	4	0	3	0
King	17	0-4	1-2	1	1	2	1
Lett	3	1-1	0-0	0	0	2	2
Totals	265	42-87	30-37	44	24	39	117

Percentages: FG .483, FT .811. **Three-point goals:** 3-7, .429 (Jordan 2-6, Davis 1-1). **Team rebounds:** 10. **Blocked shots:** 3 (Grant, Jordan, Perdue). **Turnovers:** 19 (Pippen 8, Cartwright 3, Grant 2, Jordan 2, Paxson 2, Armstrong, Davis). **Steals:** 14 (Pippen 5, Jordan 4, Armstrong 2, King 2, Grant). **Technical fouls:** Coach Jackson, 5:40 1st; Paxson, 9:09 3rd. **Illegal defense:** None.

Cavaliers	Min	FG-att	FT-att	Reb	Ast	Fls	Pts
Bennett	20	2-4	2-2	3	1	3	6
Nance	37	4-10	3-4	7	2	6	11
Daugherty	45	2-9	6-8	9	2	2	10
Ehlo	44	10-23	3-5	9	3	6	26
Price	44	6-14	17-20	2	8	3	31
Williams	42	8-12	7-9	10	1	6	23
Brown	15	1-2	0-0	0	1	1	2
Kerr	6	0-0	2-2	0	0	0	2
Rollins	4	0-0	0-0	0	0	2	0
Morton	8	1-2	0-0	0	4	0	2
Totals	265	34-76	40-50	40	22	29	113

Percentages: FG .447, FT .800. **Three-point goals:** 5-15, .333 (Ehlo 3-7, Price 2-7, Morton 0-1). **Team rebounds:** 10. **Blocked shots:** 8 (Nance 3, Daugherty 2, Williams 2, Brown). **Turnovers:** 22 (Williams 4, Nance 3, Bennett 3, Daugherty 3, Ehlo 3, Price 3, Morton 2, Kerr). **Steals:** 11 (Williams, 5, Daugherty 2, Bennett, Ehlo, Price, Brown). **Technical fouls:** Coach Wilkens 2, 7:25 3rd (ejected). **Illegal defense:** 1.

Bulls	27	26	36	16	12	117
Cavaliers	26	24	28	27	8	113

A: 20,273. **T:** 2:43. **Officials:** Dick Bavetta, Nolan Fine, Jim Clark.

pointer at the buzzer in regulation. He actually nailed 23 of 37 from the floor and 21 of 23 free throws, plus 2 of 6 three point-ers (disappointing would-be skeptics who wanted to say Jordan scored 69 the cheap way).

While Jordan fired from all angles, he actually clinched the game by grabbing the rebound of an errant Horace Grant free throw late in overtime. He was fouled and made both free ones to set the final score.

Jordan was suffering from minor cold symptoms before the tip-off, but seemed to heat up just fine.

"I got my shots off early," said Jordan, who couldn't help but be pleased with himself. "I hit everything and felt myself in a great rhythm. "I shot well. When you shoot the ball and you're playing that kind of game, it seems like all parts of your game are energized, rebounding, steals [he had four], defense—everything."

Jordan strung together quite a scoring line—16 points in the first quarter, 15 in the second, 20 in the third, 10 in the fourth, and 8 in overtime—and he was keenly aware of his hot hand. Coach Phil Jackson didn't discourage him, since Horace Grant was the only other Bull in double figures, with 16.

"It was a great performance," said Jackson in his first year as head coach. "I saw Pete Maravich get sixty-eight or sixty-nine one time, and he was terrific, but Michael was equal to that and above."

Said Jordan, "I think I missed one shot in the first quarter and four at halftime. I could feel myself knocking in shots. I hit a three with no time left on the shot clock in the fourth quarter. You know when that happens, things are starting to go your way.

"I haven't felt that way since that day in Boston [when he scored 63 against the Celtics in a 1986 playoff game—see Game No. 3]. Everything seemed to fall in line, and I just tried to jump on it and ride it as long as I could ride it."

Cleveland players and fans alike were getting queasy as they were rocked by the Jordan Express. He averaged 50.5 points in four straight wins that season, which of course was on top of The Shot that ended the Cavaliers' 1989 postseason (see Great Game No. 4).

Number 19: Great Game Index

GGI Score (109 of a possible 123).

Scoring (33 of a possible 33) Sorry, MJ, no extra credit in this category.

Game Importance (17 of 20) It was only the regular season, but late enough that both the Bulls and Cavaliers were jockeying for postseason slots.

Opponent Strength (17 of 20) This Cleveland club was struggling a bit during the late season.

Historical Significance (10 of 10) Every superhuman needs a top ten of all-time—and best of recent times—performance on his resumé.

Legendary Intangibles (10 of 10) Jordan took mostly high-percentages shots that night. He was in alignment with Phil Jackson's desire to run a more disciplined offensive scheme. To his credit, on this night Jackson deferred to MJ's undeniable hot hand.

Pressure Points (10 of 10) Michael's final points in overtime clinched victory. There was no garbage time.

Defense (2 of 5) Nothing exceptional, but no missed assignments, either.

Other Offensive Contributions (5 of 5) Remarkably, MJ pulled down 18 rebounds, 11 on the offensive boards (natch).

MJ's Physical Condition (1 of 5) Not a factor, though he did play a game-high fifty minutes.

Long Odds (4 of 5) Sixty-nine is a big number, even for Michael, but clearly, big numbers are never out of his reach anytime he steps on a basketball court.

-20-

May 9, 1992

Bulls at New York Knicks Game 3, Second-Round Playoff Series

Road win sets the tone for a second title run.

This 94–86 victory was a definition game for the 1992 Bulls playoffs squad. In a tight contest against his team's biggest rival, Michael muffed a breakaway slam dunk with about four minutes left in the first half. The Madison Square Garden fans were merciless, chanting "Myyy-kel, Myyy-kel" with delighted derision. The scoreboard showed replay after replay.

"I guess I was over-pumped," said Michael.

The Knicks rode the crowd energy into halftime, scoring eight unanswered points after the Jordan miss. Pat Riley said the momentum changed sides more quickly in a game than he had ever seen.

Michael responded that he forgot about the name-calling, the suggestions to "Eat your Wheaties," and the chanting as

Game 20: Bulls 94, Knicks 86

Bulls	Min	FG-att	FT-att	Reb	Ast	Fls	Pts
Grant	35	2-4	6-8	13	2	1	10
Pippen	41	7-12	10-12	5	3	6	26
Cartwright	27	3-7	1-2	3	2	4	7
Jordan	44	12-24	7-10	9	3	2	32
Paxson	30	2-4	0-0	0	4	3	5
Armstrong	18	0-3	0-0	0	3	2	0
Perdue	16	2-3	2-2	7	0	4	6
Hodges	6	1-2	0-0	0	0	0	3
Williams	15	1-2	0-0	1	0	2	2
King	2	0-1	0-0	0	0	0	0
Levingston	6	1-3	1-1	1	0	0	3
Totals	**240**	**31-65**	**27-36**	**39**	**17**	**24**	**94**

Percentages: FG .477, FT. .771. **Three-point goals:** 5-9, .556 (Pippen 2-2, Hodges 1-1, Paxson 1-2, Jordan 1-3, Armstrong 0-1). **Team rebounds:** 8. **Blocked shots:** 6 (Perdue 2, Grant, Pippen, Cartwright, Jordan). **Turnovers:** 16 (Jordan 6, Pippen 4, Paxson 2, Perdue 2, Williams 2). **Steals:** 9 (Jordan 3, Pippen 2, Williams 2, Cartwright, Paxson). **Technical fouls:** Illegal defense, 10:19, 2nd. **Illegal defense:** 1.

Knicks	Min	FG-att	FT-att	Reb	Ast	Fls	Pts
McDaniel	37	5-10	0-2	3	2	4	11
Oakley	34	6-9	1-2	9	0	4	13
Ewing	44	12-22	3-7	11	4	5	27
Jackson	30	4-9	0-0	3	8	0	8
Wilkins	41	6-16	1-2	5	4	4	13
Mason	17	0-2	0-0	6	0	5	0
Starks	15	2-7	4-5	4	2	3	9
Anthony	18	1-4	2-4	0	6	0	5
Vandeweghe	4	0-1	0-0	0	0	0	0
Totals	**240**	**36-80**	**11-22**	**41**	**26**	**25**	**86**

Percentages: FG .450, FT .500. **Three-point goals:** 3-11, 273 (McDaniel 1-2, Starks 1-2, Anthony 1-2, Ewing 0-1, Jackson 0-2, Wilkins 0-2). **Team rebounds:** 9. **Blocked shots:** 2 (Ewing 2). **Turnovers:** 12 (Jackson 6, McDaniel 2, Wilkins 2, Starks, Anthony). **Steals:** 3 (Anthony 2, Oakley). **Technical fouls:** None. **Illegal defense:** 1.

Bulls	32	19	20	23	94
Knicks	23	27	14	22	86

A: 19,763. **T:** 2:37. **Officials:** Darell Garretson, Bob Delaney, Steve Javie.

soon as he missed the basket, figuring it no more disheartening than a jump shot that rims out.

Somehow, though, you know that isn't entirely true, and doesn't acknowledge the heat of Jordan's deeply burning competitive flame. As the game went into the final minutes of the fourth quarter, it was clearly time to erase the mistake, apply the MJ signature, and add the proper exclamation point.

The game was close, a seesaw of large bodies and small things, like good defensive position and crisp passing, that wins titles. Jordan and Scottie Pippen were hitting a high percentage of jumpers as the Knicks appeared to have placed roadblocks in the driving lanes to the basket. Jordan crashed to the floor on one attempted layup.

With four minutes left and the Bulls leading by seven, Michael was again on the outside perimeter looking in. He saw the slightest bit of daylight between Knicks players Xavier McDaniel and Patrick Ewing. A quick step could get him through in time to take a shot but probably not without getting crunched.

There was no choice for a champion.

"Sometimes you have to face the fire," Jordan said later.

Michael went up for the shot as Ewing slammed him on one side and McDaniel caught the Bulls star square on the nose. Blood was streaking down Jordan's face about the time the basketball dropped through the net. Ewing and McDaniel collided into a tangled heap on the floor. Jordan stood directly over Ewing, shaking his fist for emphasis.

Before having one of his a nostrils packed with cotton, MJ sank a free throw to complete a 3-point play and, in many respects, finish the Knicks' dreams of dethroning the Bulls. Message delivered.

"It was one of those inspirational plays," said Jordan.

"A playoff play," said Jackson.

Number 20: Great Game Index

GGI Score (108 of a possible 123)   Tiebreaker is game importance.

Scoring (31 of a possible 33)   Michael scored 32 points on the day, working hard for every basket.

Game Importance (19 of 20)   The Bulls went up 2–1 in a series that went the limit.

Opponent Strength (18 of 20)   This was a fiercely physical Knicks team that matched up well with the champion Bulls.

Historical Significance (8 of 10)   Sort of a dubious honor, but it is likely the first and last time Jordan will miss a dunk in a playoff game—especially in Madison Square Garden.

Legendary Intangibles (10 of 10)   MJ also had his first and second successful slams of the playoffs.

Pressure Points (8 of 10)   Michael and his teammates recovered from the missed dunk and 8-point Knicks run. "We made an emphasis in the second half to regain the momentum we had," said Jordan. "We pretty much retained it the rest of the game."

Defense (4 of 5)   The Bulls' typical clampdown defensive play helped calm matters.

Other Offensive Contributions (5 of 5)   MJ finished with 9 rebounds against a New York team that can be intimidating on the inside.

MJ's Physical Condition (1 of 5)   Not a factor.

Long Odds (4 of 5)   Jordan leaped over about fourteen feet of snarling men in the game's key sequence.

-21-

May 5, 1996

New York Knicks at Bulls Game 1, Second-Round Playoff Series

Michael delivers a 44-point message.

A warning signal to the rest of the NBA was transmitted in this 91–84 Bulls victory to open up the second round of the 1996 playoffs: Michael was back in top playoff form, even if his back muscles were in spasms that lingered from a first-round knockout of Pat Riley's Miami Heat. Michael combined hard drives to the hoop with feathery jump shots and some trademark slam dunks, putting up 44 points. Riley's old team, the Knicks, were not happy to encounter Michael's return to his otherworldly mode after the 1995 postseason blip on the radar screen.

The critics will say this game was no more than MJ stepping out of his team's usual offensive flow to notch 44 points and take 40 percent of the Bulls' shots. Too many other guys were standing around, true, but a closer look reveals flawed thinking.

This game turned on defense. The Knicks were one of the NBA's best defensive teams during the regular season. New York exerted great pressure on the wing players, particularly

Game 21: Bulls 91, Knicks 84

Knicks	Min	FG-att	FT-att	Reb	Ast	Fls	Pts
Oakley	43	4-9	6-7	6-13	2	4	14
Mason	45	5-11	2-2	1-5	2	4	12
Ewing	43	9-23	3-5	3-16	1	3	21
Starks	39	0-9	4-4	2-2	2	4	4
D. Harper	40	8-17	1-2	0-0	5	2	19
Ward	8	2-5	0-0	0-0	1	0	4
Davis	15	3-4	0-0	0-3	0	2	8
Reid	7	1-1	0-0	0-1	1	2	2
Totals	**240**	**32-79**	**16-20**	**12-40**	**14**	**21**	**84**

Percentages: FG .405, FT .800. **Three-point goals:** 4-15, .267 (Davis 2-3, D. Harper 2-5, Ward 0-2, Starks 0-5). **Team rebounds:** 13. **Blocked shots:** None. **Turnovers:** 17 (Ewing 5, Oakley 3, Mason 3, Davis 3, Starks, D. Harper, Reid). **Steals:** 4 (D. Harper 2, Ewing, Ward). **Technical fouls:** D. Harper, 4:49 2nd; Mason, 8:49 3rd; Oakley, 7:59 4th.

Bulls	Min	FG-att	FT-att	Reb	Ast	Fls	Pts
Pippen	43	4-15	3-3	5-10	7	0	11
Rodman	33	0-3	3-4	3-12	2	4	3
Longley	35	4-10	0-0	5-8	2	5	8
R. Harper	30	2-7	0-0	2-7	3	3	4
Jordan	41	17-35	9-9	1-5	2	4	44
Kukoc	28	1-8	5-6	1-2	5	2	7
Kerr	15	3-6	0-0	0-1	0	0	8
Salley	2	0-0	0-0	0-0	0	0	0
Edwards	7	0-0	2-2	0-0	0	2	2
Brown	2	1-2	0-0	0-0	0	1	2
Wenington	4	1-1	0-0	1-3	0	2	2
Totals	**240**	**33-87**	**22-24**	**18-48**	**21**	**23**	**91**

Percentages: FG .379, FT .917 **Three-point goals:** 3-19, .158 (Kerr 2-4, Jordan 1-5, R. Harper 0-2, Kukoc 0-4, Pippen 0-4). **Team rebounds:** 6. **Blocked shots:** 4 (Longley 2, Pippen, R. Harper). **Turnovers:** 8 (Rodman 3, Kerr 2, Pippen, Longley, Jordan). **Steals:** 8 (Pippen 2, Longley 2, Kukoc 2, Rodman, R. Harper). **Technical fouls:** Jordan, 4:49 2nd; Pippen, 7:59 4th.

Knicks	17	30	22	15	84
Bulls	25	29	19	18	91

A: 24,934. **T:** 2:24. **Officials:** Don Vaden, Joe Crawford, Eddie F. Rush.

Scottie Pippen, Toni Kukoc, and Ron Harper. In some ways, Jordan was simply taking what New York was giving—especially hitting the shots when no one else in the home white seemed able to get the job done.

"It's easy to go to Michael because he's the guy who is in

rhythm," said Bulls coach Phil Jackson. "The other part of it is the Knicks have something to do with that. They're taking away a lot of other people's offense."

"That's why Michael's so good," said Bulls center Luc Longley. "He can take those situations and make a good show of them."

Chicago played its own ferocious brand of defense, led by Jordan, Pippen, and Dennis Rodman. Leading 73–69 after three quarters, the Bulls clamped New York in the final twelve minutes. The Knicks shot 5 of 20 for the fourth quarter, and Derek Harper's jump shot with 5:15 remaining was their last field goal of the game.

"We came out and played a lot harder on defense than we did on offense," said Scottie Pippen. "When we got on offense, we kind of lost our rhythm. Early on, we just went to Michael."

One other thing: To his enduring credit, Jordan played with a serious injury that required all-day treatment until game time. The pain was lessened, but fatigue sentenced his back to a new set of painful spasms. He actually pulled himself out of the game a few times to rest his back, lying on the floor to help ease the discomfort. His scoring spree was necessary, rather than some luxury, although Michael was the first to call for more scoring participation from his teammates.

"We know we didn't play our best basketball," noted MJ. "We won the game, but we still have a lot of improvements to make."

The upgrade for Air Jordan and teammates was arranged. Chicago went on to close out the rival Knicks in five games before exacting revenge in the form of a four-game sweep against the Orlando Magic and Shaquille O'Neal.

Number 21: Great Game Index

GGI Score (108 of a possible 123).

Scoring (32 of a possible 33)　Michael hit all the clutch baskets. It marked his thirty-first playoff game with 40 or more points. He scored 25 points in the first half to set the pace for the series. He finished with 48 percent of his team's points in the game.

Game Importance (18 of 20)   This series turned on confidence. The Bulls cast doubt into a New York team that never recovered.

Opponent Strength (19 of 20)   The Knicks defense was the league's best during the regular season. The Bulls never scored more than 99 in any game of the series.

Historical Significance (8 of 10)   Another downer for Patrick Ewing, who now knew Michael's self-imposed "retirement" years were his Knicks' best chance to win a title.

Legendary Intangibles (10 of 10)   Michael carried Chicago on his back, which was sore enough for an entire planet to know.

Pressure Points (9 of 10)   Jordan took 40 percent of the Bulls' shots. Don't ask about the other 60 percent.

Defense (3 of 5)   Jordan was tireless on the both ends of the floor. Holding the Knicks to 84 points was necessary.

Other Offensive Contributions (3 of 5)   It's tough to rebound your own shots in the NBA, and even harder to get assists when your teammates are cold.

MJ's Physical Condition (4 of 5)   Jordan played forty-one minutes with a back that would sideline mere mortals—and more than a few NBA stars—for weeks.

Long Odds (2 of 5)   Michael's return to peak form, despite a bad back, was never really in doubt.

-22-

May 13, 1989

New York Knicks at Bulls Game 3, Second-Round Playoff Series

Lost weekend for the Knicks.

This performance was the opening act of a blockbuster weekend for Michael and the Bulls (see Game No. 17). After trading wins in New York, Jordan and his maturing Chicago teammates took control of the series. He reaggravated a nagging groin injury (his pain started in March) on a 360-degree spin move in the second quarter. He came up limping but with two of his 40 points on the afternoon.

Michael has rarely missed any critical minutes of important games, much less sat out the remainder of a playoff contest. He ignored searing pain to soar instead. The Bulls rampaged to a 20-point halftime lead on the strength of Michael's 16 second-quarter points. The Knicks never saw it coming.

"I don't know what happened," said Charles Oakley, the former Bull and Jordan confidant who was traded for center Bill Cartwright during the off-season. "I went out there and was trying to play hard, and the next thing I knew, we were down by twenty."

Game 22: Bulls 111, Knicks 88

Knicks	Min	FG-att	FT-att	Reb	Ast	Fls	Pts
Newman	14	0-8	0-0	0	1	2	0
Oakley	32	4-6	1-1	9	1	3	9
Ewing	35	7-13	5-7	6	2	2	19
Jackson	30	3-7	0-2	2	6	1	7
G. Wilkins	26	6-13	1-1	0	4	4	13
Tucker	0	5-12	0-0	5	3	4	14
Vandeweghe	18	1-6	6-6	1	1	0	8
Green	11	1-2	0-0	3	0	0	2
Strickland	18	2-8	4-8	2	1	1	8
Walker	17	1-3	2-2	3	0	4	4
Myers	9	0-0	4-6	3	1	1	4
Totals	**240**	**30-78**	**23-33**	**34**	**20**	**22**	**88**

Percentages: FG .385, FT .697. **Three-point goals:** 5-16, .313 (Tucker 4-8, Jackson 1-3, Newman 0-4, Wilkins 0-1). **Team rebounds:** 9. **Blocked shots:** 7 (Walker 2, Ewing, Jackson, Wilkins, Vandeweghe, Myers). **Turnovers:** 16 (Ewing 4, Oakley 3, Strickland 3, Newman 2, Jackson 2, Vandeweghe, Walker). **Steals:** 8 (Wilkins 3, Tucker 2, Oakley, Ewing, Walker).

Bulls	Min	FG-att	FT-att	Reb	Ast	Fls	Pts
Pippen	28	6-9	0-0	7	5	6	12
Grant	35	7-10	1-1	11	3	3	15
Cartwright	27	4-6	1-4	4	1	5	9
Hodges	35	4-12	2-2	1	6	2	11
Jordan	39	14-25	11-13	15	9	3	40
Davis	26	3-8	1-3	5	2	4	7
Paxson	15	3-6	0-0	1	2	3	7
Sellers	14	2-8	0-0	5	1	2	4
Corzine	9	0-1	1-2	3	0	2	1
Vincent	6	1-3	0-0	1	1	0	2
Perdue	3	0-0	0-0	2	1	0	0
Haley	3	1-2	1-2	0	0	0	3
Totals	**240**	**45-90**	**18-27**	**55**	**31**	**30**	**111**

Percentages: FG .500, FT .667. **Three-point goals:** 3-8, .375 (Hodges 1-5, Jordan 1-2, Paxson 1-1). **Team rebounds:** 14. **Blocked shots:** 4 (Pippen; Cartwright, Jordan, Vincent). **Turnovers:** 18 (Grant 4, Pippen 3, Cartwright 3, Jordan 3, Paxson 2, Corzine 2, Sellers). **Steals:** 10 (Jordan 6, Pippen 2, Cartwright, Hodges).

Knicks	20	26	21	21	88
Bulls	24	42	17	28	111

A: 18,599. **T:** 2:20.

The Bulls coasted to a 111–88 victory. MJ played four minutes longer than any teammate, then rushed off to a special muscle-stimulation device without talking to the media.

Reporters were left to hear Knicks coach Rick Pitino put a spin on the loss that would make a whirling dervish proud.

"I think one of the keys for us was, we kept Michael Jordan in the game until the end," said Pitino, as media members wondered if the coach was joking (he wasn't). Pitino reasoned that it might tire out or limit Michael for the next game, due to be played within twenty-four hours (it didn't).

The second quarter was framed by record parameters. The Bulls tied a franchise playoff record for points in a quarter, with 42. They shot 71 percent as a team, while Scottie Pippen and Horace Grant were beginning to show why they and Jordan would form the nucleus of three straight NBA title teams.

"We had the double-team on Jordan," said Trent Tucker, the sharpshooting Knicks guard who would win a championship ring with the Bulls in 1993. "But those other guys were hitting. So we got a little more hesitant to leave them, and it's difficult to guard Jordan one-on-one."

Michael did prove unstoppable—and nearly impenetrable. Along with the 40 points, he pulled down 15 rebounds, handed out 9 assists, and had 6 steals. Earlier in the week, Jordan told the *Chicago Tribune*'s Sam Smith that he was growing more enamored with his current group of teammates with every win.

"I feel like I'm very observant about the game and how it's played," said Jordan. "I try to be aware of when my team needs my creativity and scoring or my passing or rebounding.

"Last year I had to score fifty, fifty-five points to pull out a victory in the playoffs. This year it's different. That's what I mean about the maturity of players like Scottie and Horace, and [Bill] Cartwright and Craig [Hodges]. These players have taken some of the load off me."

Cartwright had showed up in Chicago with enough baggage to fill an airport carousel. He had disappointed the Knicks brass and was skewered regularly by the New York press. Jordan's reception was cool at best, especially because his pal and top NBA rebounder Oakley was sent packing.

"Frankly, I expected more from Bill because of the trade itself," said Jordan, "but he took more time than I thought to adjust to everyone on the team. I thought we were going to get off like killers. We didn't, and then everything [on offense] was geared to the middle, toward the post play. We were totally changing our outlook after winning fifty games. I disagreed with that to a certain extent. It didn't seem like we were better."

What turned the situation around was a private meeting between Jordan and Cartwright. They cleared the air, particularly focusing on how to make things work.

"I didn't know how to play with Bill," Jordan admitted. "I had to learn to play with a center like him, his likes and dislikes, where he wanted the ball and what he would do. It's something that I've had to learn with all of my teammates. I feel it's made us a better team. [My teammates] are starting to expand their roles and get closer to the expectations I had for them."

Jordan said his expectations for his own play were beyond sky-high level. He quite accurately explained his best was yet to come.

"I don't feel I've reached my peak as a player. I really feel like I'll get better as I get older, but if people think I've peaked, it will just give me more surprises for them."

The Knicks, for one, weren't anxious for any more 40-point surprise parties. Of course, they were invited nonetheless to some dozen more anyway, including the next two games of this hard-fought series.

Number 22: Great Game Index

GGI Score (107 of a possible 123) The tiebreaker is game importance.

Scoring (31 of a possible 33) The Bulls buried the Knicks—for this game and the series—in the second quarter. Michael scored more than one-third of a club record 42 points.

Game Importance (18 of 20) With the series tied 1–1, Chicago had no intention of a letdown on its home floor.

Opponent Strength (18 of 20)   The Knicks were a ferocious defensive club that made every team, including the Bulls, work for its points.

Historical Significance (8 of 10)   Michael has flattened New York so many times, some games grab a bit smaller piece of history.

Legendary Intangibles (10 of 10)   Groin injuries have made grown men cry. Jordan's response was 40 points and a big smile.

Pressure Points (7 of 10)   MJ took the pressure off himself and his teammates with such a hot first half. It likely helped his teammates gain more confidence.

Defense (5 of 5)   Six steals is one big stat.

Other Offensive Contributions (5 of 5)   Fifteen rebounds and nine assists are equally impressive numbers.

MJ's Physical Condition (4 of 5)   Right after the game, Jordan spent two hours with trainer Mark Pfeil to get ready for the next day's game. That cramped his usual eloquent style with the media, but he was far from limited on the court.

Long Odds (1 of 5)   A 40-point effort from Jordan was beginning to be commonplace.

-23-

May 14, 1991

Philadelphia 76ers at Bulls Game 5 Clincher, Second-Round Playoff Series

Jordan time runs the clock on Philly.

The Sixers had just tied the game at 92–92 with three minutes left. Charles Barkley led a charge that helped Philadelphia come back from a 10-point deficit. He and his teammates were thinking about forcing a Game 6 back at the Spectrum in Philly.

Michael Jordan had no such travel plans. He scored the Bulls' final 12 points in a 100–95 win, including 8 after the tie. Game and series, Chicago. Jordan finished with 38 points and 19 rebounds.

"He just took over when he had to," said Rickey Green of the Sixers.

"I thought we had a good shot," added Philadelphia coach Jim Lynam, "but Jordan took over."

Michael simply took the ball to the hoop, collecting layups

Game 23: Bulls 100, 76ers 95

76ers	Min	FG-att	FT-att	Reb	Ast	Fls	Pts
Barkley	45	12-20	6-10	8	7	3	30
Gilliam	45	6-13	9-9	6	1	4	21
Mahorn	21	1-2	0-0	4	0	1	2
Green	31	6-11	2-2	1	5	1	16
Hawkins	39	6-11	1-1	3	2	6	15
Anderson	28	2-9	0-0	3	5	4	4
Turner	17	1-6	0-0	2	4	1	2
Bol	7	0-1	1-2	2	1	1	1
Reid	7	2-3	0-0	0	0	1	4
Totals	**240**	**36-76**	**19-24**	**4-29**	**25**	**22**	**95**

Percentages: FG .474, FT .792. **Three-point goals:** 4-11, .364 (Green 2-2, Hawkins 2-3, Reid 0-1, Barkley 0-2, Turner 0-3). **Team rebounds:** 4. **Blocked shots:** 6 (Gilliam 4, Barkley, Bol). **Turnovers:** 6 (Gilliam 2, Barkley, Green, Anderson, Reid). **Steals:** 7 (Barkley 2, Hawkins 2, Green, Anderson, Turner). **Technical fouls:** None. **Illegal defense:** None.

Bulls	Min	FG-att	FT-att	Reb	Ast	Fls	Pts
Pippen	39	13-18	1-2	8	6	4	28
Grant	45	3-7	3-4	11	1	3	9
Cartwright	35	3-9	2-2	6	3	4	8
Paxson	31	2-3	0-0	0	2	4	5
Jordan	42	14-31	10-11	19	7	3	38
Armstrong	17	1-5	0-0	2	1	0	2
Hodges	12	0-02	0-0	0	1	1	0
Perdue	7	4-5	0-0	3	0	1	8
King	9	0-4	0-0	2	1	0	0
Levingston	3	1-1	0-0	1	0	0	2
Totals	**240**	**41-85**	**16-19**	**16-52**	**22**	**20**	**100**

Percentages: FG .482, FT .842. **Three-point goals:** 2-6, .333 (Pippen 1-1, Paxson 1-2, Hodges 0-1, Jordan 0-2). **Team rebounds:** 7. **Blocked shots:** 1 (Jordan). **Turnovers:** 9 (Jordan 4, Pippen 2, Grant, Paxson, Armstrong). **Steals:** 2 (Cartwright, Armstrong). **Technical fouls:** None. **Illegal defense:** 1.

76ers	29	22	20	24	95
Bulls	30	28	23	19	100

A: 18,676. **T:** 2:04. **Officials:** Dick Bavetta, Joe Crawford, Joe Forte.

and foul shots to sink Sir Charles, who scored 30 in the losing effort. The two stars hugged at mid-court after the final buzzer.

While Barkley was left to wonder about opportunity lost— "Charles fought like a warrior," said MJ—the Bulls were setting for a collision course with Detroit, with the Pistons getting the worst of that pending crash. This club was now 7–1 in the midst of what would be a 15–2 playoff run to its first title.

"The ultimate goal for me now is winning a world championship," said Jordan after the game, icing an ankle throbbing with tendinitis. "Your team joins a very elite class. As a team you earn a lot of respect. As a team you consider yourself the best for that one year.

"You want it for so many reasons, for the city of Chicago. A lot of reasons for playing with pain. A lot of reasons for giving all of the extra effort it will take."

With the benefit of 20-20 hindsight, it appears that Jordan was selling himself and the Bulls a bit short, but Barkley, following the defeat didn't give his friend much chance to win it all. Even Michael's best buddies were not yet convinced he could be enough of a team player to win NBA titles.

"I think the Bulls are going to be the team to beat in the Eastern Conference," said Barkley. "No one can beat Portland, though. Why not? Because they're the best team on the planet. Didn't they spank Chicago twice this year? Get used to it, brother. Chicago, I think, will be there, but no one is going to beat Portland."

Uh, sorry, Charles. Magic Johnson and the Los Angeles Lakers beat the Trail Blazers to earn the Western Conference bid to the 1991 Finals—and the right to lose in five to Chicago.

Somewhere on a golf course in America that summer, you just know Michael Jordan was chatting up Charles Barkley on the subject of prognostication. For once, Barkley might have been speechless.

Number 23: Great Game Index

GGI Score (107 of a possible 123).

Scoring (30 of a possible 33) Besides scoring the last 12 points of the game, MJ bagged 13 in the critical third quarter.

Game Importance (17 of 20) The Bulls had some margin for error, but wanted to heal up before facing the Pistons, who were still duking it out with Boston.

Opponent Strength (17 of 20)   Barkley brought Philly up a few notches.

Historical Significance (8 of 10)   More about setting up the Detroit sweep than this one game of stats.

Legendary Intangibles (10 of 10)   Jordan took over the game—and won the series—just when it was needed. He shrugged off a poor-shooting first half (6 of 16) like the champion he would soon become.

Pressure Points (10 of 10)   Philly was on a run. MJ stopped it cold with clutch layups and free throws.

Defense (3 of 5)   Another solid game.

Other Offensive Contributions (5 of 5)   Nineteen rebounds. Count 'em, Charles.

MJ's Physical Condition (3 of 5)   Michael was battling a flare-up of tendinitis in his ankle.

Long Odds (4 of 5)   The momentum and injuries pointed in Philly's favor.

-24-

May 19, 1998

Indiana Pacers at Bulls Game 2, Eastern Conference Finals

Michael's work of beauty allows an ugly win.

*I*n what appeared an ordinary 2–0 series lead on the way to winning the conference finals in the Bulls' usual six games or less, this virtuoso Jordan performance eventually stood as the only reason Chicago made it to a Game 7 in the 1998 Eastern Conference showdown.

Indiana outshot the Bulls and outplayed them most of the game. The Pacers were up 52–45 at halftime, but Chicago roared back behind Jordan in the third quarter. Michael tallied 14 points, including 8 of 10 free throws, to fuel a 4-point Bulls lead after three quarters. He finished 15 of 18 from the foul line.

The Pacers stayed close during the final twelve minutes. Michael kept hitting key jumpers and drives to choke off any sustained rally. His output of 13 of 22 from the floor only confirmed his acceptance of the league's regular season Most Valuable Player trophy before the game. Bulls fans stood as one to applaud MJ's fifth MVP award, which put him in exclu-

Game 24: Bulls 104, Pacers 98

Pacers	Min	FG-att	FT-att	Reb	Ast	Fls	Pts
Mullin	31	6-10	5-5	5	2	5	18
D. Davis	21	3-4	3-5	9	2	4	9
Smits	31	7-11	3-4	8	0	5	17
Jackson	32	4-9	0-0	8	8	1	8
Miller	41	4-13	10-11	3	3	1	19
A. Davis	33	5-9	4-5	2-7	2	3	14
McKey	18	3-7	2-2	2	1	4	9
Rose	9	1-2	0-0	1	2	4	2
Best	16	1-4	0-0	2	2	2	2
Pope	8	0-0	0-0	1	0	1	0
Totals	**240**	**34-69**	**27-32**	**11-46**	**22**	**30**	**98**

Percentages: FG .493, FT .844. **Three-point goals:** 3-12, .250 (McKey 1-2, Miller 1-3, Mullin 1-5, Jackson 0-1, Best 0-1). **Team rebounds:** 4. **Blocked shots:** 2 (Mullin, A. Davis). **Turnovers:** 19 (Jackson 7, Mullin 4, A. Davis 3, Smits, Miller, McKey, Rose, Best). **Steals:** 2 (Jackson, A. Davis).

Bulls	Min	FG-att	FT-att	Reb	Ast	Fls	Pts
Pippen	42	6-18	7-10	6	5	4	21
Kukoc	26	5-12	5-7	3	2	3	16
Longley	24	3-7	0-0	3	2	5	6
Harper	36	3-6	1-2	9	2	5	7
Jordan	42	13-22	15-18	4	5	3	41
Rodman	24	1-5	0-0	6	1	4	2
Wennington	14	3-4	0-0	1	0	3	6
Brown	5	0-1	0-0	1	0	0	0
Burrell	7	0-1	2-2	2	1	0	2
Buechler	2	0-0	0-0	0	0	0	0
Simpkins	4	0-0	0-0	1	0	0	0
Kerr	14	1-3	0-0	2	2	0	3
Totals	**240**	**35-79**	**30-39**	**12-38**	**20**	**27**	**104**

Percentages: FG .443, FT .769. **Three-point goals:** 4-16, .250 (Pippen 2-6, Kerr 1-2, Kukoc 1-4, Harper 0-1, Jordan 0-1, Rodman 0-1, Burrell 0-1). **Team rebounds:** 5. **Blocked shots:** 5 (Pippen 3, Kukoc, Harper). **Turnovers:** 6 (Pippen 2, Harper 2, Longley, Rodman). **Steals:** 15 (Pippen 5, Jordan 4, Kukoc 2, Burrell 2, Longley, Harper). **Technical fouls:** Brown, 7:44 2nd; illegal defense, :21.2 2nd.

Bulls	26	19	33	26	104
Pacers	28	24	22	24	98

A: 23,844. **T:** 2:22. **Officials:** Jim Clark, Hue Hollins, Joe Forte.

sive company with Boston legend Bill Russell. The former Celts center, known, like Jordan, for reshaping the sport, especially on the defensive end, spoke glowingly of Jordan at the previous day's press conference.

Now, another Celtics superstar, Larry Bird, was watching Jordan dissect his team's defense from his usual spot on the Indiana bench. Bird was named NBA coach of the year for his leadership of the Pacers in his first year with the team.

"Yeah, Michael hit a lot of tough shots—well, tough for anyone else," said Bird. "He's the reason they won it, no question about it."

Despite the compliments, Bird was upset about what he figured was superstar treatment of both Jordan and Scottie Pippen by the referees.

"You know what I'd like to see?" asked Bird when prompted by reporters about the officiating. "I'd like to see Scottie Pippen guard Michael Jordan full-court like Scottie guards [Indiana point guard] Mark Jackson and see how long he stays in the game.

"Tonight I thought Scottie got away with a lot more than he did in Game One. He chest-bumped a lot. It'd be pretty interesting to see Scottie get up on Michael and see how long he lasts [without fouling out]. That's why he should stay in Chicago.

"Like I tell my guys, 'You're not going to get calls in this series. You just have to play through it.' "

Well, Bird may have been posturing, but it worked. Indiana came back in the series, getting its share of calls—and dutiful complaints from Bulls coach Phil Jackson—to push the series to the limit. It was the first Game 7 for a Michael Jordan Bulls club since New York ran the table in 1992 (see Game No. 27).

For his part, Jordan noted that he and Jackson complained plenty about preferential treatment of Bird in the former Celtic great's playing days.

"Larry sounds more like a coach when he starts to complain that I'm getting more calls than his team," said Jordan with a slight smile. "Now he's truly a coach."

Jordan wasn't laughing at the Bulls' offense, which seemed out-of-sync.

"It's very dangerous," said MJ correctly, seeing the difficulties ahead. "We're relying on individual talent right now. In the past, we've always let the system and the rhythm of our offense work. Right now, we're really struggling with our rhythm to some degree.

"Somehow, we found a way, with the leadership on this team, to win this game."

Things got tougher for Jordan and the Bulls. In Game 4, Indiana assistant coach Rick Carlisle, a former Bird teammate on the Celtics, diagrammed the perfect play for Pacers star Reggie Miller to knot the series at two games apiece, but Carlisle knew that Indiana still had plenty of work remaining in these woolly finals, especially on defense.

Carlisle was assigned to cover Jordan on too many occasions for his liking. "When Michael gets the ball and comes down and looks at you in the eye, you know something is going happen," explained Carlisle. "The only good thing that can happen is he misses a shot or [his teammates] aren't ready for one of his passes.

"When he looks me in the eye, I would try to look at his stomach. It's the only part of him that doesn't move."

Number 24: Great Game Index

GGI score (106 of a possible 123) The tiebreaker is game importance.

Scoring (32 of a possible 33) MJ drained 13 of 22 shots from the floor and added 15 free throws. He scored 40 percent of his team's points on less than 30 percent of Chicago's shots.

Game Importance (19 of 20)   Without this Jordan special, the Pacers would have closed in six, eliminating the home-court advantage the Bulls worked so hard to earn during the season.

Opponent Strength (18 of 20)   Indiana was pushing 20 by the end of the series. Reggie Miller is a clutch postseason performer and seven feet, four inches tall, but quick Rick Smits is a troublesome matchup for the Bulls' big men. Travis Best emerged in this series.

Historical Significance (8 of 10)   The game set up the drama of Game 7.

Legendary Intangibles (10 of 10)   When wheels are falling off, Michael always seems to find a way to steer to safety.

Pressure Points (9 of 10)   Indiana couldn't stop Jordan on key possessions in the fourth quarter.

Defense (5 of 5)   Jordan's 41 points provided the scoreboard material, but the defense, led by MJ, Scottie Pippen, and Ron Harper, sealed the victory.

Other Offensive Contributions (2 of 5)   MJ's 5 assists might have been doubled if his teammates were on target with shots.

MJ's Physical Condition (1 of 5)   Not a factor.

Long Odds (2 of 5)   At thirty-five, MJ is still the league's dominant player. He proved it on MVP night.

-25-

May 17, 1993

Bulls at Cleveland Cavaliers
Game 4 Clincher,
Second-Round
Playoff Series

The Shot II sinks Cleveland—again.

*E*xcuse Cleveland fans if they don't appreciate greatness at every turn. When Michael Jordan's fadeaway jumper hit virtually nothing but net just before the scoreboard had nothing but zeroes at game's end, people back in Chicago were already calling it The Shot II in honor of the game-winner their hero drained on the same floor in 1989 to win the deciding game in a first-round playoff series (see Game No. 4). But Cavs followers were groaning and thinking this Jordan guy is appearing in a bad movie that won't go away.

Michael's game-winning shot closed out the Cavs in the series, 4–0. It marked the fourth time in six postseasons that Chicago eliminated Cleveland. New York and the Knicks were next up in the Bulls' "three-peat" voyage.

The "Jordan Stopper" could only look on in awe as MJ imposed his will in the Bulls' sweep of the Cavaliers. *Reuters/Jeff Haynes/Archive Photos*

Game 25: Bulls 103, Cavaliers 101

Bulls	Min	FG-att	FT-att	Reb	Ast	Fls	Pts
Grant	33	7-10	3-4	10	1	4	17
Pippen	44	7-16	3-3	4	4	4	17
Cartwright	29	7-11	0-0	5	0	3	14
Jordan	40	11-24	7-9	9	6	2	31
Armstrong	32	2-4	0-0	0	2	4	4
King	15	2-4	5-6	2	1	2	9
S. Williams	18	2-2	4-6	4	2	4	8
Paxon	17	1-11	0-0	1	1	2	3
Tucker	10	0-4	0-0	0	0	2	0
Walker	1	0-0	0-0	0	0	0	0
Perdue	1	0-0	0-0	0	0	0	0
Totals	**240**	**38-76**	**22-28**	**35**	**17**	**27**	**103**

Percentages: FG .513, FT .786. **Three-point goals:** 3-6, .500 (Jordan 2-2, Paxon 1-1, Pippen 0-1, Armstrong 0-1, Tucker 0-1). **Team rebounds:** 5. **Blocked shots:** 4 (Grant, Pippen, Jordan, S. Williams). **Turnovers:** 12 (Jordan 4, Pippen 2, King 2, S. Williams 2, Cartwright). **Steals:** 8 (Pippen 4, Jordan 2, Grant, Armstrong). **Technical fouls:** None. **Illegal defense:** None.

Cavaliers	Min	FG-att	FT-att	Reb	Ast	Fls	Pts
Nance	36	7-12	4-4	5	1	5	18
Wilkins	39	10-19	1-8	2	6	2	22
Daugherty	41	8-2	9-10	13	1	6	25
Ehlo	31	2-0	2-4	7	4	2	6
Price	25	2-5	0-0	1	6	3	6
J. Williams	30	3-7	5-7	4	4	2	11
Brandon	26	3-6	4-4	2	4	0	11
Ferry	12	1-2	0-0	2	1	3	2
Totals	**240**	**36-72**	**25-32**	**36**	**27**	**23**	**101**

Percentages: FG .500, FT .781. **Three-point goals:** 4-9 .44 (Price 2-2, Wilkins 1-2, Brandon 1-2, Ferry 0-1, Ehlo 0-2). **Team rebounds:** 10. **Blocked shots:** 8 (Daugherty 3, J. Williams 3, Nance, Ehlo). **Turnovers:** 15 (Daugherte5, Price 3, Wilkins 2, Nance, J. Williams, Brandon, Ferry, team). **Steals:** 9 (Wilkins 3, Price 2, Nance, Daugherty, Ehlo Brandon). **Technical fouls:** None. **Illegal defense:** None.

Bulls	23	25	27	28	103
Cavaliers	27	25	30	19	101

A: 20,274. **T:** 2:22. **Officials:** Dick Bavetta, Bill Oakes, Eddie F. Rush.

"Does this man live his own commercials?" asked *Chicago Tribune* columnist Bernie Lincicome about the 103–101 victory.

"I had all ball," said Gerald Wilkins, who was assigned to MJ on the final sequence. Earlier in the series, Wilkins proclaimed himself a Jordan stopper.

"It seemed like he went back a couple of inches and let it go," continued Wilkins. "I said, 'No way,' and it went down."

Doubting Michael Jordan is seriously misplaced business—especially if you are wearing a Cleveland jersey.

"The other one [Shot I] was tougher," said Jordan, "because if I miss that, we lose."

Hall of Famer Lenny Wilkens could only watch with begrudging admiration from the Cavs' bench: "He knew it was going in and end our season. That's what great players do."

For his part, Bulls coach Phil Jackson was not pleased with his team's effort, perhaps affected by a dominant series lead and two NBA titles already in house.

"We weren't good tonight, we were lucky," said Jackson. "We were lucky we could hang around for three-and-a-half quarters so that we could play like that at the end of the game, and we're lucky Michael can do what he does at the end of ball games. It was a miracle shot."

The game was tied 101-all with 18.5 seconds left and the Bulls had possession. Jordan got the ball from B. J. Armstrong with 8.5 seconds remaining. He lost his dribble to a clean Gerald Wilkins knock-away at 3.9 seconds, but Jordan recovered the ball himself, turned, and faded back, letting fly from eighteen feet.

"There's not too many times when you have a chance to duplicate something like this," said Jordan, knowing that Magic Johnson, Larry Bird, and Isiah Thomas before him never won three consecutive NBA titles. "I'm going to church on Sunday because I am very, very fortunate to be able to respond to challenges that some people may not be able to respond to."

Jordan accomplished it all with a sore and sprained right wrist that hampered his start. He notched only 8 points by halftime, then finished strong for a game-high 31 points. The Cleveland sweep afforded nearly a week of rest before New York awaited.

Armstrong didn't have the pleasure of seeing The Shot I. He liked this version. "I was just frozen in time," he said. "It took an instant before I realized what happened out there."

Same goes for the Cavaliers and their fans.

Number 25: Great Game Index

GGI Score (106 of a possible 123).

Scoring (32 of a possible 33)   MJ hit the big shot with everyone knowing who would have the ball with time running down. His 31 points was right on his average for the series.

Game Importance (17 of 20)   The Bulls had room for error, but winning afforded needed time off for Michael's wrist.

Opponent Strength (17 of 20)   Cleveland carried the mental burden of getting knocked out by the Bulls four times in the last six postseasons.

Historical Significance (9 of 10)   Cavs fans would be glad to practice some revisionist history.

Legendary Intangibles (10 of 10)   When a game is on the line, there is no one else in basketball history to whom any experienced coach would entrust the ball.

Pressure Points (9 of 10)   The last shot was not make-or-break, but not as easy as MJ makes it look.

Defense (4 of 5)   Another solid game. Jordan and the Bulls clamped Cleveland for only 19 points in the fourth quarter to stage a 7-point rally.

Other Offensive Contributions (3 of 5)   Michael and Scottie Pippen tied for the team lead in assists in the series.

MJ's Physical Condition (4 of 5)   A sprained right wrist is tough on a right-handed shooter.

Long Odds (1 of 5)   The incredible was old news for Jordan.

-26-

February 7, 1988

NBA All-Star Game at Chicago

Michael writes an All-Star script.

*T*he coronation went down as dramatically as one of Michael Jordan's winning entries in the All-Star weekend's slam-dunk contest. In his third All-Star Game, MJ became the go-to guy for the winning Eastern Conference squad. A decade later, Jordan was still the mid-season game's dominant player (see Game No. 36).

Down the stretch, teammates like Isiah Thomas and Larry Bird were feeding the ball to the considerably younger legend-on-the-fast-track Jordan when MJ scored 16 points in the final 5:50 to hold off a rallying West team in a 138–133 victory. He had 40 in the game, 2 points short of the NBA All-Star record set by Wilt Chamberlain in 1962.

"Near the end of the game," said Thomas, the Detroit Pistons star who was part of a group that snubbed Jordan in the 1985 All-Star Game, "I look up and I see Michael has thirty-six points. I say, 'Let's get forty.'" Michael says, 'Nah, nah.' I say, 'Go for forty.'"

Michael clarified the on-court conversation: "What I said to Isiah was, 'What are you trying to do, wear me out for Tues-

Game 26: East 138, West 133

West	Min	FG-att	FT-att	Reb	Ast	Fls	Pts
English	22	5-10	0-0	3	4	0	10
K. Malone	33	9-19	4-5	10	2	4	22
Olajuwon	28	8-13	5-7	9	2	3	21
Johnson	39	4-15	9-9	6	19	2	17
Lever	31	7-14	3-4	4	3	4	17
Aguirre	12	5-10	3-3	1	1	3	14
Abdul-Jabbar	14	4-9	2-2	4	0	3	10
Robertson	12	1-3	0-0	0	1	1	2
McDaniel	13	1-9	0-0	2	0	1	2
Drexler	15	3-5	6-6	5	0	3	12
Worthy	13	2-8	0-1	3	1	1	4
Donaldson	8	0-0	2-2	6	1	2	2
Totals	**240**	**49-115**	**34-39**	**65**	**34**	**27**	**133**

Percentages: FG .426, FT .872. **Team rebounds:** 12. **Total turnovers:** 9 22 (Johnson 8, Olajuwon 4, Malone 3, Aguirre 3, Robertson 2, McDaniel, Drexler). **Steals:** 11 (Malone 2, Olajuwon 2, Johnson 2, Robertson 2, English, Aguirre, Drexler). **Blocked shots:** 7 (Olajuwon 2, Johnson 2, Donaldson 2, Worthy).

East	Min	FG-att	FT-att	Reb	Ast	Fls	Pts
Bird	32	2-8	2-2	7	1	4	6
Wilkins	30	12-22	5-6	5	0	3	9
M. Malone	22	2-6	3-6	9	2	2	7
Thomas	28	4-10	0-0	2	15	1	8
Jordan	29	17-23	6-6	8	3	5	40
Ewing	16	4-8	1-1	6	0	1	9
Rivers	16	2-4	5-11	3	6	3	9
McHale	14	0-1	2-2	1	1	2	2
Barkley	15	1-4	2-2	3	0	2	4
Ainge	19	4-11	1-2	3	2	1	12
Daugherty	15	6-7	0-0	3	1	4	12
Cheeks	4	0-0	0-0	2	1	1	0
Totals	**240**	**54-104**	**27-38**	**58**	**32**	**29**	**138**

Percentages: FG .519, FT .711. **Team rebounds:** 6. **Turnovers:** 22 (Thomas 6, Rivers 3, Barkley 3, Bird 2, Malone 2, Jordan 2, McHale 2, Ewing, Ainge). **Steals:** 11 (Bird 4, Jordan 4, Thomas, Barkley, Ainge). **Blocked shots:** 11 (Jordan 4, McHale 2, Bird, Wilkins, Barkley, Daugherty, Ewing).

West	32	22	35	44	133
East	27	33	39	39	138

Three-point goals—Ainge 3, Aguirre.

A: 18,403. **T:** 2:28. **Officials:** Darrell Garretson, Jake O'Donnell.

Since the All-Star Game was being played on Michael's home floor, his Eastern Conference teammates simply decided to see how high he could fly. *UPI/Corbis-Bettmann* day [when the Bulls and the rival Pistons were due to meet at the Stadium].'"

With thirty-seven seconds remaining, Thomas dished a pass to Jordan, who pulled up for the seventeen-foot jump shot. Points 39 and 40 were delivered on a resounding one-handed slam off a lob pass from Isiah Thomas. The 18,403 hometown fans yelled and cheered with delight. In the last seconds, Thomas was waving Jordan to cut for a backdoor layup and a tie with Chamberlain's record, but Michael just stood to the side and laughed.

"I was happy with what I had done," Jordan said. "I didn't want to seem greedy. I wanted the clock to tick off. I was embarrassed. I didn't want things handed to me. I get embarrassed when things are handed to me. My first thirty-six points were earned. The last four were respectfully given to me."

"Everybody came to see the Michael Jordan show," said Thomas, who grew up in the Chicago area. "I was glad I could help."

It seems the NBA stars themselves were watching.

"A lot of older guys think you have to pay your dues," said Bird. "I think Michael Jordan has done the job."

"Perhaps he was feeling his way and didn't want other players thinking he wanted to show them up," said Kevin McHale, Bird's Boston teammate and fellow All-Star. "I told him, 'This is your city.' This is what I came here for, to watch him."

"What impressed me is how he got his forty, in how many shots." said Magic Johnson of the Lakers, whose streak of three regular season MVP awards in four years would come to an end with Michael's first such honor, for the 1987–88 season.

Jordan hit 17 of 23 in twenty-nine minutes of play. MJ was the scoring and emotional leader of a future Hall of Fame starting lineup, with Thomas, Bird, Dominique Wilkins (at the peak of his high-flying game), and Moses Malone.

"Like a script," said Jordan after being voted unanimous MVP, the first of three times to be named star of Stars. "I was aware of the expectations—win the slam dunk, have fun. Play well, have fun, win the game, be the MVP. I wish the All-Star Game was here in Chicago every year."

Number 26: Great Game Index

GGI Score (106 of a possible 123).

Scoring (32 of a possible 33)   Just one basket short of Wilt with a shooting percentage at 74 percent. Michael's 18 points in the first half matched his total output in his first two All-Star Games.

Game Importance (15 of 20)   Not a win-or-else proposition.

Opponent Strength (18 of 20)   Karl Malone sparkled with a West-high 22 points in his first of many All-Star appearances in a Hall of Fame career. Magic Johnson was in the final season of his run of titles with the L.A. Lakers.

Historical Significance (10 of 10)   While MJ had already put opponents on notice about his once-in-a-lifetime talents, this league-wide gathering ushered in the future of the NBA—at least in the 1990s—according to Michael.

Legendary Intangibles (10 of 10)   When Larry Bird and Isiah Thomas defer, you are something extraordinarily special.

Pressure Points (8 of 10)   It is just an All-Star Game, but Jordan still had high expectations from the home crowd and national media.

Defense (5 of 5)   On an All-Star Game scale, Michael's defensive prowess has always been at the top of the charts.

Other Offensive Contributions (4 of 5)   He got into foul trouble or might have contributed even more.

MJ's Physical Condition (1 of 5)   Not a factor.

Long Odds (3 of 5)   In only his third full season, Jordan was already standing at the top of his sport.

-27-

New York Knicks at Bulls Game 7 Clincher, Second-Round Playoff Series

Michael knocks in 42, knocks out the Knicks.

*T*his game exemplifies the ferocious Knicks-Bulls rivalry during the 1990s: Body on body, sneer for sneer, defense by defense squared.

Unexpectedly, New York took Chicago to the limit of a seventh game in the 1992 Eastern Conference semifinals, though the Bulls nipped any final suspense by building a 15-point lead at the end of three quarters. The final score was 110–81, and sighs of relief were heard all around in the cramped Chicago locker room in the basement of old Chicago Stadium. There were murmurs of a sweep before the series started.

"I didn't want to wake up and read how we had disappointed a whole city," said Michael Jordan. "You've got to give New York credit. They woke us up, if anything. We went through the series sleepwalking, we came out of this game with

140

Game 27: Bulls 110, Knicks 81

Knicks	Min	FG-att	FT-att	Reb	Ast	Fls	Pts
McDaniel	42	6-15	2-2	7	0	3	14
Oakley	30	0-3	4-4	10	0	2	4
Ewing	40	8-19	6-8	9	1	5	22
Jackson	36	4-9	2-2	3	11	4	10
Wilkins	29	3-12	0-2	2	1	5	7
Starks	30	6-13	4-6	3	5	6	18
Mason	19	0-1	4-4	2	0	1	4
Anthony	12	0-1	0-0	0	3	2	0
Winchester	2	1-1	0-0	0	0	0	2
Totals	240	28-74	22-28	36	21	28	81

Percentages: FG .378, FT .766 **Three-point goals:** 3-12, .250 (Starks 2-5, Wilkins 1-5, Jackson 0-2). **Team rebounds:** 11. **Blocked shots:** 2 (McDaniel, Mason). **Turnovers:** 17 (McDaniel 4, Ewing 3, Starks 3, Oakley 2, Jackson 2, Anthony 2, Mason). **Steals:** 9 (Starks 4, Jackson 2, Wilkins, Mason, Anthony). **Technical foul:** McDaniel, 2:53 1st. **Illegal defense:** 1.

Bulls	Min	FG-att	FT-att	Reb	Ast	Fls	Pts
Pippen	45	7-11	3-4	11	11	3	17
Grant	41	6-10	2-3	6	4	3	14
Cartwright	32	2-3	1-3	5	2	5	5
Paxson	20	1-4	0-0	0	4	5	2
Jordan	42	15-29	12-13	6	4	3	42
Armstrong	24	5-7	1-2	1	5	1	12
Levingston	7	0-0	1-2	1	0	1	1
Williams	5	1-2	0-0	2	0	2	2
Hodges	12	3-4	0-0	0	1	1	7
Perdue	2	0-0	0-0	0	0	0	0
King	10	3-4	1-1	2	0	0	8
Totals	240	43-74	21-28	13-34	31	24	110

Percentages: FG .581, FT .750. **Three-point goals:** 3-4, .750 (Armstrong 1-1, King 1-1, Hodges 1-2). **Team rebounds:** 9. **Blocked shots:** 8 (Grant 4, Jordan 3, Levingston). **Turnovers:** 14 (Pippen 5, Jordan 5, Grant, Cartwright, Levingston, King). **Steals:** 13 (Grant 4, Pippen 3, Jordan 2, Hodges 2, Levingston, Williams). **Technical fouls:** Jordan, 2:53 1st; illegal defense, 2:51 3rd. **Illegal defense:** 1.

Knicks	25	26	13	17	81
Bulls	30	26	23	31	110

A: 18,676. **T:** 2:29. **Officials:** Hue Hollins, Jake O'Donnell, Ed T. Rush.

our backs to the wall and we responded. It seemed like the old Bulls that everyone expected."

A big part of the nostalgic package was Michael's 42 points. He raced out to a fast start with 18 points in the first quarter, including 8 of 8 from the free-throw line as he repeatedly drove to the basket, despite the usual hard shoves and bumps from such Knicks as Xavier McDaniel and Patrick Ewing. Jordan scored 16 of his team's first 25 points and finished the first half with 29.

James Jordan, Michael's late father, may have played the key role without even suiting up.

"I was debating with my father all morning as to how I was going to approach the game in terms of coming out aggressive or coming out passive, trying to evaluate how the other guy was going to play," said MJ. "His advice was like most parents: be aggressive, go out and do it and make it happen and they'll take your lead. That's exactly what happened."

Part of the strategy was to draw foul calls on the Knicks. Bulls coach Phil Jackson was quite vocal about the virtual muggings by New York's big men, and the first quarter proved a testing ground for how closely this game would be called. The lead whistle belonged to veteran referee Jake O'Donnell, known for calling games tight.

"It was on my mind just to come out of the blocks quickly," said Jordan. "Everybody was a little nervous. I was a little nervous because it's a one-game series. Anything can happen."

Jordan's example inspired teammates beyond his scoring touch. He finished the clincher with 6 rebounds, 4 assists, 3 blocked shots, and 2 steals. Defense is at the heart of every game he plays, and especially those among his 50 greatest.

The critical moments came early in the third quarter. New York had just rattled off 6 straight points to make it a mere 60–57 lead for Chicago. Coach Phil Jackson called a time-out, and the Bulls seemed to collect themselves.

"We couldn't drive or hit the gaps that were there earlier," said Knicks coach Pat Riley. "Their defense picked up big-time. It was a defense I hadn't seen from them all series, to be quite frank."

"Our whole defensive effort in the second half rose to a higher level," said Jackson.

The results were evident. The Bulls went on a 10–2 run and outscored the Knicks, 19–7, for the remainder of the quarter. Another big 18–6 spurt in the fourth quarter brought down the house and the series. By game's end, Jordan and triumphant mates like Scottie Pippen and Horace Grant were breathing easy on the bench.

After a tooth-and-nail-and-grit series, the Knicks were gracious in defeat. "Trying to repeat [as NBA champions] is the toughest thing they'll do," said Riley, who didn't figure on the next year's "three-peat" voyage. "Having twenty-seven teams running at you all season takes an emotional toll. What they have is what we're all playing for. Maybe this will get them started."

"Michael was Superboy today," said Gerald Wilkins, who drew Jordan for a defensive assignment most of the series. "He had more power and force and energy, but at the beginning of the game we were not allowed to play him, to put the body on him, like we did all series.

"Hey, Mike knows the game. When he knows the referees are going to let us play, he's not going for those spectacular plays and dunks. We didn't see that the whole series, but today he sees the referees are calling that and now he can go. I knew it. He knew it."

The mental fatigue of a seven-game series outweighs the hard screens, flying elbows, sore muscles, and bruises.

"This team had nothing to lose," said Michael. "It was mentally draining every day to wake up and play against this physical, brutal team and know what you had to face."

Come that next Monday morning, Jordan and the Bulls were glad to look themselves in the mirror.

Number 27: Great Game Index

GGI Score (105 of a possible 123)   Tiebreaker is game importance.

Scoring (32 of a possible 33)   MJ's 42 points was one for every minute he played. He propelled his club to a fast start by scoring 29 points in the first half.

Game Importance (20 of 20)   Nothing gets more important than one-game-takes-all.

Opponent Strength (17 of 20)   This Knicks team, a collection of bruising defenders, was hampered by Patrick Ewing's sprained ankle.

Historical Significance (8 of 10)   A close call allowed the second title run to continue.

Legendary Intangibles (10 of 10)   All eyes were on Michael early in the game, and, as usual, he delivered.

Pressure Points (9 of 10)   A Game 7 scenario is nervewracking. Jordan scored 16 of the Bulls' first 25 points to put everyone at ease.

Defense (5 of 5)   Three blocked shots and two steals was just the beginning.

Other Offensive Contributions (2 of 5)   Solid, if not spectacular.

MJ's Physical Condition (1 of 5)   Not a factor.

Long Odds (1 of 5)   A sign of Michael's greatness: scoring 42 points in a Game 7 is not unlikely.

-28-

April 28, 1988

Cleveland Cavaliers at Bulls Game 1, First-Round Playoff Series

One scary moment, 50 big points.

For these 1988 playoffs, another 250-some fans somehow squeezed into Chicago Stadium, that gloried barn since leveled for parking. The capacity-crowd noise was deafening—until Michael stretched for a full-court Charles Oakley pass and landed wrong from a foul by Cleveland defender Scott Ehlo with 7:10 remaining in the game. He crumpled in a heap of superstar. There was silence and enough quiet to hear Jordan groaning in the second-balcony cheap seats.

"Michael Jordan was down, which is not his usual direction," wrote *Chicago Tribune* columnist Bernie Lincicome. "The future, as the Bulls know it, passed before the eyes of gathered witnesses. A Bulls game without Jordan is a night without dawn."

After several minutes, that seemed more like an hour, Jordan lifted himself off the floor. He walked to the bench, eyes rolling and tongue wagging, as he sighed with the relief of not

Game 28: Bulls 104, Cavaliers 93

Cavaliers	Min	FG-att	FT-att	Reb	Ast	Fls	Pts
Nance	42	8-16	1-1	8	3	3	17
Sanders	24	7-9	4-5	4	1	5	18
Daugherty	38	4-10	4-5	4	1	4	12
Price	42	6-14	5-6	5	12	0	17
Ehlo	44	9-18	3-5	6	6	3	21
Williams	27	2-7	0-0	6	1	1	4
Curry	11	1-3	0-0	1	2	1	2
Hubbard	12	1-5	0-1	3	0	0	2
Totals	240	38-82	17-23	37	26	17	93

Percentages: FG .463, FT .739. **Team rebounds:** 8. **Turnovers:** 17 (Sanders 5).
Steals: 9 (Ehlo 4, price 2). **Three-point goals:** 0.

Bulls	Min	FG-att	FT-att	Reb	Ast	Fls	Pts
Sellers	16	1-4	1-1	4	1	2	3
Oakley	44	6-14	2-2	15	3	3	14
Corzine	38	2-7	2-3	11	1	1	6
Vincent	26	8-14	1-1	1	22	3	17
Jordan	44	19-35	12-12	7	2	3	50
Pippen	19	0-5	0-0	2	2	4	0
Paxson	27	3-6	0-0	0	7	5	6
Grant	26	4-7	0-0	10	3	3	8
Totals	240	43-92	18-19	50	21	24	104

Percentages: FG .467, FT .947. **Team rebounds:** 5. **Turnovers:** 16 (Jordan 5). **Steals:** 9
(Oakley 2, Jordan 2). **Three-point goals:** 0.

Cavaliers	29	19	28	17	93
Bulls	23	30	20	31	104

A: 18,676. **T:** 2:08. **Officials:** Hue Hollins, Jack Madden, B. Alexander.

having suffered a major knee ligament injury. He had come down with a straight-kneed right leg, but the subsequent medical report was a mildly strained hamstring.

Once MJ appeared merely shaken up rather than hurt, the Bulls fans booed and called out Ehlo, but Jordan himself bailed out the Cavs player.

"I felt a little push on my back, but it wasn't enough to cause the injury," said MJ. "Once I calmed down, I told [trainer] Mark Pfeil I just wanted to rest a little."

One fallout: Jordan said he lost some confidence in his play after that fall.

"I wasn't sure if I could move laterally," said Jordan. "Hopefully, I'll get my confidence back before Sunday."

This could have fooled Ehlo, who chased Jordan all day without much help because Cavaliers teammate and top defender Ron Harper was sitting out with a knee problem. Jordan returned to action by sinking three free throws, two for the personal foul and one more shot courtesy of a technical foul called on Ehlo for arguing the call. The free throws were at the tail end of a 14–0 run that converted a 77–75 deficit into the makings of the first franchise playoff win since 1985.

Jordan finished the game with 50 points in a 104–93 win. It erased the claims of some doubters who figured Cavs coach Lenny Wilkens had devised an ideal way to contain Jordan, as proven in the previous week's 107–103 regular season loss to Cleveland. The basic concept was to run Jordan into a funnel of shot-blockers—Larry Nance, John Williams, and Brad Daughtery.

MJ's three-point play in the face of Nance settled matters with 1:40 left. A 55-point effort in Game 2 of the series—against Harper (see Game No. 17)—knocked a huge hole in the Stop 23 Flight Plan.

"Against Michael, you have to play good position defense," said Wilkens, a Hall of Fame defender in his own playing days and coach of the 1979 NBA champion Seattle Supersonics. "He's so good that if you let up on him, he'll be around you before you know it. Then he's hanging in the air, dishing off or doing whatever he likes.

"To play at that intensity at this level, I haven't seen any player do it. To play up in the air that much, I've never seen it. Elgin Baylor [the Lakers great], he could hang up in the air like that, but he wasn't as quick as Michael."

The second quarter proved most impressive. Jordan scored 20 points while the entire Cleveland team tallied 19. The Cavs were beginning to learn about Michael Time.

"Everyone seemed to be spinning their wheels," said MJ. "I had to show my leadership. I had to step up and get something going to relax them. I try not to let this team lose. This is the playoffs. My knee is a little sore, but it will be all right."

Number 28: Great Game Index

GGI Score (105 of a possible 123)   Tiebreaker is game importance.

Scoring (32 of a possible 33)   Michael scored almost 50 percent of his team's points, including more than the whole Cavs team in second-quarter stats.

Game Importance (18 of 20)   The Bulls hadn't won a playoff game since MJ's rookie year. It was important to start off on the right note, especially at home.

Opponent Strength (18 of 20)   Cleveland was a squad with good shooters and intimidating shot-blockers.

Historical Significance (9 of 10)   It marked a magic-number total for the young Jordan, outdone only by the 63-point Boston game (see Game No. 3).

Legendary Intangibles (9 of 10)   After a frightful fall, Jordan calmly sank three free throws to steady fans' nerves and rattle the Cavs.

Pressure Points (9 of 10)   He hit all the big shots, particularly in the second quarter, when no other Bulls were shooting well.

Defense (3 of 5)   The typical solid game. Jordan's defensive skills were partly why he won the league's regular season MVP award.

Other Offensive Contributions (2 of 5)   His scoring dominated the night.

MJ's Physical Condition (3 of 5)   He played hard in the final 7 minutes, especially on defense.

Long Odds (2 of 5)   Every feat was starting to become less surprising than the next.

-29-

April 3, 1988

Bulls at Detroit Pistons Regular Season

MJ's two free throws, and 59-point effort finish the Pistons.

T he playoff breakthrough against Detroit was still three seasons away, but this game would be a confidence-builder for Michael Jordan and an omen for the Pistons. The thrilling 112–110 victory was the Bulls' third straight in a late-season surge—all on the road—while it marked Detroit's fourth consecutive loss, moving Chicago within three-and-a-half games of the first-place Pistons.

Michael put on his Easter Sunday best before a sellout crowd and national television audience. He scored 59 points, including two foul shots with 4 seconds left. His shooting line was 21 of 26 from the field and 15 of 17 free throws. There seemed to be no stopping him.

"He was on fire," said Pistons guard Vinnie Johnson, nick-named Microwave for his ability to get into hot shooting streaks. "He was in his own little funk, and there was no way I could get him out of it. He hit a few shots that I know even he had to be impressed with himself."

Johnson paused to pick out one head-shaking play.

Game 29: Bulls 112, Pistons 110

Bulls	Min	FG-att	FT-att	Reb	Ast	Fls	Pts
Sellers	28	1-3	0-0	2	1	5	2
Oakley	35	5-12	4-6	11	1	3	14
Corzine	41	3-6	6-6	12	0	3	12
Jordan	42	21-27	17-19	4	6	4	59
Vincent	42	9-20	0-0	6	13	4	18
Pippen	12	0-2	0-0	1	1	2	0
Grant	20	0-5	1-4	3	0	3	1
Paxson	13	2-4	0-0	0	1	1	4
Walters	4	0-0	0-0	1	0	2	0
Turner	3	1-1	0-0	0	0	0	2
Totals	**240**	**42-80**	**14-26**	**40**	**29**	**27**	**112**

Percentages: FG .524, FT .800. **Team rebounds:** 13. **Turnovers:** 13 (Vincent 4, Oakley 3, Grant 3). **Steals:** 5 (Jordan 2). **Blocked shots:** 6 (Vincent 2, Jordan 2). **Technical fouls:** 0.

Pistons	Min	FG-att	FT-att	Reb	Ast	Fls	Pts
Dantley	31	4-13	10-12	7	4	0	18
Mahorn	23	3-5	2-4	4	2	5	8
Laimbeer	35	9-16	0-0	8	1	5	18
Dumars	34	7-16	4-5	2	9	3	18
Thomas	40	11-24	2-4	4	8	2	24
Salley	26	2-3	0-0	4	2	4	4
Johnson	18	4-11	0-0	3	1	2	8
Edwards	7	2-3	0-0	1	0	0	4
Rodman	23	2-8	4-4	9	2	4	8
Lewis	3	0-0	0-0	0	0	2	0
Totals	**240**	**44-99**	**22-29**	**42**	**29**	**27**	**110**

Percentages: FG .444, FT .759. **Team rebounds:** 3. **Turnovers:** 10 (Thomas 4, Laimbeer 2, Johnson 2). **Steals:** 2 (Dantley, Thomas). **Blocked shots:** 3 (Thomas, Laimbeer, Rodman). **Technical fouls:** 0.

Bulls	30	33	30	29	112
Pistons	33	33	26	18	110

A: 23,712. **Officials:** Paul Mihalak, Hue Hollins.

"There was this one drive to the hole," Johnson continued. "Three of our guys jumped at him. We swiped at him, spun him around, fouled him, and it still fell in.

"We played him man-to-man in the first half unless he posted up. He got thirty-two points. We tried double-teaming him in the second half, but by that time he was extremely hot. He felt like he could do anything out there, which is what he did."

For his part, Jordan was simply showing a career-long tendency to play larger than life in big games.

"I don't think too many people could have stopped me, not the way I was today," said Jordan. "My jumper was just on, really felt inspired. It was a CBS game, and we had to establish that we could beat Detroit in case we faced them in the playoffs. That was a challenge for me."

The game marked Jordan's third appearance on the Columbia Broadcasting System (CBS) network telecasts. He was now averaging 45 points per national-TV game. The Bulls coach was comforted by Jordan's demeanor. "There was a look in Michael's eye that said he wasn't going to let us lose this game," Doug Collins said. "This was the most vocal he has been the whole season with his teammates. He was spectacular."

Pistons coach Chuck Daly, on the other hand, was unsettled by the raging Bull. "No matter what we did or tried to put on him, nothing worked," said Daly. "He's Superman. I don't know how he does it, where he gets that energy, his intelligence, his instinct for the game. It's like Philadelphia when Julius Erving was there. I'm telling the people of Chicago: You're seeing something here that only comes around once in a lifetime. Better enjoy him while you can."

To Michael's credit, he was hustling on both ends of the court, diving for loose balls, switching fluidly on defense, and disrupting the Pistons offense. He blocked an Isiah Thomas shot with twenty-four seconds left and the game tied at 110.

With ten seconds remaining, he applied defensive pressure with teammates Dave Corzine and Brad Sellers. MJ grabbed a deflected pass and was fouled by Pistons center Bill Laimbeer. Michael promptly ruined Easter dinner for Pistons fans.

Number 29: Great Game Index

GGI Score (105 of a possible 123) Tiebreaker is opponent strength.

Scoring (33 of a possible 33) A near-perfect night.

Game Importance (16 of 20)   More a battle of wills than places in the standings.

Opponent Strength (19 of 20)   Detroit was rounding into a form that would lead to NBA titles in 1989 and 1990.

Historical Significance (9 of 10)   Fifty-nine points and the last-second win makes it a keeper.

Legendary Intangibles (10 of 10)   Michael's last-minute heroics were evident on both offense and defense.

Pressure Points (9 of 10)   He sank two free throws with a tie score and 4 seconds left. He also bagged 10 points in a third-quarter stretch in which the Bulls wiped out a 7-point Pistons lead.

Defense (4 of 5)   Isiah Thomas was likely wondering what happened to the rookie Jordan, who was easier to fake.

Other Offensive Contributions (1 of 5)   It was Michael's night with the ball. He scored nearly 53 percent of the Chicago points.

MJ's Physical Condition (1 of 5)   Not a factor.

Long Odds (3 of 5)   Notching 59 points in Detroit was not unattainable, but still eye-popping this late in the season against a seasoned defensive club.

-30-

March 4, 1987

Bulls at Detroit Pistons Regular Season

Jordan hits 61 in an overtime win.

You knew something special was happening when the Detroit fans were cheering Michael Jordan at game's end, with the Bulls standing victorious 125–120 in overtime. Even Isiah Thomas appreciated his foe's 61 points.

"Hey, it was a good time," said the Bad Boy guard. "They made the big plays, so they won and we lost, but we have fun."

Thomas was actually smiling when he explained his feelings long after the game, as if getting up to go home would diminish the battle. The two NBA heavyweights traded offensive punches all night. Isiah scored 31 points, dished out 18 assists, and barely missed a three-pointer that would have sent the game into double overtime.

Joe Dumars drew the task of guarding the young Jordan, who clearly had zoomed onto the league's elite players and least-wanted-to guard list. "I played him fairly tough," said Dumars. "You can play him tough and he still makes the shot."

"With guys like him, Kareem [Abdul-Jabbar], [Kevin] McHale, all you can do is hope they miss," said Thomas.

Michael's 61 points broke the club record of 58, which the Bulls star had set just the week before against New Jersey

Game 30: Bulls 125, Pistons 120

Bulls	Min	FG-att	FT-att	Reb	Ast	Fls	Pts
Banks	40	3-6	2-3	8	2	4	8
Oakley	31	3-12	4-2	16	4	4	7
Corzine	36	5-7	1-1	8	5	3	11
Jordan	43	22-39	17-18	7	3	0	61
Paxson	38	4-12	0-0	1	5	4	9
Brown	14	2-6	2-2	3	0	1	6
Threatt	33	9-15	1-1	3	6	4	19
Poquette	13	1-2	0-0	2	2	3	2
Turner	12	1-4	0-0	3	0	0	2
Sellers	3	0-0	0-0	0	0	1	0
Totals	**265**	**50-104**	**24-27**	**57**	**27**	**24**	**125**

Percentages: FG .481, FT .889. **Team rebounds:** 4. **Turnovers:** 19 (Oakley, Jordan 5).
Steals: 7 (Jordan 3). **Blocked shots:** 7. **Three-point goals:** 1-4 (Paxson 1-3).

Pistons	Min	FG-att	FT-att	Reb	Ast	Fls	Pts
Dantley	46	13-20	6-6	6	4	2	32
Green	28	3-8	0-0	10	1	3	6
Laimbeer	38	9-15	0-0	7	3	1	18
Dumars	43	8-15	3-5	4	2	5	19
Thomas	45	14-24	3-4	5	18	2	31
Mahorn	8	0-2	0-0	0	0	3	0
Johnson	17	1-6	1-2	1	2	0	3
Salley	27	4-8	1-2	7	0	1	9
Rodman	6	0-0	0-0	2	0	3	0
Nimphius	10	1-1	0-0	3	0	1	2
Totals	**265**	**53-99**	**14-19**	**45**	**30**	**21**	**120**

Percentages: FG .535, FT .737. **Team rebounds:** 8. **Turnovers:** 20 (Dumars 5).
Steals: 7. **Blocked shots:** 8 (Salley 5). **Three-point goals:** 0-1. **Technical fouls:** 2
(illegal defense).

Bulls	28	27	23	33	14	125
Pistons	29	22	33	27	9	120

A: 30,281. **T:** 2:27. **Officials:** Darrell Garretson, Ned Wadsworth.

(sinking 26 free throws in the process). Jordan also set the Silverdome scoring mark, formerly held by the Pistons and Notre Dame sharpshooter Kelly Tripucka.

The Jordan Express was rolling three seasons into Michael's pro career. This game marked the second time he recorded more than 60 points (the other being the famed 63 at Boston Garden), to go along with three 50-plus games and nine 40-plus games.

Not surprisingly, MJ didn't stop with his offensive output. He added 7 rebounds and 3 blocked shots. After tying the game at 111 on a fall-away jump shot at a seemingly impossible angle, he made a key steal with seconds left in regulation to send the unforgettable performance into an overtime period. The 30,281 fans likely couldn't wait for another one of those hanging reverse layups, in which Michael somehow triple-clutched before shooting. A flying dunk or two might also be in order. Whatever Michael might create seemed possible on this night.

"No one's ever unstoppable," said Jordan, "but I felt close to it."

Number 30: Great Game Index

GGI Score (105 of a possible 123).

Scoring (33 of a possible 33)   MJ scored the Bulls' first 13 points of the fourth quarter, and notched 26 of their 33 overall.

Game Importance (16 of 20)   Chicago already (and correctly) knew the road to playoff success routed through Detroit. This victory was a confidence-builder.

Opponent Strength (17 of 20)   Isiah Thomas and Joe Dumars were the league's best one-two punch at guard.

Historical Significance (9 of 10)   On any given night, against any team, 61 points is head-turning. He did it against Atlanta earlier in the season—even scoring 23 straight points in one stretch—but the Bulls lost the game.

Legendary Intangibles (10 of 10)   Michael was winning over fans in every NBA city, but gaining favor with Pistons loyalists was on par with Duke fans cheering the North Carolina alum during the 1984 Olympics.

Pressure Points (9 of 10)   Every shot counts when the game ends up in overtime.

Defense (4 of 5) Michael swatted away an Isiah Thomas pass to force overtime. He didn't rest on the defensive end, as evidenced by his three blocked shots.

Other Offensive Contributions (3 of 5) In overtime, Jordan repeatedly passed the ball to Sedale Threat, who had the hot hand with four baskets.

MJ's Physical Condition (1 of 5) Not a factor.

Long Odds (3 of 5) It remains a short list when any NBA player scores more than 60 points in a game.

-31-

May 29, 1992

Bulls at Cleveland Cavaliers Game 6 Clincher, Eastern Conference Finals

Michael arrives in crunch-timely fashion.

*T*he Bulls were down by 7 points early in the fourth quarter, staring at the distinct possibility of a Game 7 back in Chicago. No Chicago player wanted another night with an inspired Cavaliers team.

It may be hard for some Bulls fans to remember, but this series was pressure-packed and filled with considerable consternation. Exhibit A for worriers was Cleveland's 107–81 drubbing of the Bulls in Game 2 at Chicago.

MJ struggled during the first three quarters of Game 6 at the Richfield Coliseum—not his usual Cleveland-clobbering self—managing only 13 points on 5-of-20 shooting. He looked out-of-sync and unable to find the rhythm he so often refers to after a spectacular performance.

"I was fighting myself because I wanted to win so badly,"

Game 31: Bulls 99, Cavaliers 94

Bulls	Min	FG-att	FT-att	Reb	Ast	Fls	Pts
Grant	45	7-11	6-6	9	0	4	20
Pippen	42	11-23	7-8	12	5	5	29
Cartwright	41	5-11	0-0	9	2	1	10
Jordan	44	10-27	9-9	8	8	3	29
Paxson	29	2-3	0-0	2	0	4	4
Armstrong	18	2-5	0-0	0	2	1	4
Levingston	11	1-3	1-2	2	0	3	3
S. Williams	10	0-1	0-0	1	0	3	0
Totals	**240**	**38-84**	**23-25**	**43**	**17**	**24**	**99**

Percentages:FG .452, FT .920. **Three-point goals:** 0-2, .000 (Pippen 0-1, Paxson 0-1). **Team rebounds:** 4. **Blocked shots:** 10 (Pippen 4, Grant 2, Cartwright 2, Levingston, S. Williams). **Turnovers:** 12 (Pippen 5, Jordan 3, Grant, Paxson, Levingston, S. Williams). **Steals:** 7 (Pippen 4, Jordan 2, Cartwright). **Technical fouls:** None. **Illegal defense:** None.

Cavaliers	Min	FG-att	FT-att	Reb	Ast	Fls	Pts
Nance	46	11-20	3-4	16	5	5	25
Sanders	14	3-6	0-0	0	1	5	6
Daugherty	46	6-13	6-7	13	6	4	18
Ehlo	43	3-10	3-4	6	5	2	11
Price	38	5-18	3-4	1	8	1	14
J. Williams	38	6-11	4-6	9	4	5	16
Brandon	10	0-2	0-0	0	2	1	0
Battle	5	2-2	0-0	0	0	0	4
Totals	**240**	**36-82**	**19-25**	**45**	**31**	**23**	**94**

Percentages: FG .439, FT .760. **Three-point goals:** 3-9, .333 (Ehlo 2-5, Price 1-3, Nance 0-1). **Team rebounds:** 8. **Blocked shots:** 8 (Nance 3, Daugherty 2, J. Williams). **Technical fouls:** None. **Illegal defense:** None.

Bulls	26	19	27	27	99
Cavaliers	21	24	27	22	94

A: 20,273. **T:** 2:28. **Officials:** Joe Crawford, Bill Oakes, Paul Mihalak.

said Jordan. "I was trying to calm myself down, take my time, and relax."

The Bulls star was quick to acknowledge the play of his teammates, especially Scottie Pippen and the other starters: "My teammates hung in there while I shot really bad, and when I was back on my feet, they were still there."

Michael's return was a bit more high-flying than he lets on. Suddenly he was slashing to the basket, hitting feathery jumpers and knocking down important foul shots. He tapped his trademark combination of poise, will, skill—and rhythm. He hummed for 16 points while keeping his teammates in the flow. The Bulls tied the game with five minutes remaining.

"Somehow I found my confidence in the fourth quarter to the point where I could lead this team to victory," said Jordan about the 99–94 cliff-hanger that advanced defending champion Chicago to its second NBA Finals.

The Bulls didn't take their first lead of the final quarter until two minutes were left. MJ hit two free throws at the 1:32 mark to put the Bulls up, 93–90. Then the Cavs' Mark Price answered with a three-point jumper that electrified the crowd. The game was knotted at 93 with forty-seven seconds left.

"The last thing I wanted to see was Price coming down and hitting that three-pointer," said Bulls coach Phil Jackson. "It just shows the kind of effort Cleveland had in this series, and the heart they have."

Not that his own team didn't have plenty. The next possession brought that old familiar feeling and the first bona fide thoughts about meeting Portland in the NBA Finals. The offensive set cleared a lane for Michael, who promptly drove to the basket by cutting through heavy traffic and game tension. He made the shot while drawing a foul from inside intimidator Larry Nance. Jordan made it look easy. There was no sign of the mere mortal Michael anymore. Superman was on hand.

Cleveland couldn't answer (Price dribbled the ball off his foot) and both Jordan and Pippen hit clinching free throws down the stretch. Game 6 was the first close outcome of the hard-fought series.

"It was a great game between two divisional opponents who have met each other so many times," said Jackson. "A fitting ending right down to the wire, a classic game"—that only Michael could finish.

Number 31: Great Game Index

GGI Score (104 of a possible 123)   Tiebreaker is game importance.

Scoring (29 of a possible 33)   Forget the first three quarters. 16 points in crunch time helped him tie MJ for game-high honors with Scottie Pippen.

Game Importance (19 of 20)   There was one game left in the quiver, but nobody wanted to be down to the last arrow after the seven-game series with New York in the second round.

Opponent Strength (18 of 20)   Cleveland would have been even tougher this night if center Brad Daugherty hadn't been struggling with a painful jammed middle finger on his shooting hand.

Historical Significance (9 of 10)   This game got them back to the Finals for the much ballyhooed repeat, which now looked almost minimal in retrospect.

Legendary Intangibles (10 of 10)   Michael didn't just turn it on in the fourth quarter, he found a way to look past his 25 percent shooting for the first three quarters. He is fearless and believes in his shot.

Pressure Points (10 of 10)   Cleveland was not going down easy. Every point was precious in the last five minutes. MJ twice broke ties in the final minutes.

Defense (4 of 5)   No letup on this end.

Other Offensive Contributions (3 of 5)   Some key rebounds in the fourth quarter.

MJ's Physical Condition (1 of 5)   Not a factor.

Long Odds (1 of 5)   A 16-point quarter is almost normal for Michael.

-32-

May 27, 1989

Detroit Pistons at Bulls Game 3, Eastern Conference Finals

Michael shakes Rodman, rattles the Pistons.

The Bulls didn't win this series, but this game marked a maturation point for the young team and a sign of good times ahead. Rather than fold to a Detroit team that would go on to win back-to-back NBA titles, the Bulls matched them shot for shot, defensive stand for defensive stand. Then it was time for heroics only Michael Jordan can deliver.

With twenty-eight seconds left, the game was tied at 97. Detroit called a time-out for coach Chuck Daly to design a play. The call was a pick-and-roll between Pistons Isiah Thomas and Bill Laimbeer. One of the two stars would get a shot at winning the game and put Detroit up in the series, two games to one.

"A very safe play, one of our bread-and-butter plays," said assistant coach Brendan Suhr. "That's why we chose it."

Jordan had other ideas. As the clock ticked to eleven seconds, Thomas began dribbling right from the top of the key while Michael slid laterally with him—until bumping into Bill

The fates of Michael Jordan and Dennis Rodman became intertwined when MJ hit the game-winner over Dennis to beat the Pistons. *UPI/Corbis-Bettmann*

Laimbeer. Referee Bill Oakes promptly whistled an offensive foul. The ball turned over to Chicago.

"I know anytime Michael Jordan is involved in a play, you have to watch yourself," said Laimbeer, noting the lofty status of Jordan with the league's court officials. "You make sure you stay clear of him, but I didn't worry about that [at the moment].

Game 32: Bulls 99, Pistons 97

Pistons	Min	FG-att	FT-att	Reb	Ast	Fls	Pts
Aguirre	36	9-16	6-8	3	4	3	25
Mahorn	12	4-6	1-2	4	0	3	9
Laimbeer	32	2-9	0-0	6	5	4	4
Dumars	29	3-8	6-7	2	4	4	12
Thomas	39	2-8	1-2	5	11	3	5
Salley	19	4-4	0-0	3	0	3	8
Rodman	26	4-6	0-0	13	0	5	8
Johnson	25	6-14	5-5	3	1	2	19
Edwards	19	2-3	0-0	1	2	4	4
Long	3	0-0	3-3	0	0	0	3
Totals	240	36-74	22-27	40	27	31	97

Percentages: FG .486, FT .815. **Three-point goals:** 3-14, .214 (Johnson 2-4, Aguirre 1-5, Dumars 0-1, Thomas 0-1, Laimbeer 0-3). **Team rebounds:** 7. **Blocked shots:** 1 (Laimbeer). **Turnovers:** 16 (Thomas 4, Dumars 3, Rodman 3, Aguirre, Mahorn, Laimbeer, Salley, Johnson, team). **Steals:** 4 (Thomas 2, Laimbeer, Salley). **Technical fouls:** Mahorn, 7:46 1st; Coach Daly, 4:52 3d. **Illegal defense:** 1.

Bulls	Min	FG-att	FT-att	Reb	Ast	Fls	Pts
Pippen	43	2-10	2-4	8	4	5	7
Grant	33	2-5	3-4	3	1	4	7
Cartwright	34	5-6	5-6	4	1	4	15
Hodges	25	1-7	0-2	0	5	3	2
Jordan	45	16-26	14-15	7	5	2	46
Davis	13	3-4	0-0	3	0	2	6
Paxson	26	6-9	0-0	1	4	5	12
Corzine	16	2-4	0-0	3	0	2	4
Vincent	5	0-2	0-0	0	1	0	0
Totals	240	37-73	24-31	29	21	27	99

Percentages: FG .507, FT .774. **Three-point goals:** 1-9, .111 (Pippen 1-2, Jordan 0-3, Hodges 0-4). **Team rebounds:** 10. **Blocked shots:** 5 (Corzine 3, Pippen, Cartwright). **Turnovers:** 10 (Pippen 3, Cartwright 2, Jordan 2, Grant, Corzine, Vincent). **Steals:** 9 (Jordan 5, Pippen 4). **Technical fouls:** Coach Collins, :31 2d.; Illegal defense, :18 3d. **Illegal defense:** 1.

Pistons	28	28	21	20	97
Bulls	27	18	21	33	99

A: 18,676. **T:** 2:31. **Officials:** Jack Madden, Bill Oakes, Ed T. Rush.

I worried about doing my job properly. I did my job properly. I set a regular screen, like I do a thousand times a year."

The whistle surprised all of the Pistons. It would be the first of many times that opponents suspected preferential treatment for Michael.

"I didn't know what the call could possibly be," said Thomas after the game. "I thought maybe a fan ran down from the stands and was stopping the game."

Oakes explained it in the referees' locker room: "Basically, the offensive player must give the defensive player an opportunity to go around a screen. In this instance, the offensive player ran into the defensive player and did not give that room."

Detroit did give Michael and his teammates a chance to get back in the game. The Bulls made up a 14-point deficit in the final 8 minutes, inspired by 17 fourth-quarter points from Jordan, who scored 46 in the game and added 7 rebounds, 5 assists, and 5 steals.

Now it was Chicago's ball with :09 on the scoreboard. Only one player was going to be assigned the final shot by coach Doug Collins. The Pistons would do all they could to keep the ball out of Jordan's hands.

"Michael chased out to half-court to get the ball," explained Suhr. "He took it to us from there."

Jordan dribbled right. Dennis Rodman, as Detroit's best defender, drew the assignment to cover MJ. Rodman stayed chest on chest, while Thomas leaped over to double-team. Michael managed to jump up, shift his torso just enough to get off a clean shot, and bank in an eight-foot game-winner with 3 seconds on the clock.

"I'm sayin' nothin'," Rodman said—or didn't say.

Detroit teammate John Salley was more than willing to dissect Jordan's final excising. "I love Magic [Johnson] to death," said Salley, who himself would become a Jordan teammate on an NBA championship club, "but after facing Michael, he should be the MVP. That man, he's unstoppable."

Detroit eventually recovered and won the series, but was reeling from losing a 14-point lead with less than 8 minutes remaining.

"This was a stolen basketball game," said Jordan. "It's kind of shocking. It really is hard to believe."

The Pistons were still up by 91–83 with four minutes left. Michael drove for a basket, then drew a foul and converted two free throws on the next possession. After exchanging baskets, it was still a 4-point game at the 1:10 mark. MJ beelined for the hoop, gliding by three Pistons. Two-point game. Horace Grant hit a pair of foul shots to tie things before Michael finished off the stunning comeback for the 99–97 victory.

Number 32: Great Game Index

GGI Score (104 of a possible 123).

Scoring (31 of a possible 33)   Michael scored 12 of his team's final 16 points and 17 in a quarter featuring a 16-point reversal.

Game Importance (18 of 20)   The victory gave the Bulls a 2–1 advantage in the series.

Opponent Strength (19 of 20)   Isiah Thomas and teammates went on to win this series and the NBA crown.

Historical Significance (8 of 10)   Michael was building an impressive file of game-winning shots in the postseason; he was only three weeks removed from The Shot at Cleveland.

Legendary Intangibles (10 of 10)   Hitting the game-winner is difficult on any court and level of basketball.

Pressure Points (10 of 10)   Michael was already amazing opponents, including the Pistons. But most fearsome was Jordan's ability to stay composed at the most critical parts of games. He won with big shots or defensive stops or both, but his greatest weapon was smart decision-making.

Defense (4 of 5)   Five steals and lots of worried looks among Pistons on the offensive end.

Other Offensive Contributions (2 of 5)   A solid if not spectacular night.

MJ's Physical Condition (1 of 5)   Not a factor.

Long Odds (1 of 5)   The Bulls were starting to believe they could beat Detroit. Things didn't seem so insurmountable anymore.

-33-

December 12, 1987

Houston Rockets at Bulls Regular Season

Jordan chops down tall timber in Sampson and Olajuwon.

A sellout crowd, soon to become habit-forming for the Bulls brass, witnessed more than spectacular offensive fireworks. Michael shot arcs from all over the floor to gather 44 points, but he saved his most impressive play for the defensive end.

Chicago was facing the fourteen-foot, four-inch combination of big men, Hakeem Olajuwon and Ralph Sampson. Jordan finished with 5 blocked shots, or three more than Olajuwon and Sampson combined. Plus, he rejected an offering from each, despite giving up almost a foot in height to the seven-foot, four-inch Sampson. It turned out to be Sampson's last game as a Rocket; he was traded later in the day to Golden State for Joe Barry Carroll.

Michael wreaked havoc on the two Rockets the whole game. He seemed to always appear in time to force an altered

With 44 points, and five blocked shots to the Twin Towers' two, MJ began to redefine the center-dominated style of play that had prevailed for decades. *UPI/Corbis-Bettmann*

Game 33: Bulls 112, Rockets 103

Rockets	Min	FG-att	FT-att	Reb	Ast	Fls	Pts
McCray	29	1-3	3-4	8	2	2	5
Sampson	40	7-15	6-7	12	3	3	20
Olajuwon	34	12-25	7-10	8	1	4	31
Leavell	42	6-15	2-3	2	15	3	15
Short	29	3-8	0-0	2	1	2	6
Reid	8	0-3	0-0	3	1	2	0
Petersen	20	2-4	0-0	4	0	2	4
Johnson	18	2-6	2-3	3	4	2	6
Free	17	6-1	4-4	2	1	3	16
Conner	2	0-0	0-0	0	0	0	0
Harris	1	0-0	0-0	0	0	0	0
Totals	240	39-90	24-31	44	28	23	103

Percentages: FG .433, FT .774. **Team rebounds:** 11. **Total turnovers:** 17 (McCray, Free 4). **Steals:** 7 (Johnson, Free 2). **Blocked shots:** 6 (Petersen 2). **Technical foul:** Illegal defense.

Bulls	Min	FG-att	FT-att	Reb	Ast	Fls	Pts
Grant	28	4-5	3-3	8	2	5	11
Oakley	41	8-15	3-4	14	8	3	19
Gilmore	20	1-2	2-6	2	1	4	4
Paxson	38	6-11	0-0	1	9	1	14
Jordan	40	16-28	12-12	3	9	3	44
Pippen	23	5-8	2-4	1	2	3	12
Corzine	28	2-6	0-0	2	0	2	4
Sparrow	6	0-1	2-2	2	0	0	2
Threatt	5	0-2	0-0	0	1	0	0
Sellers	11	1-4	0-0	3	0	0	2
Totals	240	43-82	24-31	36	33	23	112

Percentages: FG .524, FT .774. **Team rebounds:** 8. **Turnovers:** 14 (Oakley, Pippen 4). **Steals:** 11 (Jordan 5). **Blocked shots:** 7 (Jordan 5).

Rockets	25	24	29	25	103
Bulls	37	17	31	27	112

A: 18,096. **Officials:** J. O'Donnell, E. Middleton.

field goal attempt. Olajuwon was particularly bothered by MJ's interruptions.

"They don't know where I'm coming from, and that's my advantage," explained Jordan after the 112–103 win, which upped the Bulls' record to 14–6, just percentage points behind Detroit for best in the NBA. "It's like David sneaking up on Goliath. I can't block their shots looking them straight in the face. The best way to do it is sneak up from behind."

Jordan's offensive skills were plain to see for a national television audience, though his game was beginning to feature less sheer, brute one-on-three type rushes to the basket. He was feeling more confident in new teammates such as Scottie Pippen, Horace Grant, and John Paxson, as evidenced by 9 assists to complement his 44 points.

"I'm not afraid to admit I was extra pumped about the national TV," said Jordan. "I wanted to show the difference between my play this year and last year. I wanted to show I can play defense and that I don't shoot as much as Larry Bird would say"—the Boston Celtics star had criticized Jordan for taking too many shots—"It was a great opportunity to express what we already know: this is not a fluke. This is something new, the improved Bulls."

Jordan was turning an individual slight into a team benefit. His defensive play seemed even more inspired in this game and during the entire early season because he was left off the NBA's all-defensive team the previous year, despite being the first guard ever to record more than 200 steals and 100 blocks in the same season. He wouldn't say much to reporters, but privately he couldn't believe the omission.

There was no denying Jordan by the end of the 1987–88 campaign. He not only made the all-defensive team, but was named Defensive Player of the Year to become the only scoring leader who was also honored as best on defense.

Nothing seemed out of reach for Michael, even the extra-long wingspan of seven-footers like Sampson and Olajuwon.

Number 33: Great Game Index

GGI Score (104 of a possible 123).

Scoring (29 of a possible 33) Nothing shabby about 44 points, including a key basket and four clutch free throws in the final two minutes to seal the victory.

Game Importance (16 of 20) It was still early in the NBA regular season. The national TV audience, however, did mean something to Jordan.

Opponent Strength (18 of 20)   Houston was a contending club with extraordinary potential in the pivot. Olajuwon, who since fashioned a Hall of Fame career, was still learning.

Historical Significance (8 of 10)   This was a perfect checkpoint game for the theorists who didn't think NBA teams could consistently win games—or multiple championships—without a dominant big man.

Legendary Intangibles (10 of 10)   MJ knows not to preen but to perform at his best when the most cameras are pointed his way.

Pressure Points (10 of 10)   He hit four free throws with the game on the line.

Defense (5 of 5)   Michael showed why his defense is unmatched for a star with his offensive skills, and that his repertoire included forwards and centers, as well as guards.

Other Offensive Contributions (4 of 5)   Nine assists, mostly to budding teammates Scottie Pippen and Horace Grant.

MJ's Physical Condition (1 of 5)   Not a factor.

Long Odds (3 of 5)   Michael was entering new territory each time he took over games from the guard position, especially as a defender.

-34-

May 31, 1993

New York Knicks at Bulls Game 4, Eastern Conference Finals

MJ scores 54; Chicago evens the series after an 0–2 start.

*E*ven though Chicago broke into the win column in Game 3 of this series, Michael was a dismal 3 of 18 from the field. His teammates scored 81 of the Bulls' 103 victorious points. In fact, Jordan had not been his usual shooting self during the entire conference finals.

The slump lasted no longer.

Michael started Game 4 with 17 points in the first quarter. He added 10 more by halftime. The third quarter was even better and hotter. MJ heated up old Chicago Stadium for old time's sake in this last title run before the place was leveled to become a parking lot for United Center.

Jordan has always professed to prefer the Stadium—and why not? The Bulls were 32–4 there in the postseasons of the the 1990s, though he did solve his long-standing problem of not feeling comfortable in the new building. This night, Michael scored 18 of the Bulls' 24 third-quarter points. He added 5

Pat Riley's Knicks played their brand of aggressive, physical defense, but it was once again no match for Jordan, who scored 54 points.
Reuters/Sue Ogrocki/Archive Photos

Game 34: Bulls 105, Knicks 95

Knicks	Min	FG-att	FT-att	Reb	Ast	Fls	Pts
Oakley	33	4-9	3-4	12	1	5	11
Smith	32	4-6	7-8	6	4	2	15
Ewing	42	10-20	4-6	9	1	5	24
Rivers	33	1-6	0-0	1	5	5	2
Starks	47	9-17	2-2	3	7	3	24
Mason	35	6-10	4-6	6	3	5	16
Anthony	15	0-3	0-0	0	3	3	0
Blackman	2	1-3	0-0	0	0	1	3
Davis	1	0-0	0-0	0	0	2	0
Totals	**240**	**35-74**	**20-26**	**37**	**24**	**31**	**95**

Percentages: FG .473, FT .769. **Team rebounds:** 12. **Technical fouls:** Ewing, 9:12, 1st; Oakley, 3:13, 2nd. **Illegal defense:** None.

Bulls	Min	FG-att	FT-att	Reb	Ast	Fls	Pts
Pippen	43	4-14	5-6	7	4	3	13
Grant	41	7-9	0-0	6	2	3	14
Cartwright	32	0-4	4-6	6	3	2	4
Armstrong	35	3-7	6-7	4	2	2	12
Jordan	39	18-30	12-14	6	2	5	54
Perdue	2	0-0	0-0	0	0	0	0
King	12	1-2	0-0	1	0	1	2
Williams	9	0-1	1-2	4	1	4	1
Paxson	16	0-2	1-2	0	2	2	1
Tucker	11	1-3	1-2	1	2	1	4
Totals	**240**	**34-72**	**30-39**	**35**	**18**	**23**	**105**

Percentages: FG .472, FT .769. **Team rebounds:** 8. **Technical fouls:** None. **Illegal defense:** None.

Knicks	29	23	25	18	95
Bulls	33	28	24	20	105

A: 18,676. **T:** 2:42. **Officials:** Dick Bavetta, Darrell Garretson, Jack Nies.

more right at the start of the fourth quarter for a nice, fat, round 50 points against the league's best defensive team.

"He kicked my butt," admitted the Knicks' Starks, assigned the impossible task of guarding a supremely-motivated Jordan.

Michael's scoring line featured 18 of 30 field goals, including 6 of 9 three-pointers, for a 54-point total. It was the most points ever scored in the playoffs against a storied New York franchise. This time, Michael scored more than half of his team's points in a 105–95 win to even the series. It marked his sixth 50-plus game in the playoffs.

Always finding new ways to win by adapting his game to the moment, Jordan notched the big performance with the help of only one layup and zero dunks. His fadeaway jump shot was now deadly and virtually unstoppable.

The only thing that slowed Jordan was foul trouble. He was whistled for his fifth personal with 6:58 left and the Bulls up by 7 points. Coach Phil Jackson elected to pull Jordan until about four minutes remained, figuring he might need MJ to hold off the Knicks in the final possessions.

Jackson didn't like substituting for his star: "When Michael's hot like that, it's a show of his own. He's in a different space. "We told him in this series that probably a game of ten assists is going to be just as valuable as a game of forty points. I can't say the same about fifty. That was a little better."

Scottie Pippen and B. J. Armstrong hit key shots in Michael's absence. The lead was intact when Jordan returned.

"That stretch was real important, especially defensively," said John Paxson. "It showed we could hang defensively without Michael. You're always going to miss something offensively whenever he's not on the floor."

New York was the team missing out by game's end. The Knicks had squandered a 2–0 series lead and never won again. Game 5 in New York was especially heartbreaking for Phil Jackson's old team. Charles Smith couldn't make one of four consecutive close-in shots in the fleeting seconds, while Michael had another spectacular night on both ends of the court (see Game No. 15). The Bulls closed out their rivals in Game 6 back at the Stadium. Charles Barkley and the Phoenix Suns would be next, in the NBA Finals.

Number 34: Great Game Index

GGI Score (103 of a possible 123)   Tiebreaker is game importance.

Scoring (32 of a possible 33)   MJ always seemed to hit the shots to halt any New York momentum. "He bailed us out with a number of great shots in rhythm and finding a way to keep us up ten, eleven points when we'd slide back to eight," said coach Phil Jackson.

Game Importance (19 of 20)   Going down 3–1 in the series would have likely meant the end of the "three-peat" campaign. This game broke New York's swagger.

Opponent Strength (19 of 20)   The Knicks were beneficiaries of Patrick Ewing's best postseason of his NBA career. He averaged 25.8 points and more than 11 rebounds per game for the series. Ewing also led a swarming defense for coach Pat Riley.

Historical Significance (8 of 10)   Other games in the series are better remembered, mostly because MJ and his teammates decided this one by third-quarter's end. No drama allowed.

Legendary Intangibles (10 of 10)   Michael took extra shooting practice at the morning shoot-around. It paid off, especially from the three-point arc. He tied his own postseason record of most three-pointers—six—which he first achieved against Portland in the 1992 NBA Finals. He stayed after practice for extra shooting that morning, too.

Pressure Points (8 of 10)   Jordan's hot hand didn't let the Knicks get close or even put together one strong run.

Defense (3 of 5)   Another solid game, especially in the second half.

Other Offensive Contributions (2 of 5)   Isn't 54 points enough?

MJ's Physical Condition (1 of 5)   Not a factor.

Long Odds (1 of 5)   Scoring 50 in a must-win playoff game was no unusual feat for Michael. More rare was the Bulls being in many must-win games.

-35-

November 30, 1995

Bulls at Vancouver Grizzlies
Regular Season

Mike puts on a late, late show.

While much of Chicago slept the Bulls were getting whipped by the expansion Grizzlies early in Michael's first full season after his comeback. It seemed improbable, though the Grizzlies did have Byron Scott and Greg Anthony (the former Knicks nemesis scored 29 points) in the backcourt. Both were veterans of playoff showdowns with Chicago, but to be losing to a team that was barely a month old and just back from a long road trip? It didn't seem possible for the Bulls, who were 4–1 on their own road trip and playing crisp basketball against Western Conference foes.

Enter America's superhero, who had scored 55 against the Knicks at the Garden since his return to basketball. Michael Jordan was still feeling the sting of the past spring's playoff elimination by the Orlando Magic, and Vancouver was about to get blindsided by some fragments of that fury.

He scored 19 points in the time remaining and made several stops including a pair of steals. One occurred with 33 seconds left; Michael sprinted the length of the floor for a

Game 35: Bulls 94, Grizzlies 88

Bulls	Min	FG-att	FT-att	Reb	Ast	Fls	Pts
Pippen	36	6-15	2-4	6	8	2	14
Simpkins	22	5-8	0-0	8	1	0	10
Longley	35	0-6	2-2	10	3	5	2
Jordan	39	14-26	1-2	3	4	1	29
Harper	26	4-7	2-2	2	4	4	10
Wennington	13	4-5	0-0	5	0	3	8
Kukoc	23	3-10	1-2	8	5	3	8
Brown	9	1-1	0-0	0	2	2	2
Kerr	22	2-6	3-4	0	0	1	9
Caffey	12	1-3	0-0	3	0	1	2
Buechler	3	0-0	0-0	1	0	0	0
Totals	**240**	**40-87**	**11-16**	**44**	**27**	**22**	**94**

Percentages: FG .460, FT .688. **Three-point goals:** 3-13, .231 (Kerr 2-5, Kukoc 1-2, Harper 0-1, Jordan 0-2, Pippen 0-3). **Team rebounds:** 9. **Blocked shots:** 3 (Longley 2, Simpkins). **Turnovers:** 15 (Pippen 3, Harper 3, Wennington 2, Jordan 2, Caffey 2, Simpkins, Kukoc). **Steals:** 13 (Pippen 3, Jordan 3, Harper 3, Kukoc 2, Caffey 2). **Technical fouls:** None. **Illegal defense:** None.

Grizzlies	Min	FG-att	FT-att	Reb	Ast	Fls	Pts
King	40	4-8	2-2	2	1	3	10
Harvey	35	4-8	1-3	8	1	1	9
Reeves	37	3-7	5-6	7	1	4	11
Edwards	35	4-12	0-0	4	2	2	9
Anthony	34	8-13	9-12	1	7	2	27
Scott	23	3-6	4-4	3	5	4	11
Avent	22	2-5	0-0	4	2	4	4
Martin	14	3-8	0-1	0	0	1	7
Totals	**240**	**31-67**	**21-28**	**29**	**19**	**21**	**88**

Percentages: FG .463, FT .750. **Three-point goals:** 5-11 .455 (Anthony 2-2; Martin 1-2, Edwards 1-2, Scott 1-3, Reeves 0-1, King 0-1). **Team rebounds:** 11. **Blocked shots:** 6 (Harvey 2, Reeves, Edwards 4, King 2, Anthony 2, Scott 2, Avent 2, Harvey, Martin). **Turnovers:** 19 (Reeves 5, Edwards 4, King 2, Anthony 2, Scott 2, Avent 2, Harvey, Martin). **Steals:** 7 (Reeves 2, Anthony 2, King, Harvey, Martin). **Technical fouls:** Anthony, 8:29 3rd. **Illegal defense:** 1.

Bulls	25	19	18	32	94
Grizzlies	23	19	22	34	88

A: 19,193. **T:** 2:11. **Officials:** Roy Gulbeyan, Robby Robinson.

cradle-dunk and an 8-point lead—a turnaround of 16 points in six minutes.

Chicago won, 94–88, and the Vancouver crowd actually gave Jordan a standing ovation. His Bulls teammates sang the "Be Like Mike" jingle from a Gatorade commercial.

One could only imagine that opponents around the NBA were swallowing hard upon seeing the ESPN sports channel highlights—and Chicago fans were wishing they had stayed up past midnight to see the furious finish. When the Bulls played a January 1997 game in Vancouver, one local newspaper recalled the masterful performance with a full-page spread headlined "Jordan's Six-Minute Workout."

"That was the game I knew he was back," said Phil Jackson, whose team was in the formative stage of a record-breaking seventy-two–win season, fueled by Michael's return to interplanetary capacity. "His will to take over a game and his will to win came forth in that game."

Bulls television announcer Red Kerr, sitting courtside, revealed that Vancouver's Cuonzo Martin made it all possible.

"The guy [Martin] made a shot and started trash-talking at the Bulls bench all the way back down the court," recalled Kerr. Jordan, taking a breather at that point, simply smiled.

"Michael shut him up pretty good," said Kerr. "I get excited all over again just thinking about it."

Big mistake by Martin, whose team, at 2–13, had nothing to brag about. After scoring only 8 points on 4-of-11 shooting, MJ played perhaps his best basketball in more than two years. He finished with 29 points and one eye-opening stretch—scoring 11 straight points during the run.

"He had to turn it up a notch," said Bulls coach Phil Jackson. "He's a very patient player and doesn't get upset when things don't go well."

"That was vintage Michael Jordan," said Ron Harper.

"I think it's a good sign to people that, hey, I'm not too old. I can still put up some numbers in a short amount of time."

Number 35: Great Game Index

GGI Score (103 of a possible 123)   Tiebreaker is game importance.

Scoring (33 of a possible 33)   Forget the game totals. MJ's 19 points in six minutes translates to a 152-point pace for an entire 48 minutes. Some bench rest fueled his high-octane stretch.

Game Importance (17 of 20)   The Bulls were 12-2 after this game and 5-1 for the road trip. More significant was Michael serving notice his full game was back in gear.

Opponent Strength (13 of 20)   Vancouver would have a hard time jelling the entire season.

Historical Significance (9 of 10)   One of the great offensive sieges ever witnessed—the type of run you think would happen only on a playground or in the gym (see Game No. 40).

Legendary Intangibles (10 of 10)   The West Coast late start makes this game a rare bootleg gem for the Jordan diehard fans. Rather than watch the dreadful first three quarters, edit the video for fourth-quarter viewing. Take special note of Cuonzo Martin deciding to taunt a megastar.

Pressure Points (10 of 10)   It seemed incongruous to be playing with pressure against the Grizzlies, but the Bulls needed every shot in Michael's 19-point blitz to pull out the game.

Defense (4 of 5)   He's always working on his defensive assignments, particularly when he doesn't shoot well (he was 4 of 11 in the first half).

Other Offensive Contributions (2 of 5)   Nothing spectacular.

MJ's Physical Condition (1 of 5)   Not a factor.

Long Odds (4 of 5)   Nineteen points in six minutes seems nearly impossible for any NBA star.

-36-

February 8, 1998

NBA All-Star Game
at New York

Jordan wins his third
All-Star MVP award.

T here were several reasons to think Michael was due for another big game after recording the first triple-double in All-Star history in 1997. The 1998 game was scheduled for Madison Square Garden, where Jordan seemed to draw extra strength and motivation. It was anticipated as his last of twelve All-Star appearances because of his own talk about retirement. He fell ill on the Friday of All-Star weekend, not getting out of bed for more than twenty-four hours, but Michael always seemed to play well after a flu bout.

Perhaps most importantly, there were emotions about passing the NBA torch to younger flamboyant players such as Kobe Bryant—but not too soon, nor without at least one more lesson in class acts. It started when Jordan dismissed any notion of keeping aloof from the game's upcoming players. He vowed he would be "thrilled" to help the young All-Stars to enjoy the festivities.

"They are the future," said Jordan. "You are on the other side of your career. People want to see the new faces, so it's in

Michael may have been playing in his final All-Star Game, but he wasn't quite ready to pass the torch to Kobe Bryant, who was labeled "the next Jordan." *Reuters/Ray Stubblebine/Archive Photos*

Game 36: East 135, West 114

West	Min	FG-att	FT-att	Reb	Ast	Fls	Pts
Malone	17	2-4	0-0	3	2	1	4
Garnett	21	6-11	0-0	4	2	0	12
O'Neal	18	5-10	2-4	4	1	2	12
Bryant	22	7-16	2-2	6	1	1	18
Payton	24	3-7	0-0	3	13	0	7
Baker	21	3-12	2-2	8	0	1	8
Jones	25	7-19	1-2	11	1	1	15
Robinson	22	3-4	9-10	6	0	1	15
Richmond	17	4-11	0-0	1	2	0	8
Kidd	19	0-1	0-0	1	9	2	0
Duncan	14	1-4	0-0	11	1	0	2
Van Exel	20	5-14	2-2	3	2	0	13
Totals	**240**	**46-113**	**18-22**	**61**	**34**	**9**	**114**

Percentages: FG .407, FT .818. **Three-point goals:** 4-23 .174 (Bryant 2-3, Payton 1-3, Van Exel 1-6, Garnett 0-1, Duncan 0-1, Richmond 0-2, Jones 0-7). **Team rebounds:** 8. **Blocked shots:** 3 (Robinson 2, Garnett). **Turnovers:** 18 (Payton 4, Garnett 3, O'Neal 2, Robinson 2, Kidd 2, Duncan 2, Van Exel 2, Bryant). **Steals:** 13 (Malone 2, Garnett 2, Bryant 2, Payton 2, Jones 2, Robinson 2, Baker). **Technical fouls:** None. **Illegal defense:** None.

East	Min	FG-att	FT-att	Reb	Ast	Fls	Pts
Hill	28	7-11	0-0	3	5	1	15
Kemp	25	5-10	2-2	11	2	2	12
Mutombo	19	4-5	1-2	7	0	3	9
Jordan	32	10-18	2-3	6	8	0	23
A. Hardaway	12	3-5	0-0	0	3	0	6
T. Hardaway	17	3-8	0-0	1	6	0	8
Williams	19	2-3	0-0	10	1	2	4
Smits	21	3-7	4-4	7	4	3	10
Miller	20	6-8	1-2	0	0	2	14
Rice	16	6-14	0-0	1	0	0	16
Smith	16	6-12	0-0	3	0	0	14
Walker	15	2-8	0-0	3	3	0	4
Totals	**240**	**57-109**	**10-13**	**13-52**	**32**	**13**	**135**

Percentages: FG .523, FT 769. **Three-point goals:** 11-25 .440 (Rice 4-6, T. Hardaway 2-5, Smith 2-5, Hill 1-1, Jordan 1-1, Miller 1-2, Kemp 0-1, A. Hardaway 0-1, Walker 0-3). **Team rebounds:** 5. **Blocked shots:** 3 (Smits 2, Mutombo). **Turnovers:** 15 (T. Hardaway 6, Kemp 4, Jordan 2, A. Hardaway, Rice, Walker). **Steals:** 10 (Kemp 4, Jordan 3, Hill, Miller, Walker). **Technical fouls:** None. **Illegal defense:** None.

West	25	33	33	23	114
East	33	34	34	34	135

A: 18,323; **T:** 2:04; **Officials:** Hue Hollins, Bernie Fryer, Bob Delaney.

my best interests not to have any animosity toward Kobe or Grant Hill or Anfernee Hardaway. That's what I learned."

Jordan came to the knowledge in difficult fashion, getting the freeze-out treatment from Isiah Thomas, Magic Johnson, and George Gervin in his rookie All-Star appearance in 1985. He went to the game in hopes of being accepted by the league's brightest lights, but unknowingly ticked off the other stars by showing up for the slam dunk contest in Nike gear rather than then-standard team uniforms.

"With the Air Jordan apparel and the necklaces in the dunking contest, which seemed to be very innocent from my standpoint, it seemed to be more of a thing to the veteran players," recalled Jordan before the All-Star Game thirteen years later. "I think it showed some of the competitive jealousies and animosities among the veteran players with the young guys.

"I felt my first All-Star Game, first and foremost, was a privilege. I went with the notion of trying to fit in, not trying to stand out and gain any notoriety from the veterans who earned the right to be there. I didn't want to ruffle any feathers. Lo and behold, that's what happened."

No such hazing awaited the game's new young stars, but Jordan didn't overdo the politeness either. He anticipated the media hype pitting him against Bryant of the Lakers. The game started with Bryant attracting attention with his high-flying play, but MJ jumped into his own flow. He posted up on Bryant in two early possessions, hitting jump shots both times. He finished the mini-lesson with a quick slam dunk.

By first-quarter's end, the Eastern Conference All-Stars owned a double-digit lead keyed to Jordan's 9 points. The East expanded the margin with a 135–114 victory.

"I was trying to fend off Kobe as much as I could," said Jordan. "He came at me pretty early, which I would too if I were him. If I see someone that's sick or whatever, you have got to attack him. You know, I like his attitude."

Jordan was merely being polite again. He finished with 23 points, 8 assists, 6 rebounds, and 3 steals in arguably the best all-around effort ever turned in by an NBA All-Star.

"What really set the tone was when Michael started post-ing up on Kobe," said East All-Star Reggie Miller of the Indiana Pacers. "That got us going."

New York's Madison Square Garden was again the setting for Jordan magic. "I love this place," said Jordan. "I love the arena. I have always had high respect for this place and the fans."

"Give it to Michael and get out of the way," said Larry Bird, the legendary All-Star who was coaching the East because of his first-place Indiana Pacers squad. "That's the way it usu-ally happens."

Bird urged Michael not to retire at season's end. He even recommended him becoming a rival coach: "I think he'll do very well [as a player-coach]. It's good for us to have him in the game."

After the game, Michael wasn't biting on any player-coach scenarios (he repeatedly rejected the idea over the years). He was more willing to reflect about his evolution as an athlete since first winning the All-Star MVP in Chicago in 1988.

"My game has elevated from just being a spectacular dunker or player," said Jordan. "It's more about moving the ball, trying not to be a one-dimensional player.

"I'm the best basketball player I can be, aside from all of the dunking, creative shots, back to the basket. Coming into the league, sure I had those qualities. I think I'm better than I was five years ago."

That was the end of the 1991–93 "three-peat" and the beginning of Michael's sabbatical. Bulls fans—and even NBA Commissioner David Stern—could only hope the similarities stopped at "three-peats" and not retirement.

"I'm only going to allow him to have this [MVP] award if he promises to come back and do it again," said Stern. "Michael is the star of Stars."

Number 36: Great Game Index

GGI Score (103 of a possible 123).

Scoring (30 of a possible 33) Michael has the highest All-Star scoring average—21.1 points per game—of any player in NBA history.

Game Importance (15 of 20) It is only an exhibition game, but the players want to win. Jordan's work ethic doesn't allow for nonchalance.

Opponent Strength (18 of 20) The Western Conference All-Star squad was skewed toward youth—Bryant was nineteen years old—but still highly talented.

Historical Significance (10 of 10) This game was billed as Michael's last All-Star Game. Somehow, future games will never be the same.

Legendary Intangibles (10 of 10) Jordan was sick enough to beg off playing. Instead, he struggled out of bed to make sure Kobe Bryant and the other young stars didn't get too confident. One might imagine Jordan was sending a message for any postseason opponent.

Pressure Points (7 of 10) MJ's early scoring put this game out of reach and tension-free by the fourth quarter.

Defense (5 of 5) Three steals in a game that traditionally features little defense.

Other Offensive Contributions (5 of 5) Eight assists and 6 rebounds was an indicator of hustle.

MJ's Physical Condition (2 of 5) Michael overcame a flu that marred his All-Star weekend, but he did get to play golf on his day off before traveling to New York.

Long Odds (1 of 5) Another All-Star Game, another MVP award.

-37-

July 1, 1984

U.S. Olympic Team vs. NBA All-Star Squad at Minneapolis

Exhibition A: Michael turns some impressive heads.

*T*he most obscure of Jordan's greatest games, and symbolic of the first on-court, sneaker-to-sneaker impression Michael made with his future NBA colleagues, came during a barnstorming tour of games between the 1984 Olympic team and pro stars like Magic Johnson and Kevin McHale.

Say what you want about an exhibition mentality or the holiday mood of a July 4 weekend, but the idea of these games was to toughen up the Olympians, who were all college players back then. The Soviet Union was not planning to attend the L.A. Games, but the U.S. Olympic Committee and U.S.A. basketball were taking no chances. A gold medal was mandatory.

Further proof of the competitive nature of these games was the presence of Johnson, the game's top star, who certainly could have found other things to do with his summer vacation. Isiah Thomas was on hand, along with Mark Aguirre. The NBA squad's coach was Lenny Wilkens, who has never been one to

Game 37: U.S. Olympic Team 94, NBA All-Stars 90

U.S. Olympic Team	FG	FT	Pts
Wood	1-5	0-0	2
Robertson	4-10	0-1	8
Koncak	1-3	2-2	4
Mullin	6-17	0-0	12
Perkins	5-10	6-8	16
Alford	2-4	3-4	7
Ewing	2-7	8-15	10
Fleming	3-5	2-2	8
Jordan	5-13	2-2	12
Kleine	1-3	0-0	2
Tisdale	3-8	3-3	9
Turner	1-4	0-0	2
Totals	**34-89**	**26-37**	**94**

NBA All-Stars	FG	FT	Pts
McHale	8-17	2-4	18
Olberding	1-1	5-7	7
Breuer	5-6	3-5	13
Williams	0-6	0-0	0
Tucker	3-4	0-0	6
Aguirre	4-7	1-2	9
Engler	0-1	0-0	0
Johnson	2-3	5-5	9
Breuer	0-1	0-0	0
Roundfield	4-5	5-8	13
Totals	**32-59**	**26-38**	**90**

Halftime: USA 52, NBA 40. **Total fouls:** NBA 28, USA 25. **Fouled out:** None. **Technical fouls:** USA bench. **Team rebounds:** NBA 39 (McHale 14), USA 38 (Fleming 7). **Assists:** NBA 16 (Roundfield 5), USA 15 (Fleming 6). **A:** 19,038.

take competition lightly. Plus, Bob Knight was running a tight ship with the Olympians. Each game was part of a grand plan, and no minute of any game was wasted.

Jordan did not disappoint on any level. In the first minute, the Olympic captain blocked a Johnson layup and knocked the Lakers legend to the hardwood in the exchange. Johnson, maybe hiding his amazement while recognizing greatness when he smacked up against it, lifted himself off the floor to high-five Jordan.

The two megastars were destined to meet seven years later in the 1991 NBA Finals, known as the Michael-Magic Show. They eventually became friends—after an All-Star skirmish (see Game No. 36)— kidding through the years over who had the most championship rings or consecutive titles. Jordan was one of the first people Magic called after doctors told Johnson he tested positive for HIV. Johnson didn't want Michael to learn about it from anyone but him.

Jordan didn't stop with Magic in the exhibition game. He ripped a defensive rebound out of the formidable arms of McHale, the Boston Celtics stalwart playing before his home-town crowd. MJ promptly put the ball back up for 2 of his 12 points. He added 6 rebounds in the Olympians' 94–90 win before 19,038 fans. It was the third straight over NBA foes for Knight's squad, and Jordan was a central figure.

He blocked a sure two points by the taller Jim Brewer (another University of Minnesota favorite), appearing suddenly and without any warning. Brewer was left looking too surprised to be mad.

At the end of the first half, Michael swiped a pass by the often undetectable Johnson, and then sprinted the length of the court to sink a buzzer-beater jump shot.

"There were some times when we really lost our concentration and didn't play so well," said Jordan after the game, "but the big thing is we really stuck it out and kept our poise at the end."

The NBA star squad made no mistake about the game's top star.

"Somebody guard the guy with the wallet," yelled McHale to his NBA teammates while taking a breather on the bench.

A reporter asked Lenny Wilkens if any Olympic players impressed him, and might worry him in the pro season ahead (the Hall of Fame guard and coach would eventually lead a Cleveland team that you-know-who haunted more times than Cavs fans wanted to recall).

"Jordan," said Wilkens, naming no one else among a group of Olympians who turned out to be a solid group of pros. "I think Michael Jordan will be a great player in the NBA."

As the Olympic team prepared to win its gold medal at the Summer Games in Los Angeles, Knight was also impressed by Jordan, especially the practice ethic of the two-time college player of the year. The Indiana taskmaster, known as the General, named Jordan captain of the illustrious squad early in the team's formation. He knew Jordan was going to be creative and flamboyant in some ways, but also knew enough to recognize a team player when he saw one. Perhaps three years with University of North Carolina coach Dean Smith was enough credentials for the captaincy.

In short order, Jordan's teammates were looking up to him. "Playing with Michael was like going to the circus," Olympic teammate and Oklahoma star Wayman Tisdale told *Sports Illustrated* in 1984. "You'd come to practice and never know what he'd pull off."

There's a story about how Jordan communicated with Knight, who made no friends among the players by cutting a popular, talented, but sometimes disrespectful Charles Barkley of Auburn University before the gold-medal fun started in Los Angeles. Minutes before the game, the U.S. team anticipated some final words from Knight, who was called into the hallway. Jordan walked up to the chalkboard and wrote a short message that said: "You've gotten us ready, and we know what we have to do."

Some players figured Knight would blow an emotional fuse, but the coach walked into the locker room, read the note, and simply said, "Guess there's nothing else to say. Let's go."

Jordan credited Knight for his improved outside shooting, which was one alleged drawback of Michael's game. He said Knight helped him concentrate and "do things without a lot of lollygagging."

America took notice of Jordan during those star-spangled Games, about a month later than the NBA stars in Minneapolis. Michael himself was moved by the patriotic juxtaposition of wearing a gold medal and listening to the national anthem.

"My eyes were misting from almost tears but my heart was so happy I could feel and hear it beating loudly," wrote Jordan in a college term paper about the experience (he finished his final year of education during NBA off-seasons).

On that night in Minneapolis, MJ admitted to anticipating his future with the Bulls, despite the scrutiny and single-mindedness of Knight.

"Once in a while I catch myself daydreaming about what it will be like in the NBA and playing all the time against these guys," Jordan told the *Chicago Tribune's* Mike Conklin, who was sent to file a story about this young kid who seemed to be putting up some good numbers with the Olympians, and was the first Chicago sportswriter Jordan saw or heard from since draft day. "You can start thinking, 'Hey, look at me. I'm out here against all these All-Stars.' We're all young and we're all in college or about to go to the NBA. I guess we all want to show the NBA players something—that we belong."

Number 37: Great Game Index

GGI Score (102 of a possible123).

Scoring (29 of a possible 33)   Twelve points doesn't seem like much, until you realize Bobby Knight was shuffling lineups and not making any one player the focal point of offense.

Game Importance (16 of 20)   The Olympians were supported by the toughening and tuning only NBA opponents could provide. The collegians were anxious to show their abilities.

Opponent Strength (19 of 20)   Michael took control of a game with some of the NBA's best players. He set the tone, swarmed all over the court, and stayed within Bob Knight's system.

Historical Significance (8 of 10)   Jordan "introduced" himself to Magic Johnson. It was subtle and without the klieg lights of future games played before the Hollywood set, yet Michael clearly nudged Johnson firmly enough to make room at the top.

Legendary Intangibles (10 of 10)   Michael hit key shots and passed superbly, but made his biggest mark in offensive boards and on defense.

Pressure Points (7 of 10)   MJ played well in a close game.

Defense (5 of 5)   Nobody was better on the floor, on either team.

Other Offensive Contributions (4 of 5)   Jordan knew ball distribution was coach Knight's credo.

MJ's Physical Condition (1 of 5)   Not a factor.

Long Odds (3 of 5)   The shot blocks by a guard were most unexpected. All of the NBA was going to be forced into adjustments to cope with Jordan's pioneering style of play.

-38-

May 19, 1989

New York Knicks at Bulls Game 6, Second-Round Playoff Series

Jordan's 40 closes out Ewing—again.

T his Eastern Conference semifinal harbors three of Michael Jordan's 50 greatest games (see Game Nos. 17 and 22). No one could blame Knicks center Patrick Ewing if he daydreamed occasionally about playing a few years behind or ahead of Jordan as a pro.

Once again, Jordan closed out Ewing's championship hopes. He did it in the 1982 NCAA championship game by hitting the game-winning jump shot, and eliminating New York would become a habit in the 1990s. This 113–111 thriller propelled the Bulls into the conference finals for the first time since the Jerry Sloan–Norm Van Lier team did it in 1975. Detroit would be the opponent.

"I don't think there is a person in the world who thinks we can beat the Pistons, said Chicago coach Doug Collins, whose team was the underdog against New York but won the series in

Game 38: Bulls 113, Knicks 111

Knicks	Min	FG-att	FT-att	Reb	Ast	Fls	Pts
Newman	34	6-12	5-6	4	1	3	17
Oakley	32	1-2	4-6	6	2	2	6
Ewing	44	9-15	4-5	13	6	3	22
Jackson	41	5-8	9-11	2	12	3	22
G. Wilkins	34	9-22	4-4	2	3	6	22
Vandeweghe	10	1-2	0-1	0	0	0	3
Tucker	17	5-6	1-1	1	2	1	14
Green	13	0-1	1-2	3	0	3	1
Walker	6	0-1	0-0	1	1	1	0
Myers	1	0-0	0-0	0	0	0	0
Strickland	7	2-3	0-0	0	3	2	4
E. Wilkins	1	0-0	0-0	0	0	0	0
Totals	**240**	**38-72**	**28-36**	**32**	**30**	**24**	**111**

Percentages: FG .528, FT .778. **Three-point goals:** 7-12, .583 (Jackson 3-3, Tucker 3-4, Vandeweghe 1-1, G. Wilkins 0-1, Newman 0-3). **Team rebounds:** 12. **Blocked shots:** 3 (Ewing 3). **Turnovers:** 20 (Jackson 5, G. Wilkins 5, Tucker 4, Ewing 2, Oakley, Vandeweghe, Walker, Strickland). **Steals:** 11 (Oakley 4, Ewing 2, Tucker 2, Newman, Jackson, G. Wilkins). **Technical fouls:** None. **Illegal defense:** 1.

Bulls	Min	FG-att	FT-att	Reb	Ast	Fls	Pts
Pippen	27	6-7	3-4	4	2	4	19
Grant	43	3-6	5-5	7	3	4	11
Cartwright	41	7-10	2-4	8	3	5	16
Hodges	39	6-11	0-0	1	6	3	15
Jordan	45	14-22	11-12	5	10	3	40
Corzine	6	0-2	0-0	1	1	0	0
Paxson	23	4-7	0-0	0	0	4	8
Davis	2	0-0	0-0	0	0	0	0
Vincent	1	0-0	0-0	0	0	0	0
Sellers	13	2-6	0-0	1	2	4	4
Totals	**240**	**42-71**	**21-25**	**27**	**27**	**27**	**113**

Percentages: FG .592, FT .840. **Three-point goals:** 8-14, .571 (Pippen 4-4, Hodges 3-6, Jordan 1-3, Paxson 0-1). **Team rebounds:** 4. **Blocked shots:** 10 (Jordan 4, Pippen 3, Grant 2, Cartwright). **Turnovers:** 16 (Jordan 6, Pippen 2, Grant 2, Cartwright, Hodges, Paxson, Davis, Sellers, team). **Steals:** 10 (Paxson 3, Hodges 2, Pippen 2, Grant, Cartwright, Vincent). **Technical fouls:** Sellers, 6:24 2nd. **Illegal defense:** None.

Knicks	31	30	18	32	111
Bulls	32	27	27	27	113

A: 18,676. **T:** 2:27. **Officials:** Jake O'Donnell, Darell Garretson, Ed T. Rush.

six games. "They have all the weapons, and no one has come close to touching them yet. But I've said this before: Anytime you have a Michael Jordan on the floor, anything can happen."

Point proven against the Knicks. Jordan notched 40 points, including 8 of the last 10, the final 6 on clutch free throws. The Bulls were up 101–94 with 3:33 left, but New York battled to a tie with intense defense at the two-minute mark.

From there, Jordan drove to the hoop on two of Chicago's next three possessions, drawing fouls and sinking four free throws. Good thing, too, because Ewing and Gerald Wilkens hit key shots for the Knicks.

New York blinked first on offense, and John Paxson hit a jumper to extend the Bulls lead to 4, but Ewing kept his team close with a bank shot to make it 109–107 with thirteen seconds left. Jordan hit his second pair of free throws and it appeared time to celebrate—or at least start thinking about Detroit.

Maybe not. Trent Tucker, another former foe who would eventually come to Chicago to be part of a championship team, improbably swished a three-pointer and was fouled on the shot by Craig Hodges. Tucker made the free throw. Tie game. Hush at Chicago Stadium.

Six seconds remained, plenty of time for a Michael miracle. On the inbounds play, Jordan jumped out to take the pass from John Paxson. MJ cut across the court and Wilkens quickly fouled him. The Bulls star calmly sank two free throws with 4 seconds on the clock.

New York attempted one last gasp to force a Game 7 at Madison Square Garden. Johnny Newman didn't miss a 3-point attempt by much. Chicago breathed on.

"I'm very elated," said Jordan, "but I'm still kind of shocked. I was very scared when they made that four-point play. I thought maybe it was not for us tonight.

Jordan said he felt "good rhythm" on his jumpers and free throws. He added 10 assists and 4 blocked shots to his outstanding game. One imagines Patric Ewing didn't have many good dreams—or much sleep—that night.

Number 38: Great Game Index

GGI Score (101 of a possible 123)   Tiebreaker is total game performance, which includes scoring, defense, and other offensive contributions.

Scoring (30 of a possible 33)   Michael carried the primary load with 40 points, especially after Scottie Pippen was ejected for fighting with Kenny Walker in the third quarter.

Game Importance (19 of 20)   Nobody on the Chicago side wanted a Game 7 winner-take-all in New York.

Opponent Strength (18 of 20)   The Patrick Ewing Knicks were still in development, but their defense was already suffocating.

Historical Significance (8 of 10)   The beginning of the best rivalry of the 1990s.

Legendary Intangibles (8 of 10)   Sound fundamental basketball: hit your free throws, play scrappy defense, win games.

Pressure Points (8 of 10)   Michael hit 4 of 4 free throws in the final twenty-three seconds. It's harder than it looks.

Defense (5 of 5)   Four blocked shots are just one indicator of hard-nosed play.

Other Offensive Contributions (3 of 5)   Ten assists is impressive.

MJ's Physical Condition (1 of 5)   No factor.

Long Odds (1 of 5)   A 40-point game was no big deal for Jordan, even in the postseaon.

-39-

June 5, 1998

Bulls at Utah Jazz Game 2, NBA Finals

━━━━━━

Just like 'old times'; Bulls tie the series.

━━━━━━

*T*here was lots of talk. Talk is cheap (or completely free if you listen to sports radio).

Talk can also be wrong. Dead wrong. Many experts were writing off the 1998 postseason Bulls as a bit too old and lacking their usual killer instinct, having lost their previous four games when the outcome was in doubt during the final minute of play. Another proposed problem was their third-quarter leads that dwindled in fourth quarters.

Guess somebody forgot to tell Michael Jordan. It wasn't an artistic masterpiece, but MJ's mental edge outmuscled Karl Malone and the Jazz, 93–88, to knot this sixth Bulls title run at one game apiece with the next three bound for Chicago. Michael finished with a game-high 37 points, while Malone suffered his second straight poor shooting night, finishing with 16.

The Bulls actually should have won Game 1 too, but they lost in overtime on turnovers. This night, there would be no such dribbling and fumbling.

"A lot of people were talking about our age, how many

Game 39: Bulls 93, Utah Jazz 88

Bulls	Min	FG-att	FT-att	Reb	Ast	Fls	Pts
Pippen	41	7-13	7-7	6	4	3	21
Kukoc	43	6-16	0-2	9	2	1	13
Longley	17	2-2	0-0	2	2	6	4
Jordan	40	14-33	9-10	5	3	2	37
Harper	24	1-4	1-2	2	3	1	3
Rodman	27	1-1	1-2	9	1	5	3
Kerr	27	1-5	4-4	1	2	1	7
Buechler	2	0-0	0-0	0	0	1	0
Burrell	15	2-5	0-0	1	0	1	5
Wennington	4	0-1	0-0	1	0	0	0
Totals	**240**	**34-80**	**22-27**	**36**	**17**	**21**	**93**

Percentages: FG .425, FT .815. **Three-point goals:** 3-16, .188 (Burrell 1-2, Kerr 1-4, Kukoc 1-6, Harper 0-1, Pippen 0-1, Jordan 0-2). **Team rebounds:** 7. **Blocked shots:** 3 (Pippen, Jordan, Wennington). **Turnovers:** 7 (Kukoc 3, Pippen 2, Rodman, Kerr). **Steals:** 10 (Kukoc 2, Harper 2, Rodman 2, Pippen, Longley, Jordan, Burrell). **Technical fouls:** None. **Illegal defense:** None.

Jazz	Min	FG-att	FT-att	Reb	Ast	Fls	Pts
Russell	37	4-7	0-0	5	1	2	11
Malone	39	5-16	6-9	12	4	5	16
Foster	13	0-1	0-0	3	0	2	0
Hornacek	32	7-11	4-4	1	2	6	20
Stockton	31	4-5	0-0	3	7	5	9
Eisley	24	4-10	0-0	2	7	3	9
Morris	15	1-2	0-0	4	0	3	2
Anderson	24	4-7	4-5	2	0	1	12
Carr	9	1-2	0-0	1	0	0	2
Ostertag	7	3-4	1-1	3	0	0	7
Keefe	9	0-2	0-0	2	1	1	0
Totals	**240**	**33-67**	**15-19**	**38**	**22**	**28**	**88**

Percentages: FG .493, FT .789. **Three-point goals:** 7-13, .538 (Russell 3-5, Hornacek 2-3, Eisley 1-2, Stockton 1-2, Anderson 0-1). **Team rebounds:** 8. **Blocked shots:** 5 (Malone 3, Eisley, Morris). **Turnovers:** 19 (Malone 4, Russell 3, Hornacek 3, Stockton 3, Eisley 3, Keefe 2, Anderson). **Steals:** 3 (Stockton 2, Russell). **Technical fouls:** None. **Illegal defense:** None.

Bulls	23	27	20	23	93
Jazz	20	26	27	15	88

A: 19,911. **T:** 2:35. **Officials:** Joe Crawford, Danny Crawford, Bill Oakes.

minutes I've been playing and whatever," said the perfectly dressed, sweat-free Jordan in the press conference after another cool and collected postseason performance. "But we're here and we beat some good teams to get here, so if that's what they consider to be dead, I don't mind being dead for a little while longer. I believe in what we can accomplish, no matter what the disadvantages people think we may have."

What the Bulls got done early was attacking on offense. Jordan, Scottie Pippen, and Toni Kukoc scored all the first-quarter points for a 23–20 lead. An offense that had struggled now seemed to have the major cogs in place. During the next three quarters, other spark plugs and connections were tuned up, as Luc Longley and Scott Burrell hit some big shots.

Steve Kerr made the play of the night with fifty seconds left in the game, missing on an open three-point attempt and then slashing between Malone and Utah's other perennial All-Star, John Stockton, for the rebound. He flipped a short pass to an open Jordan, who converted and drew the foul. The free throw made it 88–86, Chicago. Kerr also canned a pair of free throws with 19.9 seconds left for a 4-point lead.

But it was Jordan who inspired his teammates, hitting the tough shots and standing calmly at the foul line to make clutch free throws. He fought through some of his own struggles—4-of-9 shooting—to lead the team with 13 points in the final quarter. He also contributed his usual stifling defense, as Chicago held the Jazz to 1 point during the first seven minutes of the quarter. A 3-point Utah lead turned into a 7-point deficit.

Perhaps even more importantly, Jordan was smiling during breaks in play. He patted teammates on the back and looked confident. His swagger was back, if in fact it had ever vanished. Defense and poise win championships—and must-win games.

"You don't become champions five times without having some type of mental advantages," explained Jordan. "We are mentally strong and confident about what we want to accomplish."

Utah seemed to take notice. Jeff Hornacek, the leading Jazz scorer with 20 points on a gimpy Achilles tendon, sat glumly in the interview room. "They're still the champs until somebody beats them," he said. "We knew they'd be good tonight and not want to be down two-zero. We didn't meet the challenge."

Hornacek hit a three-pointer to make it 86–85 in Utah's favor with 1:46 left. Then Bulls fans were the glum ones.

"I thought we were in dire straits there," admitted Chicago coach Phil Jackson, "but we found a way to win. This is a team that does that."

Kerr said his critical rebound off the missed 3-point jumper was "just a lucky play."

Jordan put his own spin on the game action: "True desire and the kind of thing we had to do down the stretch."

True enough. Dennis Rodman was a prime example, with 9 second-half rebounds, a key twenty-foot jumper when nobody else could connect, and, most of all, airtight defense on Karl Malone. Jordan's most significant work might have been in the first quarter, when he was 4 of 7 from the field, for 8 points. He also beat whatever double-team was thrown his way, dishing to open men like Pippen and Kukoc (and later Kerr, Burrell, and Longley) when the situation demanded.

"You come out and attack," said Jordan.

Jerry Sloan, the honest-to-goodness Utah coach and former Bulls great, knew that Jordan's leadership won the night.

"I'm concerned about the first quarter, that's where the game is established in my opinion," Sloan said. "I know it's not always won there, but that's how you establish who you are as a team. They did that against us [with six more shots and six more offensive rebounds in the first quarter]. They established that right at the beginning of the game."

Number 39: Great Game Index

GGI Score (101 of a possible 123)   Tiebreaker is game importance.

Scoring (29 of a possible 33)   Michael didn't have a great shooting night (14 of 33) from the floor, but his 9 of 10 free throws included several game-breakers.

Game Importance (19 of 20)   The only good thing about being down 2–0 would have been the schedule calling for the next three games in Chicago, but Utah proved itself a tough road team.

Opponent Strength (19 of 20)   The Jazz were working with a year of experience, becoming the only team to make a second appearance against Chicago in the Finals.

Historical Significance (8 of 10)   Hold the obituaries, fellas.

Legendary Intangibles (10 of 10)   Jordan was sinking jumpers and getting in position to draw the fouls. His defense was a clinic for superstar or rec league player alike. He enjoyed the process, while Karl Malone looked hesitant. "Anytime we lose a game, Chicagoans are going to worry," said Jordan after the pregame morning shoot-around. "We have a good feel for where we are, and we just have to come out and make adjustments."

Pressure Points (8 of 10)   MJ converted two 3-point plays down the stretch. That sort of clutch shooting instills confidence in the entire team.

Defense (4 of 5)   Forget the thirty-five-year-old legs stuff.

Other Offensive Contributions (2 of 5)   Nothing spectacular, but 3 assists at strategic moments.

MJ's Physical Condition (1 of 5)   Not a factor, unless you want to believe hysterical radio show hosts. Much was made of Phil Jackson saying Michael looked tired and MJ denying it. This was not a new wrinkle that developed after Jordan's thirty-fifth birthday in February. Jackson, as is his right, has watched his star player's minute count for years.

Long Odds (1 of 5)   Though Chicago was an underdog in these Finals, nobody should have been surprised about the outcome of Game 2. Jordan and his teammates certainly were not.

-40-

April 29, 1998

Bulls at New Jersey Nets
Game 3 Clincher,
First-Round Playoff Series

Bulls feast on Jordan's 'zone' diet.

*T*he thoughts were similar to those heard in other locker rooms of the conquered, but the voices were different. The New Jersey Nets, a team that looked to be on the rise, had just been grounded for the season by Michael Jordan's 16-of-22 shooting night. MJ finished with 38 points as Chicago swept the opening round series with a 116–101 win.

"You're just trying to make it as hard as you can," said Kerry Kittles, the young defender who drew the short straw on guarding Jordan. "That's all you can do. He was active, getting the ball, driving it, creating for himself."

"When he gets going, you can send as many guys as you want at him," said Keith Van Horn, a rookie who has All-Star stamped on him for many seasons ahead. "You're not going to stop him."

"You've got to run at him," said John Calipari, the Nets coach whose emotions never veered far from his sleeve. "Even when you make it hard, sometimes it doesn't matter.

"When you play Michael, it's like playing blackjack and

201

The young, improved Nets offered a strong first-round challenge, but
with 23 points in the first half, MJ proved he was up to the task.
Reuters/Ray Stubblebine/Archive Photos

Game 40: Bulls 116, Nets 101

Bulls	Min	FG-att	FT-att	Reb	Ast	Fls	Pts
Pippen	44	2-12	9-10	5	10	2	13
Kukoc	27	6-10	0-0	3	3	2	13
Rodman	43	5-13	0-0	17	6	6	11
Jordan	44	16-22	4-5	4	3	2	38
Harper	23	5-6	0-0	2	2	2	12
Burrell	24	9-11	2-2	3	0	4	23
Kerr	23	2-5	0-0	1	1	2	4
Wennington	4	1-1	0-0	0	0	0	2
Simpkins	2	0-1	0-0	0	0	2	0
Brown	5	0-1	0-0	0	1	0	0
Buechler	1	0-0	0-0	0	0	0	0
Totals	240	46-82	15-17	35	26	22	116

Percentages: FG .561, FT .882. **Three-point goals:** 9-16, .563 (Burrell 3-5, Jordan 2-2, Harper 2-2, Rodman 1-1, Kukoc 1-2, Pippen 0-1, Kerr 0-3). **Team rebounds:** 9. **Blocked shots:** 2 (Jordan, Harper). **Turnovers:** 13 (Harper 3, Kukoc 2, Rodman 2, Jordan 2, Pippen 2, Wennington, Brown, team). **Steals:** 8 (Rodman 2, Jordan 2, Pippen, Kukoc, Harper, Burrell). **Technical fouls:** None. **Illegal defense:** 1.

Nets	Min	FG-att	FT-att	Reb	Ast	Fls	Pts
Gill	25	8-13	1-2	3	0	4	17
Van Horn	32	5-9	8-11	0	0	2	18
Williams	36	1-3	1-2	10	3	2	3
Kittles	44	5-8	4-4	3	4	1	16
Douglas	45	9-15	0-0	0	8	1	19
Harris	15	2-3	0-0	0	1	3	4
Gatling	28	7-12	4-6	3	1	3	18
Seikaly	9	1-1	2-3	1	0	1	4
Cassell	3	1-1	0-0	0	0	0	2
Evans	2	0-0	0-0	1	0	0	0
Vaughn	1	0-0	0-0	0	0	0	0
Totals	240	39-65	20-28	21	17	17	101

Percentages: FG .600, FT .714. **Three-point goals:** 3-8, .375 (Kittles 2-5, Douglas 1-2, Harris 0-1). **Team rebounds:** 7. **Blocked shots:** 5 (Williams 2, Kittles, Cassell, Vaughn). **Turnovers:** 12 (Gatling 3, Gill 2, Kittles 2, Douglas 2, Van Horn, Williams, Seikaly). **Steals:** 7 (Williams 2, Harris 2, Kittles, Douglas, Gatling). **Technical fouls:** Douglas, 9:34 2d. **Illegal defense:** 1.

Bulls	35	26	32	23	116
Nets	28	24	24	25	101

A: 19,889. **T:** 2:10. **Officials:** Jim Clark, Steve Javie, Nolan Fine.

he's the dealer. If he deals himself an ace and a king, there ain't no push. He was going over us, going under us, everything. I'm looking at Kerry and feeling sorry for him."

"He's the best athlete in the world and he's got the best team in the world," said Jayson Williams, one of the league's scrappiest rebounders. "He had that look in his eye from the beginning. Everyone says he's lost something, but he hasn't lost a thing."

Williams and the Nets, especially Calipari, should have known what was coming. Jordan hit a three-pointer just two minutes into the game and started his own brand of courtside chatter. He had an animated conversation with Calipari during the entire first quarter. Even a few fans heard some of it, along with Bulls teammates who needed—ahem—to be encouraged.

"He was in a zone," said Ron Harper about the early game outburst of points and pointers. "The only thing we had to do then was hit some shots and let him do his thing."

Kittles called it Jordan's "comfort zone." After hitting only 42 percent of his shots in the Bulls' first two 1998 postseason wins, Jordan was good nearly 73 percent of the time this night.

Michael's first half was a hoops work of art. He hit 9 of 10 shots, including an eighteen-foot jump shot right before the buzzer after dribbling off most of the twenty-four-second shot clock. He finished with 23 points for the first twenty-four minutes.

To make it worse for New Jersey, when Jordan was double-teamed, he would pass frequently to reserve Scott Burrell, who went 9 of 11 for 23 points.

"My rhythm was in synch early, and then I just let my game come to me," said Jordan. "I made some easy shots and I made some tough shots. I used my head-and-shoulder fake to get open, but when I'm in rhythm, it's doesn't really matter. I just go with the flow."

Harper didn't mean to deflate the fans' enjoyment, but did want to make one thing clear about his workout pal Jordan (they share the same personal trainer, Tim Grover of A.T.T.A.C.K. Athletics): "Understand this. Everyone's oohing and aahing when Michael does what he did tonight, but we see it every day. You see it only in games. He goes at us that hard every day in practice."

Number 40: Great Game Index

GGI Score (101 of a possible 123)   Tiebreaker is game importance.

Scoring (32 of a possible 33)   Michael's near-perfect 23-point first half put the Bulls in charge by halftime, 61–52. It ended the series before three games were even played.

Game Importance (17 of 20)   The Bulls needed some rest to heal Luc Longley's knee injury, plus get some practice time to work on an offense that needed some tuning.

Opponent Strength (17 of 20)   New Jersey played better ball than the franchise's reputation. It was encouraging enough for future seasons under John Calipari.

Historical Significance (9 of 10)   One series down, three to go in the attempt for a sixth NBA title.

Legendary Intangibles (10 of 10)   Jordan never missed an opportunity to school younger players about hard knocks. "I remember one play," said Nets star Jayson Williams. "They had been driving down the middle, so I said I'd take a hard foul on Michael. The next time down he hit me in the side of the head and said, 'Don't think I forgot about that.' He's one of the most amazing men I've ever met, along with my father and Bill Cosby."

Pressure Points (7 of 10)   MJ's early entry in his personal shooting zone took much of the suspense out of this game.

Defense (4 of 5)   Michael finished with a blocked shot and 2 steals. He didn't let up all night on the defensive end.

Other Offensive Contributions (3 of 5)   A solid night.

MJ's Physical Condition (1 of 5)   Not a factor.

Long Odds (1 of 5)   No Jordan shooting streak is improbable.

-41-

1984–85 Regular Season

Bulls vs. Bulls Practice

Seeing red, wearing white.

S tarting with his freshman year at the University of North Carolina, Jordan was known as the hardest worker in practice on every club on which he played. North Carolina coach Dean Smith said he had no player who worked or competed harder. Chicago general manager Jerry Krause said he knew only one player, Bulls great Jerry Sloan, who was even in Jordan's class during practice time.

Bulls teammates know that some of Michael's greatest moves and "games" were in practice. The most notable performance was during Michael's rookie season.

Kevin Loughery was coaching the Bulls. He had a habit of ending each workout with a five-on-five scrimmage to eleven baskets. The losing team had to run an extra fifteen laps.

One day, Jordan's red-shirted team was leading comfortably, 7–2, but Loughery, who knew Jordan was a special player, decided to shake up his young star. He ordered Jordan to turn his shirt inside out and join the white-shirted squad.

MJ was livid. He didn't see any reason why he was switching sides (it was strictly Loughery's whimsy). He nearly left the gym, but instead took up the challenge.

Even in his rookie season, Jordan put the Pistons, and the rest of the league, on notice that he was a force to be reckoned with. *UPI/Corbis-Bettmann*

The raging Bull walked out to his position. He proceeded to score seven straight baskets and make about that many defensive stops. His white team won, 11–8, and a chapter was added to the legend book.

"I was trying to test him," explained Loughery years later.

Jordan, who was miserable losing forty-four games his rookie year, over the years softened on his first pro coach. "Loughery may have been the best coach I've had here, for me," Jordan said before winning a fistful of titles with Phil Jackson. He pushed me to limits I didn't think I could reach."

Jordan couldn't save Loughery's job, however. The veteran coach was fired during the off-season, when new owner Jerry Reinsdorf installed Krause as the general manager. Jordan continued to go all-out in practices for, first, Stan Albeck, and then Doug Collins, before Phil Jackson arrived.

Michael's hard-driving style was an intriguing match with Jackson's more spirituality-steeped approach to game preparation. Both men seemed to learn something from each other.

"Michael has always maintained he didn't need any of 'that Zen stuff' because he already has a positive outlook on life," writes Jackson in his book *Sacred Hoops,* coauthored with Hugh Delehanty. "Who am I to argue? In the process of becoming a great athlete, Michael has attained a quality of mind few Zen students ever achieve. His ability to stay calm and intensely focused in the midst of utter chaos is unsurpassed. He loves being in the center of a storm. While everyone else is spinning madly out of control, he moves effortlessly across the floor, enveloped by a great stillness."

Jackson, privy to so many of Jordan's great games and metaphysical moments, said he first clicked on Michael's special place in basketball history during an ordinary workout.

"We wound up with Michael at power forward one day in practice [during Jackson's first year as an assistant coach to Doug Collins]" said Jackson. "The big guys couldn't get past him. So [now] we know he can play four positions, and we hadn't tried him at center yet."

Number 41: Great Game Index

GGI Score (101 of a possible 123)   Tiebreaker is total game performance, which includes scoring, defense, and other offensive contributions.

Scoring (32 of a possible 33)   MJ wiped out a five-basket lead with seven straight baskets for a scrimmage team that was obviously struggling—until they stop having to guard and score on their super-talented teammate.

Game Importance (12 of 20)   It was practice, though a war of wills between coach and star player.

Opponent Strength (12 of 20)   Every NBA player is formidable to some extent.

Historical Significance (10 of 10)   This story made the rounds throughout the league.

Legendary Intangibles (10 of 10)   Though willing his scrimmage squad to win, perhaps Jordan's best move was not stalking off the gym floor. That's leadership no one can teach, except maybe your parents.

Pressure Points (9 of 10)   This wasn't a game, but there was little margin between victory and error—fifteen laps.

Defense (5 of 5)   Jordan was tenacious and only bound to get better. Many stars tend to coast on defense some days in practice. Not Jordan, and, consequently, not his teammates.

Other Offensive Contributions (5 of 5)   Michael grabbed practically every rebound and loose ball during his white-shirted fury.

MJ's Physical Condition (1 of 5)   Not a factor.

Long Odds (5 of 5)   MJ was doing things daily that Loughery and then–general manager Rod Thorn (who went on to become a top league executive) would not have believed if they hadn't seen it. This practice day was at the top of their lists.

-42-

Detroit Pistons at Bulls
Regular Season

MJ returns the 'favor' to Thomas.

M ichael put on a clinic, and this time Isiah Thomas was the one taken to school. Jordan dunked, drove, and feathered jump shots to reach a single-game, career-high 49 points. The Bulls won their first contest after the All-Star Game, which MJ started as a rookie, overpowering the Pistons in overtime, 139–126.

Thomas claimed to be slowed by a bruised thigh, while Michael was dealing more with a sore ego. After explaining his less-than-spectacular All-Star performance as a case of the jitters ("I've never had that feeling before, never been nervous"), the Bulls hot hand discovered that several NBA stars had conspired to freeze out Jordan at the star proceedings. It seems that Isiah and George Gervin—and, rumor had it, Magic Johnson—were not enamored with Jordan's decision to wear his Nike sweat pants longer than usual during the Saturday slam-dunk contest. There was also some confusion over whether Jordan snubbed Thomas in an elevator at the All-Stars hotel in Indianapolis. Jordan said the elevator ride was without incident; Thomas said the alleged ride never happened (though a

Game 42: Bulls 139, Pistons 126

Pistons	Min	FG-att	FT-att	Reb	Ast	Fls	Pts
Benson	40	3-4	3-3	13	0	6	9
Tyler	23	1-5	2-2	5	1	3	4
Laimbeer	40	7-19	5-8	3	1	5	19
Long	40	12-20	2-2	1	0	3	26
Thomas	33	5-15	7-8	3	9	6	19
V. Johnson	26	12-18	3-4	2	7	6	28
Campbell	19	5-6	0-0	4	2	3	10
Cureton	31	3-7	0-0	6	0	3	6
M. Jones	6	1-2	1-1	0	0	0	3
Steppe	7	1-4	0-0	1	0	3	2
\Totals	240	50-100	23-28	38	20	38	126

Percentages: FG .500, FT .821. **Team rebounds:** 10. **Turnovers:** 19 (Laimbeer 4). **Steals:** 6 (Campbell 2, Cureton 2). **Blocked shots:** 7. **Three-point goals:** 3-9 (Thomas 2-6, V. Johnson 1-1).

Bulls	Min	FG-att	FT-att	Reb	Ast	Fls	Pts
Green	38	6-10	4-4	15	3	3	16
Woolridge	48	11-20	9-10	6	4	3	31
Corzine	40	3-7	0-0	7	3	6	6
Jordan	45	19-31	11-13	15	5	5	49
Matthews	28	5-9	4-6	1	5	2	14
Dailey	33	6-13	9-11	2	5	5	21
Oldham	13	1-1	0-2	2	0	1	2
Higgins	5	0-1	0-0	0	0	1	0
Greenwood	15	0-0	0-0	3	0	2	0
Totals	240	51-92	37-46	51	25	28	139

Percentages: FG .554, FT .804. **Team rebounds:** 6. **Turnovers:** 22 (Jordan 6). **Steals:** 7 (Jordan 4). **Blocked shots:** 4. **Three-point goals:** 0-0.

Pistons	31	30	37	25	3	126
Bulls	41	26	28	28	16	139

A: 13,363. **T:** 2:26. **Officials:** Paul Mihalak, Walter Rooney.

Thomas adviser, Dr. Charles Tucker, told the *Detroit Free Press* that Isiah said Jordan had an "attitude problem").

Michael was bewildered by the All-Star snub: "I went to the All-Star Game to enjoy and observe. I knew I was a rookie, and I didn't feel comfortable at all. I felt kind of odd, with all those legends, like I shouldn't be there."

In fact, Jordan said the weekend was salvaged by such things as having dinner with Moses Malone and blocking one of big man Ralph Sampson's shots.

In the hour before game time against the Pistons, Jordan was not confused or looking for consolation, only focused on a measure of revenge. He was pedaling furiously on a stationary bicycle to get warmed up in more ways than one.

"I won't forget what happened or who did it to me," confided Jordan to nearby onlookers.

Chances are, Thomas didn't forget Michael's payback effort. With his parents watching from the Stadium stands, Jordan added to the family scrapbook by scoring 24 points in the second half and another half dozen in overtime, but his most jaw-dropping points occurred on a 3-point play in the second quarter. Michael quick-stepped past Thomas, leaped by two more Pistons before yet more Detroit bodies got in the way. MJ merely switched the ball from right to left and banked it in while drawing the foul.

Jordan engaged in no trash talk or even a hint of revenge after the Bulls' victory. "I felt Isiah was weakened with his injury," said Jordan. "You have to go to the weak point of a player, and I just used that."

Maybe, but there was a determination in Jordan's all-around play that was hard for the 13,363 fans to miss. His passes seemed to have a little more zip, his rebounds a bit more elbow.

Number 42: Great Game Index

GGI Score (101 of a possible 123).

Scoring (32 of a possible 33)   Michael hit 19 of 31 from the floor, a significant turnaround from 2-for-9 shooting at the All-Star Game.

Game Importance (12 of 20)   A regular season contest in February.

Opponent Strength (18 of 20)   Detroit was a solid title contender; the Bulls were simply trying to revive a franchise.

Historical Significance (8 of 10)   The biggest impact was the impressions made between future contenders for several NBA crowns.

Legendary Intangibles (10 of 10)   Payback is a dog—for Motown's Thomas. Keep in mind that Jordan didn't flaunt his night's performance, but the message was reverberating.

Pressure Points (9 of 10)   MJ put back his own miss to tie the game late in regulation.

Defense (3 of 5)   Four steals keyed a solid defensive effort.

Other Offensive Contributions (4 of 5)   It was a vintage Jordan line: 49 points, 15 rebounds, 5 assists.

MJ's Physical Condition (1 of 5)   Not a factor.

Long Odds (4 of 5)   Remember, this was Michael's rookie season. The league was fully aware of the Jordan speed traps in the road ahead.

-43-

April 29, 1992

Bulls at Miami Heat Game 3 Clincher, First-Round Playoff Series

Michael's message: look out below.

O pponents should have considered themselves warned for the 1992 postseason: Michael was in rare form, traveling in his own dimensions. "The playoffs are Michael's special time," said Bulls coach Phil Jackson.

Fans were glad Michael chose to share it with them, but Miami players were not as enthused. Jordan rocket-fueled the Heat with 56 points to sweep this opening-round series. It was the first step to another trip to the high-altitude climes of Championship Mountain.

The Bulls trailed by a point entering the fourth quarter, which tends to be Michael's special time within a special time. He hit a fall-away jumper to put Chicago ahead, 98–96, with 5:30 left. He pumped in a dozen more down the stretch, including two clinching free throws with 9.5 seconds remaining to set the final score at 119–113.

"I was hitting everything," said Jordan, who finished 20 of 30 from the field and 16 of 18 at the foul stripe. "Everything

215

Game 43: Bulls 119, Heat 114

Bulls	Min	FG-att	FT-att	Reb	Ast	Fls	Pts
Grant	42	4-9	0-0	8	3	2	8
Pippen	45	12-23	7-8	8	5	5	31
Cartwright	33	0-3	1-4	5	2	5	1
Jordan	43	20-30	16-18	5	5	3	56
Paxson	22	1-5	0-0	1	2	3	2
Armstrong	23	4-7	4-4	4	4	2	13
Williams	9	0-3	0-0	6	0	3	0
Hodges	4	2-3	0-0	0	0	2	6
Perdue	7	1-1	0-0	0	1	1	2
Levingston	12	0-2	0-0	3	1	2	0
Totals	**240**	**44-86**	**28-34**	**40**	**23**	**28**	**119**

Percentages: FG .512, FT .824. **Three-point goals:** 3-5, .600 (Hodges 2-2, Armstrong 1-2, Pippen 0-1). **Team rebounds:** 7. **Blocked shots:** 4 (Pippen 2, Jordan 2). **Turnovers:** 9 (Pippen 2, Jordan 2, Grant, Cartwright, Paxson, Williams, Levingston). **Steals:** 8 (Jordan 4, Grant 2, Armstrong, Perdue). **Technical fouls:** Illegal defense, 3:03 2nd. **Illegal defense:** 1.

Heat	Min	FG-att	FT-att	Reb	Ast	Fls	Pts
Long	44	7-15	3-6	2	3	5	17
Rice	42	10-26	4-5	6	1	2	25
Seikaly	46	4-9	14-16	12	1	5	22
Shaw	37	7-12	3-4	6	6	3	19
Smith	32	7-11	0-1	5	6	1	18
Askins	9	0-1	0-0	2	2	1	0
Coles	16	2-2	5-7	2	1	1	9
Edwards	12	1-1	2-4	2	1	0	4
Ogg	2	0-0	0-0	1	0	2	0
Totals	**240**	**38-77**	**31-43**	**38**	**21**	**20**	**114**

Percentages: FG .494, FT .721. **Three-point goals:** 7-15, .467 (Smith 4-4, Shaw 2-3, Rice 1-6, Long 0-2). **Team rebounds:** 14. **Blocked shots:** 6 (Seikaly 5, Ogg). **Turnovers:** 12 (Seikaly 3, Shaw 2, Coles 2, Edwards 2, Long, Rice, Smith). **Steals:** 5 (Long 2, Shaw, Smith, Coles). **Technical fouls:** Coach Loughery, 6:23 3d. **Illegal defense:** 1.

Bulls	19	32	28	40	119
Heat	33	23	24	34	114

A: 15,008. **T:** 2:28. **Officials:** Jess Kersey, Ronnie Nunn, Derrick Stafford.

seemed to be in rhythm. I was not hesitating at all. I always knew what I was going to do, and I utilized it all.

"If they gave me the drive, fine, I took it. If not, I took the jump shot—and boom!"

Indeed, Jordan sandblasted Miami with 17 points in the

third quarter and 18 in the final twelve minutes to send the foes packing for summer picnics at the nearby beach. The points were important because the Heat, led by Kevin Loughery, Jordan's first NBA coach, stayed close until the final seconds.

"It's just a great feeling," said Jordan. "You see the basket very well, and you don't see anything else. I don't even know how to describe it myself."

Loughery praised his team for its tenacity, but Miami center Rony Seikaly was not so inclined. He recognized trouble and treachery when he saw it on his team's home court. He didn't buffer his words.

"Michael is like a grenade without a pin," said Seikaly. "He could score whatever number he wants. He could score one hundred points if he wants to."

Fifty-six was enough. It marked Jordan's second highest postseason total and the third-best in NBA history.

Number 43: Great Game Index

GGI Score (100 of a possible 123)   Tiebreaker is game importance.

Scoring (32 of a possible 33)   MJ scored 47 percent of Chicago's impressive total of 119 points. After a slow start, he tallied 17, 17, and 18 for the next three quarters.

Game Importance (18 of 20)   Chicago wanted to get some rest after the rigors of a regular season in which every opponent was gunning for the champs.

Opponent Strength (17 of 20)   Miami was a young team with some talented players, such as Brian Shaw, Glen Rice, and Seikaly.

Historical Significance (8 of 10)   This was a setup for the Bulls' second title run.

Legendary Intangibles (9 of 10)   Michael was already sending clear signals to any approaching opponent.

Pressure Points (8 of 10)   MJ hit key baskets down the stretch, though the Bulls had some room for error in the series.

Defense (4 of 5)   The usual buzz saw.

Other Offensive Contributions (2 of 5)   Nothing spectacular.

MJ's Physical Condition (1 of 5)   Not a factor.

Long Odds (1 of 5)   Fifty-six points was not hard to imagine anymore, postseason or not.

-44-

February 26, 1987

New Jersey Nets at Bulls
Regular Season

Net result: MJ busts a record,
but not a foe.

Sheer numbers demands that this game be in the Jordan 50, but there is more to its greatness: Michael pulled himself out of this 128–113 blowout of the New Jersey Nets with nearly three minutes left. He had already scored 58 points, enough to break Chet "the Jet" Walker's franchise record of 56, set in 1972. He figured enough was enough, even though the fans were screaming for more, at least 60 and maybe even 70, with a furious finish.

"I was happy with what I was doing and what the team was doing," explained Jordan. "I didn't want to be selfish. I wanted the rest of my teammates to get a chance to play. I had done well and didn't want to push it. I did want to break the Bulls' record, but I didn't want to go any further than that."

MJ called over his coach, Doug Collins, and simply said, "Take me out." He then walked off the Stadium court to a foot-stomping standing ovation that had more reverberation than any number of rock concerts held in this old barn of an arena. The fans finally started chanting, "Michael, Michael" over and

Michael flew to 58 points to beat the Bulls' franchise record, but took himself out in the fourth quarter to avoid humiliating the anemic Nets. *UPI/Corbis-Bettmann*

Game 44: Bulls 128, Nets 113

Nets	Min	FG-att	FT-att	Reb	Ast	Fls	Pts
King	17	3-5	1-2	2	0	6	7
B. Williams	32	7-15	11-12	6	1	3	25
Gminski	31	6-13	2-2	13	3	3	14
Brown	27	2-6	0-0	2	3	4	4
Washington	18	0-3	4-4	1	4	2	4
R. Williams	22	1-8	2-2	1	3	1	14
Woolridge	31	7-14	6-9	6	3	3	20
Engler	6	0-0	0-0	0	0	1	0
McKenna	12	2-3	1-2	0	1	3	6
Turner	6	2-7	1-2	3	0	0	5
Coleman	22	6-6	2-2	7	1	6	14
Wood	16	3-7	3-4	0	3	0	10
Totals	**240**	**39-87**	**33-41**	**41**	**22**	**32**	**113**

Percentages: FG .448, FT .805. **Team rebounds:** 12. **Turnovers:** 18 (R. Williams 4).
Steals: 9 (R. Williams 3). **Blocked shots:** 7 (Woolridge 3). **Three-point goals:** 2-4
(McKenna 1-2, Wood 1-2). **Technical fouls:** Coach Wohl 2 (ejected).

Bulls	Min	FG-att	FT-att	Reb	Ast	Fls	Pts
Banks	38	4-8	4-5	7	7	4	12
Oakley	36	5-18	2-2	17	7	5	12
Corzine	30	3-6	6-8	10	4	3	12
Paxson	41	6-13	4-5	2	5	5	16
Jordan	37	16-25	26-27	8	3	4	58
M. Brown	8	0-2	0-0	0	0	4	0
Sellers	23	5-7	0-0	4	1	3	10
Threatt	16	1-3	0-2	0	4	1	2
Poquette	11	3-5	0-0	2	1	3	6
Totals	**240**	**43-87**	**42-49**	**50**	**32**	**32**	**128**

Percentages: FG .494, FT .857. **Team rebounds:** 4. **Turnovers:** 14 (Oakley 4). **Steals:**
11 (Paxson and Jordan 3). **Blocked shots:** 7 (Corzine 3). **Three-point goals:** 0-3.

Nets	24	25	34	30	113
Bulls	33	37	32	26	128

A: 14,098. **T:** 2:18. **Officials:** Jack Madden, Mel Whitworth.

over, louder and louder, in desperate hopes of calling his Air-
ness back for just one more encore.

Jordan acknowledged the applause and accolades, but
then sat down on the bench as the other eleven Bulls huddled
during a time-out. MJ bowed his head, shook his fist, and
allowed himself a slight smile for what was an expansive night's
work.

Michael shot 16 of 25 from the floor and sank 26 of 27 free throws. It marked the most points of the NBA season, beating out the 57 Dominique Wilkins scored against the Bulls on December 10. Somehow one had to wonder if Jordan was thinking about Wilkins as much as Walker on this record-breaking night. The 1986–87 season marked the first of MJ's seven straight regular season scoring titles, unseating none other than Dominique Wilkins in the process.

Michael's nearly perfect free-throw total was also the third highest in NBA history, and he was second highest in free-throw percentage for one game, at 96.2. He made his first nineteen free throws.

Perhaps more significant was the number of times MJ went to the line. It showed that NBA referees were respecting his superstar status. Gripes from opponents were already beginning to develop, but the argument has always been mere folly. Michael has found countless ways to beat a team; the free-throw line is merely one possibility.

The Nets could have no complaints at all this night. Jordan showed mercy after first drilling them for 17 points in the first quarter, a repeat 17 in the second period before 11 in the third and 13 in the fourth. He scored the Bulls' first 11 points. His record-breaking points came when Jordan soared to crisscross the lane before hitting a reverse layup. He was fouled on the play. Goodbye, Chet the Jet. So long, Dominique.

"The highlight of the whole game was when he asked to come out," said Collins. "I don't know if he understood it or not, but he took a lot of pressure off my back.

"You've got fourteen thousand people [before sellouts were commonplace at the Stadium] who want to see him get 60, but I would never, ever let a record be set if a game is won. New Jersey is struggling right now, and I might be in that position some day. I'll tell you, that guy has a lot of class."

The fans were not totally disappointed. Red Kerr, the first Bulls coach and longtime announcer who saw plenty of Walker's games, rushed out to interview Michael. The TV producers had somehow hooked up Jordan and Kerr on the public-address system. Everyone enjoyed Michael's reflections, and clearly recognized that here was not just another selfish superstar.

It was actually quite a week for Michael. Before the 58 points on a Thursday night, he recorded 43 points, 8 steals, 6 assists, and 5 blocked shots against Cleveland on Sunday, then 34 points, 12 rebounds, 5 steals, and 5 blocks against Atlanta on Tuesday. It all added up to a three-game winning streak and some colossal numbers.

"I'm getting lots of rest," said Jordan when asked about his power surge during this final week of February, as he warmed up in the usual bone-chilling Chicago winter. "My endorsements and appearances are down. I wanted it that way. This is the crunch time of the season. I was on a roll and everything was falling.

"It felt a lot better than the Boston game [when he scored sixty-three points in a breathtaking postseason show during a double-overtime loss]. We won and my shooting percentage had to be better."

Number 44: Great Game Index

GGI Score (100 of a possible 123).

Scoring (33 of a possible 33)   You can't do much better than 58 points. Few players in history ever have. The free throws were a special twist.

Game Importance (14 of 20)   Regular season game.

Opponent Strength (14 of 20)   The Nets were mediocre.

Historical Significance (10 of 10)   Chet Walker was a beloved Bull and a great scorer. Michael clearly was already winning the hearts of even the most diehard loyalists of the historic Bulls teams.

Legendary Intangibles (10 of 10)   Pulling himself out of the game was an early sign of Jordan's unusual demeanor for a 1990s professional athlete.

Pressure Points (8 of 10)   MJ took a lot of suspense out of the game.

Defense (3 of 5)   Solid night, but nothing like his performance the following winter, when he recorded 10 steals in a home game against the Nets.

Other Offensive Contributions (2 of 5)   Nothing out of the ordinary.

MJ's Physical Condition (1of 5)   Not a factor.

Long Odds (5 of 5)   Chet Walker probably figured his Stadium record was unbreakable because Wilt Chamberlain had already retired.

-45-

April 27, 1997

Washington Bullets at Bulls Game 2, First-Round Playoff Series

The future is now for MJ, and Chicago.

T his second game of the 1997 postseason was a throw-back in several ways. First, MJ's 55-point barrage recalled the young Michael Jordan who once carried the Bulls offense squarely on his lone and lithe shoulders. Second, it reminded the likes of young turks on the Washington club, namely Juwan Howard and Chris Webber, why they grew up idolizing No. 23. Finally, Michael went retro-geometric by bust-ing out of his team's famed and usually fortuitous "triangle offense."

After the 109–104 victory, Jordan passed on comparing his performance with other great games; it was the eighth time he had scored 50 or more points in a postseason game and marked the thirty-seventh such overall game in his career. Instead, he deferred to the accomplishments of longtime assis-

Michael's 55 points in the first round against the Bullets proved that he still rose above the competition. *Reuters/Scott Olson/Archive Photos*

tant coach Tex Winter, the inventor of Chicago's offensive scheme that has prospered and rarely sputtered in the 1990s.

"I apologized to Tex after the game," said Michael. "I said, 'Sorry about the triangle, Tex.' I kind of forgot about the triangle. Once I got into that mode, I just couldn't turn it off."

MJ also apologized to his teammates, especially buddies like Ron Harper and Scottie Pippen.

"I saw it when I was not on this team, and I saw it while I was on this team," said Harper, who was once burned himself by a 55-point Jordan playoff effort when defending against Mike as a Cleveland Cavalier. "He told us he was very sorry for scoring all the points. I told him he had nothing to feel sorry for."

Phil Jackson called it Michael's best game of the season. He was not happy with the club's overall effort, but clearly appreciative of MJ's 20 fourth-quarter points. Scottie Pippen was the only other Bull to score in the final twelve minutes, sinking a three-pointer with 2:51 remaining for a 103–97 lead.

Game 45: Bulls 109, Bullets 104

Bullets	Min	FG-att	FT-att	Reb	Ast	Fls	Pts
Webber	40	8-13	2-6	12	6	6	21
Howard	44	6-14	6-6	6	0	3	18
Muresan	13	0-2	1-2	3	0	3	1
Strcklnd	41	5-18	6-6	5	8	3	16
Cheaney	42	10-18	6-6	5	1	0	26
Grant	11	0-2	0-0	1	0	2	0
Murray	32	6-14	10-11	5	0	3	22
Whitney	7	0-0	0-0	1	1	0	0
L. Wllms	1	0-0	0-0	0	0	0	0
Legler	6	0-0	0-0	1	1	2	0
Jackson	3	0-0	0-0	1	1	4	0
Totals	240	35-81	31-37	40	18	26	104

Percentages: FG .432, FT .838. **Three-point goals:** 3-12, .250 (Webber 3-5, Strickland 0-1, Grant 0-1, Cheaney 0-2, Murray 0-3). **Team rebounds:** 8. **Blocked shots:** 4 (Webber 2, Howard, Cheaney). **Turnovers:** 14 (Webber 6, Strickland 3, Muresan 2, Whitney, team 2). **Steals:** 6 (Cheaney 2, Webber, Howard, Muresan, Murray).

Bulls	Min	FG-att	FT-att	Reb	Ast	Fls	Pts
Pippen	42	4-10	5-6	9	4	3	14
Caffey	16	1-3	6-8	3	4	3	8
Longley	27	3-8	0-0	3	6	4	6
Harper	29	4-7	0-0	3	1	3	10
Jordan	44	22-35	10-10	7	2	3	55
Kukoc	18	2-5	2-3	2	0	2	6
Rodman	33	2-3	0-0	8	2	4	4
B. Wllms	6	1-3	0-0	1	0	5	2
Kerr	21	1-2	0-0	2	3	0	2
Buechler	2	0-1	0-0	0	0	1	0
Brown	2	1-1	0-0	0	0	0	2
Totals	240	41-78	23-27	38	22	28	109

Percentages: FG .526, FT .852. **Three-point goals:** 4-10, .400 (Harper 2-2, Jordan 1-2, Pippen 1-5, Buechler 0-1). **Team rebounds:** 7. **Blocked shots:** 7 (Pippen 2, Caffey 2, Longley, Harper, Kukoc). **Turnovers:** 11 (Pippen 3, Rodman 3, Jordan 2, Caffey, Longley, Harper). **Steals:** 7 (Jordan 2, Caffey, Harper, B. Williams, Kerr, Brown). **Technical fouls:** Coach Jackson, 8:29, 2nd; Rodman, 5:20, 2nd.

Bullets	30	35	15	24	104
Bulls	29	29	28	23	109

A: 24,267. **T:** 2:35. **Officials:** Don Vaden, Hugh Evans, Nolan Fine.

Jackson wisely called enough time-outs to give Michael needed rest from his game-high forty-four minutes.

One problem was Jordan's defensive assignments, first the formidable ballhandler Rod Strickland, and then Tracy Murray, who had a hot hand.

"Michael was struggling and desperately needed a rest there a couple of times in the fourth quarter," said Jackson.

On the other end, Washington's fourth-year player Calbert Cheaney was chasing the thirty-four-year-old Jordan.

"He kept asking me, 'Aren't you tired yet?'" Jordan said about Cheaney. "I said, 'Have we won yet? Then I ain't tired.'"

The Bullets, down 2–0 in the best-of-five series, were impressed but still clinging to the notion they could somehow wear Jordan out before Chicago could win the series.

"Michael is Michael," said Howard. "We all know that. I watched him do this for years as a kid growing up."

"Our thing is to make Michael play great," explained Webber. "To make him beat us."

The strategy didn't work. The Bulls closed out the Bullets three nights later in Landover, Maryland. The team played much better as a unit, perhaps in no small part due to Michael's raised voice in the halftime locker room during Game 2. Chicago was down by seven points at intermission.

"Washington was playing better than we were in the first half," said Michael, who is not known as a screamer by any stretch. "I just felt this is our building and we were not playing our type of basketball. Somehow that had to be vocalized. I mentioned that a little at halftime."

The Bulls outhustled Washington in the third quarter, powering to a 6-point lead with both Michael's on-court and on-target guidance.

"There weren't any adjustment made at halftime, other than an attitude adjustment," said Bulls guard Steve Kerr.

Number 45: Great Game Index

GGI Score (99 of a possible 123)   Tiebreaker is game importance.

Scoring (32 of a possible 33)   MJ tallied more than half of the Bulls points, including an incredible 87 percent of Chicago scoring in the fourth quarter.

Game Importance (17 of 20) Though the Bulls swept the series, Washington played three close games. Losing a home game might have chipped away at Chicago's confidence while significantly boosting the young Bullets.

Opponent Strength (16 of 20) Washington was one of the league's top young teams.

Historical Significance (8 of 10) A setup series for another title run.

Legendary Intangibles (9 of 10) Consider this a lesson for all up-and-coming NBA stars. All possible success still must pass through Chicago and Route 23.

Pressure Points (8 of 10) When push comes to crunch—and postup moves—count on MJ.

Defense (3 of 5) Another prime example for any young NBA millionaire or high school reserve.

Other Offensive Contributions (3 of 5) MJ grabbed some key rebounds against the likes of Chris Webber and Juwan Howard.

MJ's Physical Condition (1 of 5) Not a factor.

Long Odds (2 of 5) MJ still had to prove to himself that he could score at will in the United Center, where he never felt comfortable with the shooting background. He was partial to the old barn, Chicago Stadium. He played more than 40 games in the new arena before deciding he was comfortable enough there. (See Game No. 49.)

-46-

Feb. 15, 1988

Atlanta Hawks at Bulls
Regular Season

Lights, camera, Jordan.

C BS seemed to bring out the best in Michael Jordan. The previous time the Bulls played on national TV during the 1987–88 regular season, Michael led his surprising squad—and make no mistake, it was now his team—to a resounding victory over the Houston Rockets (see Game No. 33). This time Atlanta got caught in the camera lights in a Monday afternoon game played on the Presidents' Day holiday.

Michael was in the middle of his first Most Valuable Player regular season (he won the award five times, including 1997–98). He was also in the middle of pretty much everything on the Chicago Stadium court before another full house (November 20, 1987, marked the first of consecutive sellouts that stretched through the 1998 postseason). The Bulls won easily, 126–107.

Atlanta was the first-place club in the Bulls' Central Division and the NBA's second-best defensive club, but no match on this day. Jordan scored 32 points, cleaned the boards for 13 rebounds, dished out 8 assists, and recorded 5 steals. Chicago won the season series, three games to two, mostly because

Game 46: Bulls 126, Hawks 107

Hawks	Min	FG-att	FT-att	Reb	Ast	Fls	Pts
Levingston	33	4-11	1-2	7	2	1	9
Wilkins	34	8-21	8-10	6	5	3	25
Rollins	16	3-4	0-0	3	0	5	6
Rivers	36	4-11	7-9	2	10	2	15
Wittman	34	8-15	2-2	1	3	1	18
Willis	24	4-12	0-2	6	1	3	8
Carr	19	5-7	3-3	2	1	6	13
Webb	16	2-4	1-1	2	6	2	5
Washburn	14	2-2	0-0	5	0	0	4
Whatley	7	1-3	0-0	1	0	1	2
Hastings	7	0-2	2-2	1	0	0	2
Totals	240	41-92	24-31	36	28	24	107

Percentages: FG .446, FT .774. **Team rebounds:** 15. **Turnovers:** 11 (Rivers 3, Wilkins 2, Carr 2). **Steals:** 5 (Levingston 2). **Blocked shots:** 9 (Rollins 3). **Technical:** delay of game (11:25, 4th).

Bulls	Min	FG-att	FT-att	Reb	Ast	Fls	Pts
Sellers	42	5-11	7-10	9	8	3	17
Oakley	39	6-12	7-10	11	6	4	19
Brown	10	1-2	0-0	3	1	2	2
Sparrow	6	0-2	0-0	0	1	1	0
Jordan	38	13-22	6-8	13	8	2	32
Threatt	20	4-6	3-3	1	6	2	11
Corzine	28	7-12	2-2	4	0	2	16
Grant	15	3-7	2-2	3	0	2	8
Pippen	26	4-9	4-6	8	3	4	12
Paxson	17	4-8	0-0	1	2	2	9
Totals	240	47-91	31-41	61	35	24	126

Percentages: FG .516, FT .756. **Team rebounds:** 8. **Total turnovers:** 10 (Sellers 2, Oakley 2, Jordan 2, Pippen 2). **Steals:** 10 (Jordan 5, Oakley 3). **Blocked shots:** 7 (Jordan 2, Corzine 2, Pippen 2).

Hawks	34	21	26	26	107
Bulls	29	40	33	24	126

A: 17,704. **Officials:** Ed T. Rush, Bill Sacer.

Michael himself was learning the importance of distributing the offensive load.

"Right now, everybody thinks this is a guard-oriented team," Jordan said. "We need scoring from our forwards and centers."

A hint at the future arrived about halfway through the second quarter. Jordan and the young forward Scottie Pippen combined for all but two points in a 15–4 run that turned a 42–39 deficit into a 54–46 lead. John Paxson hit a three-pointer to beat the buzzer to establish a 69–55 halftime lead.

The Bulls never looked back, adding a 17–4 spurt in the third quarter. Michael scored the last 6 points of the quarter after earlier dishing out 4 assists. It was the beginning of what became a championship formula in Chicago, with Jordan, Pippen, Paxson, and Horace Grant all making key contributions.

"The first half was the best half of basketball we've played since I've been coach," said Doug Collins, who arrived for the 1986–87 season.

Doc Rivers, a local favorite who played guard for Atlanta, was asked about the All-Star slam-dunk contest staged at Chicago Stadium a little more than a week earlier (see Game No. 26). There were some wags who figured the Hawks' Dominique Wilkins should have won the dunking exhibition, but Rivers, wise beyond his years, wasn't biting—especially to avoid adding any more wood to Michael Jordan's bonfire season.

"Do I think Dominique beat Michael?" asked Rivers, laughing. "Hey, I'm not getting into that. I have my opinion, but I'm keeping it to myself."

Wilkins managed 25 points on the afternoon, but once again played second chair to Jordan. Over the years, MJ always seemed to hit more of the high notes than the gifted Wilkins. This game, which highlighted offensive teamwork and gritty Bulls' defense, provided some of the early reasons why.

Number 46: Great Game Index

GGI Score (98 of a possible 123).

Scoring (27 of a possible 33)   A typical day at the office on the scoring ledger.

Game Importance (16 of 20)   There have been countless important games since—okay, at least 150—but this was a big home win against a skilled Atlanta team. The Bulls' season record improved to 29–21.

Opponent Strength (16 of 20)   Dominique Wilkins was at the peak of his career.

Historical Significance (8 of 10)   The game featured solid performances from some teammates—Scottie Pippen, Horace Grant, and John Paxson—in whom Jordan would come to trust during the title years of 1991–93.

Legendary Intangibles (10 of 10)   Jordan and Wilkins had just battled for All-Star dunk and game MVP honors, both of which Michael won—but make no mistake about the intent of his 13 rebounds in this game. He could match any player, strength for strength, and then some.

Pressure Points (9 of 10)   MJ hit key shots to close out the Hawks by the end of the third quarter.

Defense (5 of 5)   Five steals inspired a team effort that was normally the Hawks' niche. This was the season Jordan won the Defensive Player of the Year award. He hasn't missed All-Defensive First Team since.

Other Offensive Contributions (5 of 5)   Eight assists and a fistful of offensive rebounds.

MJ's Physical Condition (1 of 5)   Not a factor.

Long Odds (1 of 5)   This was a representative game from Jordan's first MVP season.

-47-

May 16, 1990

Philadelphia 76ers at Bulls
Game 5 Clincher, Second-Round Playoff Series

Jordan to the emotional rescue.

Bulls coach Phil Jackson is hesitant to single out too many of Michael Jordan's greatest games. He figures there are at least a hundred of them from the playoffs alone. He does recall this game with fondness, though, especially because it occurred during his first season as Chicago's head coach.

"Scottie Pippen's father had died and he had gotten back for the game, but emotionally he wasn't there," said Jackson. "Michael took the team on his shoulders and just played an outrageous game. I don't even remember what he scored.

"You never know what he is going to bring to the game, and you always feel you have a chance to win as long as he is in there."

Jordan scored 37 to close out Philadelphia in this game. He added 9 rebounds, 8 assists, and 6 steals to cover for his

Game 47: Bulls 117, 76ers 99

76ers	Min	FG-att	FT-att	Reb	Ast	Fls	Pts
Barkley	41	6-10	5-10	13	5	5	17
Mahorn	33	5-12	0-0	7	3	6	10
Gminski	33	9-14	0-0	5	1	1	18
Dawkins	43	6-12	6-7	1	15	3	18
Hawkins	38	4-10	2-2	4	3	0	11
Anderson	34	8-12	4-4	2	0	1	20
Brooks	5	0-2	1-2	0	1	1	1
Thornton	10	0-1	2-2	1	0	3	2
Nimphius	1	0-1	0-0	1	0	0	0
Payne	1	0-1	2-2	1	0	1	2
Copeland	1	0-1	0-0	0	0	0	0
Totals	**240**	**38-76**	**22-29**	**36**	**28**	**21**	**99**

Percentages: FG .500, FT .759. **Three-point goals:** 1-7, .143 (Hawkins 1-4, Mahorn 0-1, Brooks 0-1, Payne 0-1). **Team rebounds:** 7. **Blocked shots:** 6 (Gminski 3, Mahorn 2, Thornton). **Turnovers:** 15 (Dawkins 5, Barkley 4, Hawkins 3, Mahorn, Anderson, Thornton). **Steals:** 2 (Gminski, Dawkins). **Technical fouls:** None. **Illegal defense:** None.

Bulls	Min	FG-att	FT-att	Reb	Ast	Fls	Pts
King	26	3-11	7-8	3	1	3	13
Grant	34	8-11	2-4	7	4	4	18
Cartwright	31	4-6	4-4	8	1	2	12
Paxson	24	0-3	0-0	0	9	3	0
Jordan	42	17-26	2-4	9	8	2	37
Pippen	37	13-17	2-3	6	3	2	29
Armstrong	22	2-4	2-2	2	5	1	6
Nealy	11	0-0	0-0	2	0	5	0
Hodges	10	1-2	0-0	0	0	1	2
Perdue	3	0-2	0-0	1	0	0	0
Totals	**240**	**48-82**	**19-25**	**38**	**31**	**23**	**117**

Percentages: FG .585, FT .760. **Three-point goals:** 2-6, .333 (Pippen 1-1, Jordan 1-3, Hodges 0-1, Perdue 0-1). **Team rebounds:** 5. **Blocked shots:** 3 (Pippen 2, Jordan). **Turnovers:** 12 (Jordan 4, Cartwright 3, Pippen 2, Armstrong 2, grant). **Steals:** 11 (Jordan 6, Paxson 2, King, Grant, Pippen). **Technical fouls:** None. **Illegal defense:** 1.

76ers	31	32	18	18	99
Bulls	28	34	27	28	117

A: 18,676. **T:** 2:11. **Officials:** Jess Kersey, Jack Madden, Paul Mihalak.

running mate Pippen, who got more inspired as the game developed, scoring 29 off the bench. The 117–99 rout clinched a berth in the Eastern Conference finals opposite Detroit.

As importantly, it seemed to ignite the afterburners for Chicago; Jordan and company were revved up for the Pistons.

One local columnist wrote that Michael was "playing a game of basketball in the same way that opera resembles rap; his special music is at such a high pitch that only very tall dogs can hear."

"I have never seen anyone have as great an offensive series as I've seen from Michael Jordan," marveled Phil Jackson after the game.

MJ averaged 43 points per game in the five-game series. He led the Bulls in scoring in sixteen of twenty quarters.

"We've matured and improved as a team," said Jordan. "We're ready to take on the test."

Losing to Detroit in seven games, the Bulls eventually stopped one step short of their NBA Finals goal, but there were ingredients of the ensuing 1990s dynasty on display in the Sixers game. Chicago might have been most impressive on defense.

Philly converted for only 36 points in the second half after leading 63-62 at the break. The 76ers had 8 turnovers in the third quarter alone, and Jordan's 6 steals were part of a 53–25 margin for the series.

In one lethal five-minute sequence, Jordan and Pippen both hit three-pointers as they combined with Horace Grant to outscore Charles Barkley and the Sixers, 14–1. The game and series were effectively over, and the league was officially put on alert: This trio, along with Bill Cartwright and John Paxson, would do serious damage to other teams' title hopes in the early 1990s. Later, Dennis Rodman would replace Grant, Luc Longley would move in for Cartwright, Ron Harper would take the starting guard spot, and Steve Kerr would become the designated spot-up shooter, and all would wreak similar havoc on championship dreams in the late 1990s.

"We came out hard in the second half and they started to doubt themselves," said Jordan. "They seemed very passive out there. I think some of them were ready to go on vacation."

While the next series sent the Bulls packing, that would be the last time Chicago would lose a postseason series with Jordan in the early 1990s. There was always time for Jordan's favorite hobby—golf—in July and August.

Number 47: Great Game Index

GGI Score (95 of a possible 123).

Scoring (28 of a possible 33)   MJ actually scored 6 points less than his average for this series.

Game Importance (16 of 20)   Chicago had margin for error, but every game played meant more rest for rival Detroit, which had wrapped up its semifinal series.

Opponent Strength (16 of 20)   Philadelphia's leader was Charles Barkley. He scored only 7 points in the second half.

Historical Significance (8 of 10)   If it sticks in Phil Jackson's memory, that means a lot.

Legendary Intangibles (10 of 10)   Scottie Pippen was earnest about playing—he missed Game 4 and practiced his shooting in a high school gym back home in Arkansas in between funeral events—but MJ picked up the emotional slack. He got every other teammate involved to rally around Pippen.

Pressure Points (7 of 10)   MJ and his mates supplied the knockout punch in the third quarter.

Defense (4 of 5)   More frenzy and fear for opponents, half a dozen steals for Michael.

Other Offensive Contributions (4 of 5)   An above-average night with 9 rebounds and 8 assists.

MJ's Physical Condition (1 of 5)   Not a factor.

Long Odds (1 of 5)   This savior stuff was starting to become routine.

-48-

November 1, 1986

Bulls at New York Knicks Regular Season

Opening night is a big (Jordan) hit in New York.

---

*I*n Doug Collins's first game as the Bulls coach, Michael wasn't about to let the moment wither with a Chicago loss. In fact, he added his own historical touch by breaking the all-time scoring mark of an opponent in the new Madison Square Garden with a 50-point effort on the opening night of the 1986–87 season. NBA legend Rick Barry shared the old record.

The Bulls won, 108–103, thanks in large measure to MJ's 21 points in the fourth quarter. He put the game out of reach on a layup with 22 seconds remaining, while three Knicks held on to various pieces of his body and uniform as the ball gently rippled the net. No chance, New York.

There was considerable doubt halfway through the fourth quarter, when the Knicks had roared back—inspired by the usual throaty Garden crowd—to take a 90–85 lead.

Collins called a time-out and looked understandably tense. Jordan calmly walked to the bench, looked his new boss in the eyes and said, "Coach, I'm not going to let you lose your first game."

Game 48: Bulls 108, Knicks 103

Bulls	Min	FG-att	FT-att	Reb	Ast	Fls	Pts
Cureton	34	8-16	1-2	3	1	4	17
Oakley	32	7-17	3-5	8	3	5	17
Walters	19	1-2	0-0	4	0	5	2
Colter	37	1-7	5-6	2	10	3	7
Jordan	41	15-31	20-22	6	3	2	50
Sellers	25	4-8	0-0	8	1	4	8
Corzine	28	0-3	1-2	5	2	5	1
Paxson	18	2-6	2-2	0	1	5	6
Brown	6	0-0	0-0	1	0	2	0
Totals	**240**	**38-90**	**32-39**	**47**	**21**	**35**	**108**

Percentages: FG .422, FT .821. **Team rebounds:** 5. **Turnovers:** 12 (Jordan 6). **Steals:** 8 (Jordan 4). **Blocked shots:** 6 (Jordan 3, Sellers 2). **Three-point goals:** 0-1. **Technical fouls:** 2.

Knicks	Min	FG-att	FT-att	Reb	Ast	Fls	Pts
Cartwright	38	8-12	5-7	8	1	5	21
Walker	28	2-7	9-10	2	1	2	13
Ewing	39	3-10	7-8	5	2	5	13
Sparrow	36	9-15	6-7	7	4	3	24
Wilkins	18	3-7	1-2	4	1	3	7
Cummings	22	1-8	1-1	8	1	2	3
Orr	20	1-3	4-6	5	1	0	6
Tucker	30	5-9	2-2	2	3	4	12
Granger	12	1-2	0-2	4	5	2	2
Thornton	2	1-2	0-0	2	0	0	2
Totals	**240**	**34-74**	**35-45**	**47**	**19**	**26**	**103**

Percentages: FG .459, FT .778. **Team rebounds:** 10. **Turnovers:** 20 (Sparrow 4). **Steals:** 6 (Cartwright 2, Tucker 2). **Blocked shots:** 2 (Walker, Ewing). **Three-point goals:** none attempted. **Technical fouls:** 2, Illegal defense.

Bulls	25	20	32	31	108
Knicks	13	28	32	30	103

A: 19,325. **T:** 2:21. **Officials:** Joe Crawford, Bennett Salvatore.

As good as his word, Michael immediately scored on the team's next two possessions, but Michael's work had started much earlier in the evening. He started the season by blocking shots of Gerald Wilkins and seven-foot, one-inch Bill Cartwright (who happily became a 1990s teammate) in the opening minutes. He struggled with his shooting, going only 3 for 12 in the first half, so he concentrated on playing good defense and hitting his ten free throws.

"Give credit to number twenty-three," said Collins after the victory. "He sets the tone, just like Larry Bird. He just never stops working, and the other guys see it. I can't expect him to do what he did every night."

Maybe not, but Knicks coach Hubie Brown was no less complimentary, gauging that Michael was picking up where he had left off against Bird and the Celtics the previous spring, scoring 48 points in one playoff contest and 63 in one of his greatest games ever.

"He single-handedly had Boston nervous," noted Brown. "When you have a superstar like him, all you need is the four other guys to work hard and the opportunities will come for him to win the game."

In crunch time, Brown pitted his twin giants, Cartwright and Patrick Ewing, against Jordan for offensive control. The shortest guy—only in inch count, not in vertical leap or sky-rocketing status—was the one left standing.

"I've never seen anything like Michael Jordan, ever, ever, never," gushed Collins.

Ewing, Cartwright, Brown, and 19,325 fans at the Garden were inclined to agree.

Number 48: Great Game Index

GGI Score (93 of a possible 123).

Scoring (31 of a possible 33)   MJ hit the half-century mark, with 42 percent coming in game's last twelve minutes.

Game Importance (14 of 20)   Opening night in New York is center stage.

Opponent Strength (14 of 20)   The Knicks were just starting to turn their franchise in the upward direction after a long dry spell.

Historical Significance (9 of 10)   After his only year with a major injury during an illustrious NBA career, MJ got off on the right foot.

Legendary Intangibles (10 of 10)   Michael is more sentimental than a whole lineup of other superstars. He looked out for new coach Doug Collins.

Pressure Points (7 of 10)   Plenty of key shots.

Defense (3 of 5)   Early blocks and steals offset his poor shooting in first half. He also sent a message that he is no prima donna who eases up on defense.

Other Offensive Contributions (2 of 5)   Michael scored but also distributed the ball and worked the boards.

MJ's Physical Condition (1 of 5)   Michael was basically healed from a broken left foot.

Long Odds (2 of 5)   This was the start of only Jordan's second full season as a pro. What a beginning.

-49-

March 7, 1996

Detroit Pistons at Bulls Regular Season

At United Center, he stands.

It required almost a full season at the new United Center, but this night marked the first time that Michael Jordan felt entirely at home. Scoring 53 points against an old but now bedraggled nemesis helps you find a comfort zone. The Bulls walloped the Detroit Pistons 102–81 to run their 1995–96 regular season home record to 30–0.

The perfect mark was a subject of discussion during the heat of the contest. Pistons coach Doug Collins, in his first game here since being fired by the Bulls in 1989, grew weary of what he thought were foul calls favoring Chicago. He was particularly peeved about a third personal called on young star Grant Hill (another one of the "next Michael Jordans") just before halftime.

"Jack!" Collins screamed at lead referee Jack Nies. "These guys are 30–0 here. You don't have to help them."

Jordan, who has a knack for showing up at just the right time, happened to be running by when Collins was making his plea.

Air Jordan was back for real as Michael put up his first 50-plus point effort in the new United Center. *Archive Photos*

Game 49: Bulls 102, Pistons 81

Pistons	Min	FG-att	FT-att	Reb	Ast	Fls	Pts
Hill	40	3-16	1-1	13	6	4	13
Thorpe	22	3-11	2-2	7	2	3	8
Reid	20	1-2	2-2	4	1	5	4
Houston	38	9-14	0-0	5	2	0	21
Dumars	37	4-8	2-2	2	2	2	13
Mills	30	3-9	1-3	1	0	3	10
Curry	22	2-5	2-2	2	1	4	6
Ratliff	10	1-2	0-0	5	0	2	2
Roe	3	1-1	0-0	1	0	2	2
Hunter	14	0-4	2-2	1	1	0	2
West	4	0-1	0-0	0	1	1	0
Totals	**240**	**29-73**	**13-14**	**41**	**16**	**26**	**81**

Percentages: FG .397, FT .857. **Three-point goals:** 11-24, .458 (Dumars 3-7, Houston 3-6, Mills 3-6, Hill 2-3, Curry 0-1, Hunter 0-1). **Team rebounds:** 7. **Blocked shots:** None. **Turnovers:** 22 (Hill 6, Houston 4, Mills 3, Thorpe 2, Reid 2, Dumars 2, Curry, Hunter, West). **Steals:** 2 (Reid, Curry). **Technical fouls:** coach Collins, 7:11 3d. **Illegal defense:** None.

Bulls	Min	FG-att	FT-att	Reb	Ast	Fls	Pts
Pippen	40	5-17	0-0	5	10	3	11
Rodman	32	1-4	1-4	13	1	4	3
Longley	29	6-9	1-1	5	2	4	13
Harper	27	3-8	1-2	2	2	1	7
Jordan	38	21-28	9-10	11	2	3	53
Kukoc	29	3-8	1-2	4	4	2	7
Buechler	9	0-6	0-0	1	1	0	0
Kerr	23	2-7	1-2	0	2	1	7
Brown	6	0-0	0-0	3	1	1	0
Caffey	4	0-1	0-0	0	0	0	0
Salley	3	0-3	1-2	2	0	1	1
Totals	**240**	**41-91**	**15-23**	**46**	**25**	**20**	**102**

Percentages: FG .451, FT .652. **Three-point goals:** 5-24, .208 (Jordan 2-4, Kerr 2-3, Pippen 1-7, Buechler 0-1, Rodman 0-2, Harper 0-3, Kukoc 0-4). **Team rebounds:** 10. **Blocked shots:** 4 (Longley 2, Rodman, Kukoc). **Turnovers:** 9 (Jordan 4, Pippen 2, Rodman, Longley, Salley). **Steals:** 12 (Jordan 6, Pippen 2, Harper, Kukoc, Buechler, Kerr). **Technical fouls:** None. **Illegal defense:** 1.

Pistons	15	25	28	13	81
Bulls	23	21	32	26	102

A: 23,369. **T:** 2:00. **Officials:** Lee Jones, Don Vaden, Jack Nies.

"No, we're 29–0," said Jordan as he galloped past, "but we're about to be 30–0."

Jordan later explained, "I just had to correct him."

Michael was in good spirits after hitting 14 of 16 shots in the second half, and 21 of 28 for the evening. His 53 points were a season high for the NBA, and signified Jordan's first 50-point game in the new arena. He hadn't even broke 40 there since the home opener (he had already done so five times on the road, presumably the tougher challenge). He was still scoring at a league-leading rate, but nonetheless felt sort of jinxed.

MJ remains a big fan of that rickety barn of a building, Chicago Stadium, now razed to make room for additional parking. He said his main technical trouble was seeing the baskets clearly enough at the United Center.

"Now I can truly say it's my home," said Jordan. "I proved to myself I can play well here. I didn't know when it would happen. It happened tonight."

The change in fortunes—and an old familiar feeling soon to be dreaded by NBA opponents—seemed to change as rapidly as Chicago weather in the spring. Michael started the second half with the team's first three-pointer. Then he rained down jumpers from all over the floor. He added a few easy layups and slams off of steals.

Collins tried to stop the storm, switching defenders about every time-out after Michael worked past early double-teams.

"Michael was sensational," said Collins. "I've seen that on the other side. It's not as much fun to watch when you're on the other bench, but you marvel at the guy's greatness. The other guys [on the Bulls] were struggling; he strapped them on his back and made the big shots."

Jordan was glad to be back—all the way back—from seventeen-month retirement. The United Center was finally rightside up.

"I felt confident with any shot I threw up," said Michael. "No matter which way I turned. I could have shot left-handed and felt confident I'd make it."

Number 49: Great Game Index

GGI Score (91 of a possible 123).

Scoring (31 of a possible 33)   Michael dominated the second quarter because his teammates needed bailing out. No other Bulls were shooting well—and why not pass to a guy who was 8 of 10 in the third quarter and dead-on 6 of 6 in the fourth quarter?

Game Importance (14 of 20)   Another regular season game.

Opponent Strength (14 of 20)   Detroit was energetic under Collins but lacked a consistent inside game.

Historical Significance (9 of 10)   Jordan's first 50-plus night at United Center.

Legendary Intangibles (9 of 10)   After struggling to adjust at the United Center ("struggling" by Jordanian standards—MJ still led the league in scoring and Chicago was 30-0 at home after this game) Jordan put all the shooting jinx theories to rest. He also carried his team on a night when it was necessary, a less frequent occurrence during this spectacular seventy-two–win season.

Pressure Points (7 of 10)   Michael was red-hot in the second half.

Defense (2 of 5)   Typical solid game.

Other Offensive Contributions (2 of 5)   Nothing out of the ordinary, but still better than most players in the NBA.

MJ's Physical Condition (1 of 5)   Not a factor.

Long Odds (2 of 5)   Scoring 50 is never ordinary.

-50-

October 29, 1984

Milwaukee Bucks at Bulls Regular Season

MJ hits 37 in his third game as pro.

*T*he Bulls season was three games old when Michael stamped an early imprint on a sport and league that he changed forever. In this third game as an NBA rookie, he scored 37 points, including 22 points in the fourth quarter (breaking Bob Love's club record for scoring in one quarter). He sank 20 of the Bulls' final 26 points in a 116–110 victory accomplished without Bulls star Quintin Dailey. No matter. Jordan's star would quickly rise in what technically would have been his senior year in college.

Jordan would score 45 points in a game by the end of the first month of his NBA career. By end of the season, he would score 40 or more points in seven games. MJ averaged more than 36 points per game during a tough stretch of seven games in February, usually about the time the college stars learn first-hand about the grueling physical lessons of an eighty-two–game season. He played every game of the regular season and averaged 28.2 points per game.

Jordan also led the Bulls in assists, rebounding, and free-throw percentage. He was taking care of the little things

Game 50: Bulls 116, Bucks 110

Bucks	Min	FG-att	FT-att	Reb	Ast	Fls	Pts
Cummings	36	10-20	6-10	2	7	4	26
Pressey	20	5-6	0-1	3	2	6	10
Lister	28	3-7	2-4	1	12	6	8
Dunleavy	21	2-7	2-2	3	1	3	7
Moncrief	42	11-21	6-9	3	3	4	28
Fields	17	3-6	1-2	1	2	3	7
Hodges	28	4-8	4-4	9	1	3	12
Mokeski	20	3-7	2-2	3	5	5	8
Micheaux	5	0-0	0-0	1	0	1	0
Grevey	4	0-0	0-0	0	0	1	0
Breuer	19	2-3	0-0	1	7	5	4
Totals	240	43-85	23-34	27	40	41	110

Percentages: FG .506, FT .676. **Team rebounds:** 16. **Turnovers:** 24 (Moncrief 7, Cummings 6). **Steals:** 6 (Moncrief 3). **Blocked shots:** 2. **Three-point goals:** 1-5 (Dunleavy 1-4).

Bulls	Min	FG-att	FT-att	Reb	Ast	Fls	Pts
Johnson	26	5-6	2-2	3	3	5	12
Woolridge	41	10-15	10-16	4	12	2	30
Jones	21	1-2	5-6	0	1	4	7
Jordan	34	13-24	11-13	5	4	4	37
Whatley	25	3-5	2-2	3	0	4	8
Matthews	22	4-8	3-3	4	1	2	11
Higgins	22	1-5	1-2	1	0	2	3
Corzine	20	0-1	2-2	0	5	2	2
Green	22	2-2	2-2	1	4	3	6
Oldham	7	0-0	0-0	1	1	2	0
Totals	240	39-68	38-48	22	31	30	116

Percentages: FG .574, FT .792. **Team rebounds:** 5. **Turnovers:** 22 (Johnson, Corzine 4). **Steals:** 14 (Jordan 6). **Blocked shots:** 3 (Jordan 2). **Three-point goals:** 0-1 (Whatley). **Technical foul:** Coach Loughery

Bucks	27	27	31	25	110
Bulls	25	28	23	40	116

A: 9,356. **T:** 2:27. **Officials:** Mike Mathis, Bill Oakes.

while making a big splash with fans around the league. In Chicago, attendance doubled in a matter of months; the Bulls have sold out every home game and practically every road game in the 1990s. Even Michael admits his season soared past expectations.

"Coming into an unknown situation, I was given freedom by a coach [Kevin Loughery] who really just let me go," recalls

Jordan. "That really helped me out confidence-wise, and it certainly helped my skills."

Opponents didn't need much convincing.

"All I saw were the bottoms on his shoes," said Suns player Michael Holton, after Jordan virtually single-handedly dunked Phoenix on a West Coast swing during the 1984–85 season.

Against Milwaukee in this October game, Jordan hit a 3-point play when the game was still in doubt with forty-seven seconds left. Seven-foot center Alton Lister fouled out trying to stop the successful Jordan drive. Jordan added two free throws later to seal matters.

"He was sensational," said Milwaukee coach Don Nelson. "Down the stretch, we couldn't do anything with him. We tried double-teaming him and he just jumped right over it."

"He showed tremendous poise," said Bucks guard Mike Dunleavy, who became an NBA coach and faced Jordan in the 1991 NBA finals as the Los Angeles Lakers' head coach. "Very few rookies can come into the NBA and dominate like this kid."

NBA commissioner David Stern, new to the job, attended the game. "Why am I in Chicago?" asked Stern in response to a reporter's question. "The same reason everyone else is—to see Michael Jordan."

MJ himself demurred on his expanding status.

"I'm not a superstar of this team and I don't want to overshadow anyone," he said. "I just want to mingle with the rest of the guys. I need the other eleven guys.

"A game like this, we have the feeling we can win now. I kept saying on the bench during the whole fourth quarter, 'We can win.' And they started to believe it."

Among other talents, Michael showed his flair for competition.

"We needed some enthusiasm in the fourth quarter to get everything going, and I just did the best I could," said Jordan after the game. "I saw [Milwaukee star] Sidney Moncrief limping around a little and saw a chance to go in and score. It's tough when you have to take advantage of a guy who is hurting, but that's life in the NBA."

Tell us about it.

Number 50: Great Game Index

GGI Score (90 of a possible 123).

Scoring (28 of a possible 33)   MJ would have much bigger nights, but this was still formidable for his third game as a pro.

Game Importance (11 of 20)   Early in the season, though it did temporarily put the Bulls in first place.

Opponent Strength (12 of 20)   Milwaukee was past their glory years with Kareem Abdul-Jabbar.

Historical Significance (10 of 10)   MJ's first big night.

Legendary Intangibles (10 of 10)   Jordan was already showing signs of inspiring lesser teammates and taking over games.

Pressure Points (10 of 10)   He scored every key basket.

Defense (2 of 5)   MJ was still learning on the defensive end.

Other Offensive Contributions (2 of 5)   He was still learning the Bulls offense too, though Kevin Loughery tended to let Jordan create the plays rather than stay within a system.

MJ's Physical Condition (1 of 5)   Not a factor.

Long Odds (4 of 5)   Few rookies could be this dominant, especially before October was over.

In the Locker Room: Details on the Great Game Index (GGI)

*I*n many ways, there is no finite number that can mark Michael Jordan's greatness. The Great Game Index (GGI) is simply a method to rank the superlative from the super, the excellent from the way above average

Somehow you figure Michael's worst game still has bright spots that any NBA or NCAA or Olympic player would gladly beam into his own repertoire of skills. An example? Jordan admits to not feeling his normal calm self as a rookie starter in the 1985 NBA All-Star Game—scoring a total of 7 points—but he still managed to block a shot by seven-foot, four-inch Ralph Sampson.

The dimmer outings are few and faint. There are more than 1,200 games considered here. Michael's 50 greatest games—the Jordan 50—represent about 4 percent of his total games played. It is an elite collection.

In the Game Time section of this book, each entry, Nos. 1 through 50, shows the GGI score. Remember, 100 + 23 = Perfection. Michael has come close to full 123 percent more than any player in history and certainly far beyond the cliché 110 percent reserved for mere mortal NBA players. Here is how the scores for the Great Game Index categories are determined:

Scoring

Right from the start, it is clear that Jordan demands some new thinking about putting the ball in the basket. A typical night for him, say 37 against the Miami Heat during the regular-season race for home-court advantage, doesn't even approach the outer edges of the Jordan 50. Michael's career scoring average is nearly 32 points per game during the regular season and another basket higher during the playoffs.

In fact, MJ has more than thirty postseason games in which he has more than 40 points. He broke prolific scorer Wilt Chamberlain's record for the most 50-plus games during the playoffs. He has set handfuls of scoring marks for the NBA Finals, crunching the most numbers at the ultimate crunch time (just ask Magic Johnson, Clyde Drexler, Charles Barkley, and Karl Malone, among others).

So a raw number alone won't do. There are games in which MJ has scored 60 or more points that don't qualify for the Jordan 50. Instead, the GGI looks at total points, percentage of team points; points in the second half, fourth quarter, last two minutes, and overtime; shooting percentage, and whether the points came on field goals (breaking down dunks, layups, and jump shots) or free throws (factoring in importance and sheer volume). This approach allows for interpretation of how Jordan's game has evolved, keeping him at the top of the basketball globe for so long.

Experts and fans (are they the same thing?) might argue, but the GGI says that scoring is one-third of Michael's total game, or 33 percent (on a human scale, not the Jordanian system).

The maximum value for the Scoring category is 33.

Game Importance

No competitor in any sport can ignore the Jordan penchant for rising to the occasion. In big games, Michael has set new standards that just get bigger each postseason.

The Game Importance category is a primary sorter of Michael's extra-extraordinary efforts from the extraordinary and ordinarily great. It compares playoff games to those in the regular season, key-stretch regular season and early-year games, first- and second-round games against conference and NBA finals, and, of course, any make-or-break games (of which, to Jordan and the Bulls' credit, there have been amazingly few).

The maximum value for Game Importance is 20.

Opponent Strength

This category separates the superstars from the men and boys. It judges the challenge of the opposing teams, especially the stars who are battling Michael for domination of a game.

The process can be likened to natural selection, or Darwinism. While MJ has played some spectacular college games—he was named Player of the Year twice in three seasons—the level of talent in the NCAA postseason tournament is still a cut or three below the NBA (depending on the subregionals and regionals, and whether Jordan and his University of North Carolina teammates were placed in friendly surroundings). So most of his NCAA games, though consistently fabulous, don't make the cut for the Jordan 50. This has more to do with Opponent Strength than the old joke that legendary North Carolina mentor Dean Smith is the only coach who could hold MJ to under 20 points per game by making him stay within the disciplined Tar Heel offensive system. The same goes for his two gold-medal-winning Olympic tours.

Rony Seikaly, the veteran NBA center who played for some successful Syracuse University teams, made the college-pro distinction after Chicago trounced his then–Miami Heat team in the 1992 postseason.

"You can't compare the NCAA tournament with the NBA playoffs," said Seikaly. "We're talking about grown men here. This is their living. There's pushing, shoving—everyone is so much stronger. You think it was tougher back then, but in col-

lege you blow on some guy and he thinks it's a foul. "You saw
how the Bulls came out today. They took our heads off. That's
what it's all about."

The maximum value for Opponent Strength is 20.

Historical Significance

At some point in his career (it's difficult to pinpoint exactly
when), every time Jordan stepped on the court signified a date
with history. This category concedes Michael's looming explo-
siveness on any given night to look closer at how he gained the
loftiest place in basketball history. It considers both individual
and team accomplishments. Critics didn't project Jordan as
much of a team player during Michael's first six pro seasons.
How wrong those so-called prognosticators turned out to be.

The maximum value for Historical Significance is 10.

Legendary Intangibles

There is something about great competitors that is eminently
intangible—sort of know-it-when-you-see-it proposition. This
category awards points for such nuances of Jordan greatness. It
boosts some games into surprising status in the Jordan 50.

The maximum point value for Legendary Intangibles
should be unlimited, since Michael seems to keep inventing
new intangibles and twists—not to mention court moves and
marketing strategies. To keep to the GGI math, though, the
maximum value for Legendary Intangibles is 10.

Pressure Points

Scoring in the clutch is one thing, and difficult at that, but
Michael has done much more than hit jump shots or free
throws with a game in the balance. This category recognizes
those achievements and shows why *choke* is not in Jordan's
vocabulary.

The maximum value for Pressure Points is 10.

Defense

In a perfect world, the Defense category would rate much higher in scoring the Jordan 50. Trouble is, Jordan never takes a night off on the defensive end of the court. Therefore it becomes difficult to distinguish a supremely great defensive effort from any other. Plus, the Bulls scheme of pressuring opponents makes one of three players key up-front defenders, not Jordan alone. (Scottie Pippen was one such up-front defender, so were Horace Grant and Dennis Rodman).

So, with full acknowledgment that defense wins playoff games and fueled the Bulls championship seasons, the maximum value for Defense is 5. There's just too little difference to warrant big swings among Jordan's NBA games.

Other Offensive Contributions

Similar to defense, offensive numbers beyond points make a real difference in game outcomes. Michael has set a new (and unreachable) curve for players succeeding him. Along with 30-something points, Jordan has averaged roughly 6 rebounds and 6 assists for every game of his entire pro career. It gets hard to sift out the great nights when you are that consistently superb. Nonetheless, there were some block-the-sun brilliant games, and this category helps find them.

The maximum value for Other Offensive Contributions is 5, though guys like Dennis Rodman (talk about Legendary Intangibles), Charles Oakley, Nate Archibald, and Oscar Robertson might scoff.

MJ's Physical Condition

No athlete has ever been better conditioned in the peak seasons of his career than Michael Jordan. He hired a personal trainer, Tim Grover of A.T.T.A.C.K. Athletics, long before other athletes even considered the notion. The move paid off in many fewer injuries than competitors suffered, and compared to his early seasons as a pro. Michael was wise enough to understand the value of building his upper-body strength and increasing endurance for the rough-it-up grind of the NBA season. Grover's sophisticated approach was the ideal match.

Even so, there were times when Jordan played at less than full capacity due to injury or sickness. This category identifies how greatness prevailed over everything from food poisoning to foot problems.

The maximum value for MJ's Physical Condition is 5.

Long Odds

Even the most talented superstars can face what seems to be insurmountable odds. Michael has had his share of those games, especially early in his Bulls days. This category explores that concept.

The maximum value for Long Odds is 5.

A score of 123 is the maximum value for the Great Game Index. The Jordan 50 ranges from 90 to 119. Basketball fans have never had it so great.

Final Note on the GGI: A tiebreaker system was used to rank games that were given the same number of points. The first tiebreaker is game importance. The second tiebreaker is total game performance (scoring, defense, and other offensive contributions). The third tiebreaker, necessary in some cases, is opponent strength.

Postgame Analysis

After he carried the Bulls on his highly capable back during Game 6 of the 1998 NBA Finals to make it an even half-dozen world championship titles in the last six full seasons he played, Michael Jordan was asked about his future in the postgame press conference, before he could finish a first victory cigar. He preferred to savor the present moment, an approach he had been repeating as far back as those cold January and February nights when the same broadcasters would frame the same hope-this-is-not-your-last-season questions around his locker after home games. This championship night, Michael allowed himself to reflect on the past just a bit. The future would have to wait.

"Hopefully, I've put enough memories out there for everybody to at least have some thoughts about what Michael Jordan did and put up some comparisons for kids to follow and reach for," said Jordan.

Oh, that is safe to say.

Utah Jazz coach Jerry Sloan, whose jersey number is retired in the rafters of United Center to mark his playing days in Chicago, conceded that sometimes "great players make great plays" when asked if he would do anything different to defend Jordan after losing two straight NBA Finals. Michael's career actually builds on this premise: a great player makes great plays at the right times.

So it seems. Jordan has missed shots and free throws, and

watched other team's superstars score a key basket or go on a 7–0 run, but when greatness is the deciding factor, Jordan is the only NBA player left standing at the end. Make your arguments for Bill Russell or Wilt Chamberlain, Magic Johnson or Larry Bird. Then be honest with yourself. Would you start a daydream team with anybody other than Jordan?

You shouldn't need much evidence to support your decision, but here are some statistics and achievements to keep in mind: In thirty-five NBA Finals games, Michael has scored 20 or more points each time, a record. He has led the Bulls in scoring thirty-three times and been the game-high scorer twenty-eight times. His team is 24-11 in those games. During the six title runs, he has been the team's leading scorer in 111 of 116 postseason games.

Of course, there is much more to Jordan's game than points. He led his team in minutes played during the six NBA Finals, winning the Most Valuable Player award each time. He led in steals in 1998, always finishing among the top three team rebounders but lower on the turnovers list.

Eleven of his thirty-five NBA Finals games rank in *Michael Jordan's 50 Greatest Games*, including six in the top ten and ten of the top sixteen. There's also the NCAA championship game in the top ten and six Eastern Conference finals games among the top thirty-four. Another sixteen playoff games bulk up Michael's 50. That's two-thirds of all his greatest games coming when the outcome means the most. Great players make great plays at the right times.

May appears to be MJ's favorite month, with sixteen games in the Jordan 50, though June is proportionately represented, with twelve games (in a month when fewer but the most important games are played).

Utah fans may be less enamored with the Jordan mystique. Five games from the 1997 and 1998 NBA Finals made the Jordan 50, including four in the first twelve and the top two of all time. Jordan is certainly a primary reason why John Stockton and Karl Malone rank first and second in most postseason games played without a league championship to show for it.

New Yorkers have a special respect and appreciation for Jordan's unique talents. It is not surprising to Knicks fans that ten of the Michael's 50 greatest games are against New York, including seven of the top twenty-three and three from the destiny-deciding conference semifinals in 1989.

Six games occurred against Detroit, mostly from the Isiah Thomas era. Two were played against Magic Johnson's Los Angeles Lakers and two apiece against Charles Barkley's Phoenix Suns and Clyde Drexler's Portland Trail Blazers. Another pair was against Larry Bird, one as a player—the only Bulls' loss in the Jordan 50—and one as a coach. There are six versus Cleveland, as if Cavaliers fans have to be reminded. In all, seventeen other NBA teams are part of the Jordan 50.

Numerous opponents know their chances of winning an NBA title are geometrically increased whenever Jordan exits the center stage and top of the key, but most of those same foes have never been entirely eager to see him go.

Coaches like Sloan, Bird, Chuck Daly, and even Pat Riley have publicly urged Jordan to keep playing. The Barkleys, Malones, Hardaways, and Ewings, would rather win with Jordan on the court than with Jordan watching on a giant screen at some exclusive golf resort. On the 1998 championship night, Scottie Pippen said that Michael could easily dominate the sport for another five years, fueled by both physical abilities and knowledge of the game.

There's just something about savoring the best, watching the best, and competing against the best that is hard to resist—even if it means one of Michael Jordan's 50 greatest games is played against you.